Planning Research in Hospitality and Tourism

Planning Research in Hospitality and Tourism

Levent Altinay and Alexandros Paraskevas

AMSTERDAM • BOSTON • HEIDELBERG • LONDON • NEW YORK • OXFORD
PARIS • SAN DIEGO • SAN FRANCISCO • SINGAPORE • SYDNEY • TOKYO

Butterworth-Heinemann is an imprint of Elsevier

Butterworth-Heinemann is an imprint of Elsevier
The Boulevard, Langford Lane, Kidlington, Oxford, OX5 1GB
30 Corporate Drive, Suite 400, Burlington, MA 01803, USA

First edition 2008
Reprinted 2008

British Library Cataloguing in Publication Data
A catalogue record for this book is available from the British Library

Library of Congress Cataloging-in-Publication Data
A catalog record for this book is available from the Library of Congress

ISBN: 978-0-7506-8110-0

For information on all Butterworth-Heinemann publications
visit our website at www.elsevierdirect.com

Printed and bound in *Hungary*

08 09 10 10 9 8 7 6 5 4 3 2

Working together to grow
libraries in developing countries

www.elsevier.com | www.bookaid.org | www.sabre.org

ELSEVIER   BOOK AID
International   Sabre Foundation

Contents

Preface

There are several stories about a real person, Nasreddin Hoca (pronounced Hodja), who was born in 1208 in the western part of Central Anatolia in Turkey. Hoca served as a judge, and his sense of fairness and wisdom soon made him a legend, not only in Turkey but also in neighbouring countries such as Greece, Syria and Bulgaria. One of these stories is the starting point of this 'research journey' that we will share with you.

One day, a neighbour of Hoca came to him with a complaint against another. Hoca listened to the charges carefully and then concluded, 'Yes, dear neighbour, I believe you are quite right.' The other neighbour then came to him. Hoca listened to his defence carefully and then concluded, 'Yes, dear neighbour, I believe you are quite right.' Hoca's wife, having listened to the entire proceeding, said to him, 'Husband, they cannot both be right!' Hoca turned to her and said, 'Yes, wife, I believe you are quite right too!!!'

The message behind this story is that sometimes there is no right or wrong way of doing things; there might be more than one way. There is always an alternative means – some other idea or belief – that may also be right! What is important is how you justify what you do and how you do it, and this is where this book will help. One of its main foci is to offer a balanced approach regarding the theory and practice of research methods, so that you will be equipped with the knowledge and the skills necessary to perform research and justify your approach to it. We have used a straightforward style to present and explain concepts and ideas employed by hospitality and tourism researchers, using real-life examples, and to emphasize the skills that you, as an under- or post-graduate researcher, will need to carry out your research projects, whether for coursework, consultancy or dissertation. In particular, the book offers guidance on planning a research project in hospitality and tourism by considering the specific characteristics of this industry, including the international dimension and the implications this may have regarding the research process.

We have tried to structure the book in a staged approach, both to help you to understand the basics of research and also to develop your own way of thinking, be able to justify this thinking, and appreciate that there are other, equally valid, means of approaching your research topic. In Chapter 1 we explain why we, as academics, do research, but also why it is important that you do the same during your studies in higher education. We help you to find ways of developing reasoning for undertaking research on a particular topic, and articulate the research questions that will guide your research journey.

Chapters 2 and 3 are aimed at providing the skills you will need to cope with academic reading, and a strategy to approach literature review in a manner that will be meaningful in building a strong theoretical foundation for your research project.

In Chapter 4 we introduce you to the more conceptual elements of research by presenting different philosophies, approaches and strategies that you may choose to adopt in your project.

Chapters 5, 6 and 7 concern the more technical parts of research, providing guidance regarding who you get your information from, how to obtain it, and how to prepare a research proposal that will convince your supervisor or your institution's research committee that you are able to undertake an academically rigorous research.

Chapter 8 discusses undertaking fieldwork – i.e. 'getting out there' and doing your research. The chapter aims to equip you with some strategies to deal with the real world and cope with adversity.

Chapters 9 and 10 are aimed at providing you with the basic skills required for data analysis, by introducing different approaches and techniques to perform this task. These chapters offer several examples that will help you to understand and practise these techniques before actually applying them in your own project.

Finally, Chapter 11 offers advice on writing up your project following a generally accepted structure, but also on how you can turn a successful project into a publishable academic article.

Levent Altinay
Alexandros Paraskevas

Acknowledgements

In the preparation of this book we were fortunate to receive considerable feedback from colleagues in both UK and overseas universities. We are extremely grateful to them for giving their time and sharing their ideas. We also take this opportunity to thank our families for their patience and for encouraging us in our endeavours.

Chapter 1
Getting started

All life is a great chain, the nature of which is known whenever we are shown a single link of it. Like all other arts, the Science of Deduction and Analysis is one which can only be acquired by long and patient study.

(Sherlock Holmes, in Arthur Conan Doyle's A Study in Scarlet.*)*

If we ask for a definition of 'research', the immediate reaction might be to either 'google' it or look it up in 'wikipedia'. Many students become confused regarding the various dimensions of research, which range from the simplest (such as 'basic' and 'applied') to the more complex (such as 'inductive' and 'deductive', 'qualitative' and 'quantitative' etc.). Those who look into the subject more deeply and check the research methods books in the library will find that there are several schools of thought regarding research and that, for hospitality and tourism in particular, these range from the more practical to the highly scientific.

In Doyle's (1887) quotation above, particular attention should be paid to the words: 'arts', 'long' and 'patient study'. Research is an art, and can be compared with painting a portrait using very special techniques, while the researcher is an artist. The quality of a portrait depends not only on the model, but also on how well the artist chooses paints, brushes and other equipment, and plans each stage of painting – from checking the composition to adding the final details. Similarly, the end result of a research project or a dissertation depends not only on the topic of investigation but also on how well the researcher has chosen the sample, the data collection and analysis techniques, and how he or she has planned each stage – from the literature review to the conclusions and recommendations. This whole process of painting a portrait or, in our case, doing research is one that requires – in the words of Sherlock Holmes – 'long and patient study'.

What is research and why do we do it?

We can broadly define research as being a form of systematic enquiry that contributes to knowledge. Research is essential for understanding the various phenomena that individuals and organizations encounter in their everyday activities. Consequently, research can be conducted by a wide range of individuals, teams, organizations and institutions. People do research when they want to buy a new car or a house, companies conduct research to test a product in the market, pharmaceutical labs undertake research to develop a new vaccine, and political parties use research to assess their influence in society.

Together with teaching, research is a principal activity in universities, and is often referred to as 'academic scholarship'. Traditionally, research in academic institutions has been viewed as a scholarly activity focusing on creating or reformulating knowledge regarding a particular subject. An example is provided by Roper and colleagues, who, based on the existing knowledge on centricity of multinational companies (i.e. the organization's view and/or approach to international management of its operations; see Chakravarthy and Perlmutter, 1985; Calof and Beamish, 1994), investigated the centric profile of major international hotel groups in order to identify their approach to international management and create new knowledge on business decisions in the international hospitality industry (Roper *et al.*, 1997).

The work of Ernest Boyer and the Carnegie Foundation for the Advancement of Teaching stimulated an interesting debate regarding the aims of research in universities. Boyer (1990) articulated a paradigm shift in academic research to include three dimensions:

1. Integration of knowledge by bringing together otherwise isolated knowledge from two or more disciplines or fields, thus creating new insights and understanding. Burgess and Bryant (2001), for example, integrated the literature on profitability with that on revenue management to demonstrate the key role of hotel financial management in designing and implementing cost systems, in order for revenue management to shift its emphasis from revenue to profits.
2. Application of knowledge in order to trigger change, improvement or resolution of societal and business issues. For example, Miller's work on the development of indicators that can be used to monitor movement of the tourism industry with reference to more sustainable positions aimed, among other things, to identify the factors that would trigger changes in the actions of tour operators in terms of corporate responsibility (Miller, 2001).
3. Teaching by the development of creative and original means for delivery and measuring the achievement of learning objectives, and by stimulating 'active, not passive, learning {which} encourages students to be critical, creative thinkers, with the capacity to go on learning' (Boyer, 1990: 23). All pedagogic research published in generic education or in hospitality and tourism-specific journals (such as the *Journal of Hospitality, Leisure, Sport and Tourism Education*, the *Journal of Hospitality and Tourism Education* and the *Journal of Teaching in Travel and Tourism*) falls within this category.

The first major contribution of Boyer's report comes from the fact that it is based upon the belief that everyone at university should be a discoverer and a learner, and that it is this shared mission that binds together everything that happens on campus. The second is that Boyer's identification of the realms of research offers a vocabulary for discussing the different aspects common to contemporary hospitality and tourism research. Thus, research is not just about 'discovery' but should also include the integration and application definitions as well. This view is clearly reflected in the nature of research output in the field as published in field-specific and mainstream academic journals. Looking at research output investigations – for example, that of Taylor and Edgar (1996) regarding hospitality – we could suggest three principal purposes of hospitality and tourism research:

1. To uncover and make sense of existing patterns of behaviour and phenomena within the hospitality and tourism industry
2. To identify new and better ways of managing within the hospitality industry
3. To enable hospitality and tourism faculty to educate future practitioners.

Academic research that aims at discovery, integration and application may be triggered by various factors. There might be a pressing industry-specific or wider social/management issue that needs to be resolved – for example, the development of an activity-based costing approach to hotel operations that will facilitate a more accurate customer profitability analysis (Krakhmal, 2006). Alternatively, there might be an area that academics feel needs some fresher thinking, such as the concern that traditional budgeting systems – with their typical bureaucratic encouragement of internally-focused, department-centred cost minimization – may present a significant barrier to the more flexible, responsive and empowered management structures that hospitality and tourism organizations need in order to compete successfully in the information age (Brander Brown and Atkinson, 2001). Perhaps there is a specific opportunity – for example, a mega-event in a tourism destination – that may stimulate research in various areas, from visitor perception to economic, societal, cultural and environmental impacts on the destination. An example of this is provided by Kim *et al.* (2006), who researched the impact of the 2002 World Cup on South Korea. Another stimulus for research may arise from personal experience – for example, Tony Seaton's work on thanatourism (Seaton, 1996, 1999, 2002). Finally, research might be triggered and funded by external sources, such as the industry and national or international research councils. These usually result in consultancy projects (research undertaken by the university to propose solutions to an industry-specific problem for one or a cluster of companies), collaborative research (such as a project funded, for example, by an EU initiative requiring the collaboration of three EU-based and two Asian institutions), or contract research (when a request is made by industry or a government agency for a specified project to be carried out with identified aims and objectives). The latter might include the scale of tourism both within a country (domestic and in-bound) and out-bound to other destinations measured in terms of trips made, tourism-days, and expenditure; the effect this has on the local economy and on the economies of destinations abroad; and the social effect that tourism expenditure and investment has on employment, locally and in other countries, etc.).

Triggered by a wider interest in student learning experience, in addition to the above, there is a strong stream of pedagogic research specific to hospitality and tourism which, although still at a developmental stage, has made significant contributions towards the improvement of teaching, learning and assessment practices in the field. Research of this type is published in generic as well as pedagogy-specific journals such as the *Journal of Hospitality and Tourism Education*, the *Journal of Teaching in Travel and Tourism* and the (slightly broader context) on-line *Journal of Hospitality Leisure, Sport and Tourism Education*.

The linkage between research and student learning experience does not stop with the development of innovative pedagogic practices; it is obviously expanded by the content of the learning itself. Reflecting the majority of hospitality and tourism researchers, Peter Jones, a distinguished hospitality scholar, states that:

> it is important not to see research and teaching as separate activities, and for teachers to also be researchers. Teaching, reading recently published work or conducting my own primary research all feed into one another. The products of both my primary and secondary research are employed in my teaching, whilst the discussions in my classes can influence my research. It is this seamless relationship between research and teaching that should differentiate higher and further education.
>
> (Tribe, 2004: 1)

Most research-led universities in the UK, Australia and the United States pay particular attention to ensuring this linkage into both undergraduate and postgraduate courses. The overarching idea in these institutions is that linking teaching and research goes beyond involving students in research activities, or exposing them to the research of their tutors, in that it offers many new opportunities for curriculum development (HEA – HLST, 2006).

The benefits of this approach have been acknowledged by both academics and students. Academics (Boterill, 2003) believe that there is an implicit complementarity between knowledge creation (research) and knowledge dissemination (teaching), while students believe that their understanding of the subject improves as they reach a greater appreciation of the problems faced by the industry, and that staff involved in research are more interesting and provide greater stimulation to learning (Healey et al., 2003).

Why do we need to do research at all?

Arguably, this is the most common question from both undergraduate and postgraduate students. It usually stems from their frustration with the very disciplined and detailed planning and execution processes they have to go through when undertaking research either for a project or for their dissertations. The question is usually complemented by a further one, 'how will this be useful to me after I graduate?'

Apart from the benefits stated in Healey et al. (2003), a further answer is that the dissertation is considered a perfect platform on which to display the higher-order thinking skills developed during studies. According to Lewis and Smith (1993: 136), 'higher order thinking occurs when a person takes new information and information stored in memory and interrelates and/or rearranges and extends this information to achieve a purpose or find possible answers in perplexing situations'. However, perhaps there is no need to look any farther than Marcel Proust's (1923) quotation: 'The real voyage of discovery consists not in seeking new landscapes but in having new eyes.' The key idea here is 'having new eyes'. Research is a process that requires careful planning and execution in order to find solutions to the questions or problems being investigated. It always begins with a question – Why? How? These kinds of questions are at the very heart of everyday life after a student's graduation, and every research 'exercise' students go through during their studies aims at sharpening their vision, giving them 'new eyes'.

Research allows students to appreciate better the practical applications of knowledge acquired in the classroom or the lecture theatre, to step outside their institution and learn more about the theories, resources, tools, and ethical issues scholars and professionals come across every day. Regardless of their complexity and length, student research projects usually share eight distinct characteristics (Box 1.1).

On considering the characteristics listed in Box 1.1, you will realize that the research process helps you to learn how to formulate questions, clearly identify and define problems, methodically plan ways to find answers, collect and analyse data, draw conclusions from that data, and share your findings with other researchers, scholars and practitioners. Although the overall research process appears to be very ordered and linear, it also provides the opportunity to solve unforeseen problems and to be

Box 1.1	The eight characteristics of research projects

1. Research projects originate with a question or problem. The first requirement in any such project is to identify clearly the question or the problem that will be investigated.
2. The next step is to define the aim of the research in terms of a clear statement of the problem, question or hypothesis.
3. Next, a specific plan for proceeding has to be developed.
4. The principal problem needs usually to be divided into more manageable sub-problems, to prevent the research project from becoming cumbersome and unwieldy.
5. The research is guided by the research problem, which directs the researcher to appropriate data.
6. The researcher has to make some critical assumptions. These assumptions are underlying theories or ideas about how the world works.
7. In order to resolve the problem that initiated the research, the researcher has to collect and interpret data about it.
8. Research is, by its nature, cyclical – i.e. research findings lead to other questions, which require further research.

(Source: Adapted from Leedy and Ormrod, 2005)

open to changing your conceptions of the world (Brew, 1999). Seasoned researchers know that:

> *The research process and particularly the intellectual or 'thinking' part of it is inherently 'messy'. This is because however well planned a research process is, there will always be an element of creative uncertainty'.*

> *(Clark* et al., *1998: 1)*

Cooper *et al.* (1996: 26) point out, very correctly, that 'research should have beneficial influence, not only on the body of knowledge of hospitality and tourism, but also on the personal development and career paths of those undertaking research'. There is ample anecdotal evidence that research may provide a networking opportunity within the industry, while enabling you to develop expertise in a research area and preparing you for the workplace – where people who can identify and solve problems are very much appreciated. It helps you to develop further your critical thinking skills, creativity, time-management and budget skills, and your confidence in setting and achieving challenging goals.

How does a research project start?

The saying 'a good beginning is half the battle' is very appropriate regarding research projects. A research project always starts with a research idea. However, a difficulty for many students is finding a starting point for their research. This is because the focus of their learning and assessment has so far largely been determined and directed by their teachers (Saunders *et al.*, 2007).

It is quite a leap to make the transition from the passive mode of learning that traditional lecture courses encourage to an active and critical one. Nevertheless, there are some techniques that can help you to generate ideas for research and to move on to the stage of selecting a particular topic and articulating research questions. These include:

- identifying your personal aspirations
- using your experience of the industry
- looking for industry trends
- reading existing research
- seeking advice from an active researcher.

Personal aspirations

Perhaps the best approach for selecting a research area is to ask yourself: 'What do I want from this research project and how can it help me in the future?' The word 'future' is key here; quite often students base their quest for a research topic on the career path they envisage for themselves after graduation. For these students, the research project is not only proof of the problem-solving and other skills developed during their studies, but also provides evidence of their deeper understanding of the research area.

Industry experience

Many students on hospitality and tourism courses have already some experience of the sector, as either employees or customers. Reflecting on your experiences will help you to identify broad areas that you may like to investigate further – for example, you might wish to look at operational or human resources issues you were faced with as an employee, or marketing and customer service issues you encountered as a customer. If you have worked with entrepreneurs, you may wish to research strategic, financial or entrepreneurial areas.

Industry trends

Another way of generating research ideas is to look at current thinking, developments or research streams. You may attend research seminars or conferences, consider areas discussed in current debates and 'think tanks' in the sector, or even look at the topics brought up in different Internet newsgroups and in the trade press.

Existing research

The most common source for research ideas is past and current research. You may start reading articles from the top hospitality and tourism journals, such as *Tourism Management*, the *Annals of Tourism Research*, the *Journal of International Hospitality Management* and *Cornell Quarterly*. These are available in print in most academic libraries, or may be retrieved from the institution's electronic database. By reading these sources, you will be exposed to current thinking and contemporary areas of research. Lubbe (2004) suggests that greater benefit can be obtained by, after reading the article, asking yourself 'canonical questions' about it – i.e. questions that are otherwise known as the 'wh' questions: who, what, where, when, why, and how (Box 1.2).

Further practical advice regarding how to read an article appears in Chapter 2.

Advice from an active researcher

A very helpful resource for research ideas is the 'wisdom' of existing researchers – lecturers, research assistants or PhD students in your institution, or guest speakers

Box 1.2	Canonical questions to trigger ideas from articles

- Who are the main researchers in this area, and have I read their work?
- What exactly was accomplished by this piece of work?
- Where did the author seem to draw ideas from?
- Why is this research topic an issue for the sector?
- When does it occur?
- How do various groups perceive it?
- What relationship does it have with other phenomena?
- How does it seem to relate to other work in the field?
- What ideas from related fields might be brought to bear upon this subject?
- What would be the reasonable next step to build upon this work?

and others who present their work at workshops, seminars or conferences. If you are attending research events, you may be able to approach the presenters of papers that interest you. Over coffee, you can usually get ideas for several projects. One good technique is to ask presenters how they would do their research were they to start from scratch but knowing what they know now. Similarly, if you read an interesting research paper, you may contact its authors. Authors are generally very happy to hear from people who find their subject interesting, and they often offer advice, access to unpublished manuscripts and perhaps even some consultation time.

Once the broad research area has been identified, the next decision is to choose a research topic within it. This is perhaps the most important decision that you will make, as it will impact on all the stages that follow in the research process. Since the research is more often than not a 'long and patient study', the first requirement for the topic is that it is of interest to you. This will help you to maintain momentum throughout the project even when things do not really work according to the original plan.

Then again, is finding an interesting research topic enough? The characteristics of an ideal topic may some times be conflicting. For example, an interesting topic may be a topic that has stimulated debate before and has left some unexplored areas or unanswered questions that would justify further research. On the other hand, it may be an overcrowded research area which is 'tired' after intensive research – i.e. although interesting for you, the topic is already saturated. Tung (2006: 33), paraphrasing Hambrick's quotation that 'there are three kinds of people: those who make things happen, those who watch things happen, and those who wonder what happened' (Hambrick, 1994: 16), states that the Sloan School of Management at the Massachusetts Institute of Technology (MIT) has a saying regarding three categories of research: 'Oh, gee, I wish I had done that; I'm glad somebody did that; and why on earth would someone do that?'

The topic should also be contemporary and well-timed if the research is to be used as evidence of mastering an area with potential for future work and employment. It should address fundamental management issues – those that are important today and are likely to remain significant in the future. However, you must be careful not to pursue merely 'trendy' topics – i.e. something that is 'hot' for the moment but may be just a fad that will have passed in a couple of years.

Some students have the tendency to seek a really innovative area of research, which is great in the sense that they have the opportunity to demonstrate a high level of creativity, although such research is often somewhat speculative – especially if the topic is not broad enough to generate interest among researchers – and it may be unclear at first how the ideas proposed will develop. On the other hand, research that builds on past research benefits from an already existing baseline for exploration and, in most cases, extends and improves our understanding of a phenomenon.

Finally, a topic should challenge previous understandings and findings that just don't fit together anymore, and explore something that is missing and perhaps can be found if the right research is undertaken. Kuhn (1962: 92) argues that 'scientific revolutions are inaugurated by a growing sense that an existing paradigm has ceased to function adequately in the exploration of an aspect of nature to which that paradigm itself had previously led the way'. In other words, existing paradigms persist until enough people start finding enough places where it just doesn't fit. On the other hand, the research topic should be within your reach and ability, and careful consideration must be given to the time allowed for the project, as well as access and resource constraints.

Summarizing the above, Tung (2005) suggests six questions (stemming from her six principles of research topic selection) that all researchers should answer when justifying their research topic (Box 1.3).

Box 1.3	Six questions regarding research topic selection

1. What are the significant and important trends that have broad implications for theory and practice in the future?
2. Is the topic sustainable over an extended period of time, and not just a fad?
3. Will the topic be broad enough to generate interest among a sufficiently large group of researchers?
4. How much research attention has the topic received thus far?
5. What is my competitive advantage in this area?
6. Am I truly passionate and excited about the topic?

(Source: Adapted from Tung, 2005)

It is clear that questions 1–4 relate to the popularity and sustainability of a research topic with respect to the interest and contribution it could make to a field of enquiry, while questions 5 and 6 consider not only how capable you are regarding a particular area, but also how motivated and passionate you are about it.

Formulating the broad research question

Once the research topic has been broadly identified, you need to start thinking about what the research project is going to test, explore or explain – i.e. the 'purpose' of your study. In order to make the broad research idea more tangible, a good starting point is to draft a short title for the project – a 'working title'. Many graduates, looking back at their research experience, consider this to be the first major milestone in their project. Glesne and Peshkin (1992: 131) give the example of a student who printed out her current working title on a big banner so that 'it guided her work whenever she lifted her head to reflect'. The working title provides a point of continuous reference, focus and re-focus, because it may change several times during the project as data are being collected.

A working title must – in the very first stages – describe in simple, non-academic language what the study is about (i.e. the main research area). For example: 'My study will be about crisis communications planning'. This description should include the particular focus of the study, the context (e.g. 'My study will be about crisis communications planning in destination management organizations') and the purpose of the study ('My study will be about crisis communications planning in destination management organizations (DMO) and will aim to integrate communication theories and current best practice in order to develop a clear strategy for a DMO').

Many students make the common mistake of trying to frame their working title in complex academic terms, and using unnecessary descriptions – such as 'A Study of …', 'A Survey of …', 'An Investigation of …', etc.. Even if these make sense, at this stage it is far too early to use them. Another frequent mistake is forgetting that the research is academic – so there must be either a 'theory' as a starting point or a 'theoretical angle' from which to approach their topic. This decision has to be made at the outset of the research. What is needed is a means of coupling the interest in a research area with intellectual enquiry – the kind of speculative and analytical approach that makes us question whatever we are researching. In the above example, it is clear that the theoretical basis could be organizational communication theories, marketing communications theories, or a combination of the two. Some strategic management may also need to be brought into this research with regard to strategy planning. However, a working title such as 'Corporate Social Responsibility in Tourism Organizations' begs for clarification regarding the angle from which the study is going to explore CSR, and which tourism organizations will be studied.

It is good practice, before seeing your research advisors/supervisors, to think about how you will justify the research topic selection – what we usually call the 'rationale' for the study. This is an excellent mental exercise which will make the first meeting with the supervisor much more productive, and prove to be extremely useful at the later stage of the formal research proposal (see Chapter 6). When drafting the rationale of the study, you may begin by explaining what attracted your attention to this particular research area, and then provide a brief background that will provide the supervisor with the context of your particular study. This should describe, in broad terms, what is happening in the industry that has triggered your interest in this research area. You may find the questions in Box 1.4 useful as a guide to develop a good and informed argument.

Box 1.4	Questions for the rationale of the study

1. What are the most recent facts that have shown the influence of the research area in hospitality and tourism?
2. What trends are arising in the research area, and how are these expected to affect the industry?
3. What are the problems surfacing in the industry with regard to the research area?
4. Are any other developments enhancing these problems?
5. What is the general state of knowledge in this area? Is there any industry-specific knowledge?
6. What are the deficiencies in the current studies?
7. How will the study close the gap left by these deficiencies?

For example, the student who drafted the working title described above ('My study will be about crisis communications planning in destination management organizations (DMO) and will aim to integrate communication theories and current best practice in order to develop a clear strategy for a DMO') might give the following answers to these questions:

1. The tourism industry has been hit by several crises since 2000: terrorist attacks such as 9/11 and the bombings in Bali, Jakarta, Madrid and London; epidemics such as foot and mouth disease and SARS, and the prospect of a 'flu pandemic; and natural disasters such as the tsunami in the Asia-Pacific region and the hurricanes Katrina, Rita and Wilma in the US. All of these have shown the importance of communications for tourism destinations both during a crisis and after it, in the recovery stage. There are examples of destinations that handled the whole thing very poorly and others that showed that a proper communications strategy will speed up the recovery of tourism in the affected area.

2. People want to know more about what is happening. Several crisis communications approaches have been developed, supported by different technologies. Existing tourists and their families, as well as prospective tourists, expect the DMO to be a reliable source of information. The same stands for all those involved with tourism and the tourism destination.

3. It appears that some DMOs do well in this area while others do not. There seems no consistency in their approaches, and the need for a well-planned crisis communication strategy is obvious.

4. Technological progress has led to the demand for speedy and accurate information. People can obtain it, either in print or online, for everything. The telephone is not enough anymore. However, during a crisis, technology may fail. If a DMO is not a good communicator in normal times, then in times of crisis it will be even worse. There should be alternative emergency communications systems.

5. I have identified some good research and a few books regarding this area. I looked at the university's catalogues and databases using 'crisis communications' as a keyword. I should not have much problem regarding theory. There are also some tourism-specific books and articles on the issue.

6. I have not yet come across any clear strategy for DMOs.

7. I will aim to integrate communication theories and current best practice, which I will identify through secondary and primary research, and develop a clear crisis communications strategy for a DMO.

It is evident that the student will go to the supervisor with some good ideas regarding this research. The information used came mainly from daily news, and the research undertaken in the library and the electronic databases was just a 'quick browse', probably on titles and not on content. At this stage, this is sufficient. As the student progresses – with appropriate supervisor guidance – the above 'rationale' will be refined and become the basis of a statement of purpose with both aim and objectives being clearly articulated in the research proposal.

The role of the supervisor

One of the most important ingredients in the recipe for success regarding a research project is the research supervisor. Depending of the institution's policy, the supervisor will either be assigned to you or you will have to negotiate supervision of the research project with several potential supervisors. In the latter case, you need to identify candidates for the research project supervision, considering their specialisms and their willingness to supervise such a topic. It is preferable for the supervisor to have some expertise in the research area, but other factors also need to be considered.

The first and most important of these is the supervisor's research activity. A research-active supervisor is knowledgeable regarding research methodology and data collection techniques, and will be better able to guide you through the research process. A research-active supervisor may also provide better networking access to the industry for primary research. On the downside, a research-active supervisor may have limited time for tutorials, and you will have to manage your research around your supervisor's availability – a compromise that needs to be carefully considered.

A second factor that needs to be considered is compatibility. Research supervision is a relationship that may last for a long time, and thus the right 'chemistry' is important. If at the first exploratory meeting you cannot detect this 'chemistry', then perhaps you should look for another supervisor.

The role of the supervisor is akin to that of a training coach – he or she is not there to teach you, but to help you develop your knowledge on the topic and your research skills. Supervisors will provide guidance in clarifying the research questions, finding ways to address possible gaps in your knowledge on the topic, developing a conceptual framework for your research, and deciding on methodology and data collection techniques. They will advise you on how to approach the analysis of the findings, but you need to know where the line is drawn: supervisors will neither conduct the research themselves nor write the research report or dissertation on your behalf!

The supervisor will warn you if the research is going off-course or becomes problematic and, in order to do so, needs to see and discuss your work-in-progress. Therefore, both parties will need to agree on some ground rules for the supervision, the frequency of meetings, and agendas that will make guidance and production of work more effective. Certain institutions have very strict regulations regarding the time each student is allocated for supervision. You should therefore make the most of it by being on time for your tutorials, and being prepared for them. In preparation for a tutorial, you may consider some of the issues presented in Box 1.5.

Box 1.5	Issues for consideration prior to meeting your supervisor

- What questions arising from your current stage of research work do you need to ask?
- What problems do you feel might emerge as the research progresses?
- What are the outcomes you would like to achieve from this meeting (for example, clarification of a concept you do not understand; assurance that you are 'on the right track'; feedback on a piece of work you submitted last week; advice on a problem, etc.)?
- What should the next steps/stages of you research be?

The supervisor is not the only support resource in your research experience. Increasingly, institutions encourage – either by providing online communication platforms or by organizing research-related social events – the creation of 'communities of practice' that eventually lead to peer support and collaborative learning. You will always benefit from discussing and sharing your research experiences, problems and frustrations with other researchers, regardless of whether this is done formally or informally.

The international researcher

Every aspect of your research journey has a subjective quality, and who you are cannot be divorced from what you are researching and the way you are doing it. According to Hofstede (1993: 82), 'management scientists, theorists and writers are human too: they grew up in a particular society in a particular period and their ideas cannot but reflect the constraints of their environment'. Your personality is involved in everything to do with your research project, from the definition of the research problem to the design and execution of the research and the analysis and writing-up of the project. Different 'researcher personalities' have a different impact on decisions made and practices during the various stages of the research journey. Your 'researcher personality' will also come into play when you relate to other groups or individuals in the research process (supervisors, fellow-researchers, respondents, etc.). It is mainly influenced by the following five factors, which you will need to take into consideration when conducting your research:

1. Your cultural background
2. Your age and gender
3. Your experience (both research and work experience)
4. Your educational background
5. Your learning style.

One of your first tasks when embarking on a research project is to reflect on these five elements of your personality and identify where they can be advantageous or disadvantageous in your research. If they are disadvantageous, you will need to be able to 'manage' them in order to minimize their influence.

Your cultural background may have an impact on your research design, from research philosophy to the choice of data collection techniques. For example, if you come from a culture with a high power distance rating (i.e. your culture accepts some power inequalities and places a large importance on societal hierarchies), you may find it difficult to employ data collection techniques that involve direct (face-to-face) contact with high-ranking officials in governments or companies. This is not a problem in itself, as long as you choose a research approach that is more appropriate for both your topic and you – and your supervisor will be there to help you do that. However, your cultural background may also limit your ability to study other cultures objectively during fieldwork, and your supervisor will not be there to help you with this. You must realize that the very nature of hospitality and tourism companies is international, and the first step for good research is an awareness of the socio-cultural knowledge of your participants. A major part of your preparation for the fieldwork will be to understand what socio-cultural knowledge the participants bring to and generate in your area of study. This is particularly important when you are aiming to represent your participants' voices as authentically as possible, because you will need to reach some degree of 'intimacy' with their cultural background. In order for your research to be successful, your relationship with them will not involve only the transfer of knowledge but also the creation of knowledge through the understanding and analysis of the data that you will collect, as well as of the persons who have supplied you with this data. In his book on interviews, Spradley (1979: 9) argues that a large part of any culture consists of tacit knowledge:

> *We all know things that we cannot talk about or express in direct ways. The researcher must therefore make inferences about what people know by listening carefully to what they say, by observing their behaviour, and by studying artefacts and the way they are used.*

Adaptation is therefore required, with every participant, to minimize the 'cultural distance' between them and yourself. This cultural adaptation will also help you to reduce (if not completely avoid) any possible ethnocentric bias in the interpretation of your findings. A good method for developing this skill is to try and work with fellow researchers from different cultural backgrounds in developing your research proposal and theirs. This will give you an insight into different cultures, and also the opportunity to obtain more 'expert' guidance on how to undertake research with participants from different cultural backgrounds.

Both your age and your gender will play an important role in accessing particular participant groups, especially when your research involves face-to-face interviews or observations. There is nothing wrong with being a young researcher – on the contrary, youth may give you the enthusiasm and energy to pull off research tasks that are more difficult for older age-groups. However, a problem arises when potential respondents wonder whether you are old enough and serious enough for them to share information with you. Being a young researcher working with experienced and high-ranking respondents may imply a high level of inequality in terms of status, power and influence (Welch *et al.*, 2002). On the other hand, youth gives you the chance to ask more provocative and even 'naive' questions that will help you in a deeper understanding of the research topic.

Your gender may also influence access, as well as the quality of responses to be collected. In certain cultures, being a male researcher gives you a certain freedom of movement and opportunities that would not be available to female researchers; in others, the exact opposite may be true. In recent years there has been a series of reports and works, from both male and female researchers, reporting the influence of the researcher's gender on the research process in fieldwork. Williams and Heikes (1993: 281) note that same-gender (researcher–respondent) interviews yield better results, based on 'the intuitive notion that rapport is more easily achieved', whereas in different gender contexts the 'respondents assume different shared experiences with a male and a female researcher'.

Although your age and gender are factors that may influence your research, there is not much you can do about this other than taking these factors into consideration, anticipating any limitations and planning your research accordingly. Seasoned researchers are facing similar problems, but, as Chapman (1992: 46) argues:

> *No matter what {a researcher} does, he cannot become a woman if he is a man or a man if she is a woman. He cannot, by the same token, be old if he is young or young if he is old.*

Experience of the industry and previous research will give you more confidence and will influence your choice of research design in terms of data collection and sampling techniques. Approaches and methods you have tried before and with which you are familiar will probably guide your decisions regarding the project in hand. Previous professional experience will probably help you in building a better rapport with your respondents, and your fieldwork may yield significantly richer data. However, depending on the context and country of research, you will need to be cautious in how obvious your experience or lack of it is. In certain national contexts it may be more effective for you to appear to be less experienced and allow the respondents to 'teach' you how things are, rather than being seen as a 'threatening expert' – which will make the respondents more reluctant to open up. On the other hand, experience often leads to preconceptions that may influence your findings and leave you with an uninterested, outside perspective. The more familiar you are with a research context, the more likely you are to take it for granted and to run the risk of becoming less context-sensitive.

Previous education clearly influences choices and tendencies in the research approach and design. Anecdotal evidence suggests that students with an educational background strong in numeracy tend to choose a more positivist approach in their research, focusing on highly structured research methodologies and quantifiable research that lends itself to statistical analysis. On the other hand, students from education systems that do not favour debate or the challenging of existing concepts and focus more on textbook memorization have difficulty in using qualitative approaches that involve the discovery of 'what lies beneath'. A background that is based on the Confucian tradition, focusing on the group rather than the individual, will foster a more collaborative approach in undertaking a research project, whereas the Western, individualistic model of education will render the researcher more like a 'lonely cowboy'. Your educational background will have somehow influenced, if not completely shaped, the last and certainly not the least factor of your 'researcher personality' – your learning style or learning preference. Whether you are an activist, a reflector, a theorist or a pragmatist, the research journey will take you through all the stages of Kolb's (1984) experiential learning cycle:

- When you are working on your literature review you are trying to sense and understand the theory ('abstract conceptualization'), and are applying your theorist skills.
- When you are planning your research design, contacting your participants and collecting and analysing your data, you will be personally involved with your research project, achieving a 'concrete experience' from it using your activist learning skills.
- When you are reflecting ('reflective observation') on your concrete and theory-building experiences as an individual, or discussing with your fellow researchers issues related to data collection, analysis, interpretation and presentation, you will be applying your reflector learning skills.
- When you are testing your research design and piloting your data collection tools ('active experimentation'), you will be using your pragmatist learning skills.
- When you have distilled these reflections and are starting to build and refine theories, moving from the particular research context to drawing conclusions about the sector and making generalizations for the industry ('abstract conceptualization'), you are again applying your theorist skills.

You will probably excel in the areas that are more suited to your own learning preferences, but you will most certainly have to develop learning abilities related to the other areas of Kolb's cycle as well.

Summary

- Research in hospitality and tourism is generally undertaken in order to disclose and make sense of existing patterns of behaviour and phenomena within the industry, to identify new and better ways of managing businesses, and to enable academics to educate future practitioners better.
- You are asked to undertake research projects in order for you to develop and display the 'higher-order thinking' skills. Apart from testing your self-discipline and time-management skills, the research process helps you to learn how to formulate questions, clearly identify and define problems, methodically plan ways to find answers, collect and analyse data, draw conclusions from those data, and share your findings with other researchers, scholars and practitioners.
- The main sources for generating ideas for research are your personal aspirations, your experience of the industry, looking at industry trends, reading existing research and seeking advice from an active researcher.
- The research topic should be within your reach and ability regarding investigation, and you should carefully consider the time allowed for the project, as well as access and resource constraints.
- A good starting point for your research is to draft a short title for the project – what is commonly termed a 'working title'. The next step is to develop the rationale of your study, where you will justify the research topic selection. You may begin by explaining what attracted your attention to this particular research area, and continue by identifying the 'gap' in the literature and how your study is going to fill it.
- Your project supervisor is similar to a training coach. Supervisors are not there to teach you, but to help, guide and advise you on how to develop your knowledge regarding the topic, and also your research skills.
- The research journey is not one that you have to take alone. You will always benefit from discussing and sharing your research experiences, problems and frustrations with fellow researchers.
- Your personality is involved in everything that has to do with your research project, from the definition of the research problem, to the design and execution of your research. This 'researcher personality' is shaped by your cultural and educational background, your preferred learning styles, your gender and age, and your professional and research experience.

Student experiences

Victoria, a student from Uganda, shares her experience regarding topic selection and how to manage the researcher–supervisor relationship.

Selecting a dissertation topic

My experience shows that prior knowledge or personal interest might facilitate decision-making, while consultations with the supervisor ensure precision and a clearer perception.

My choice of research topic was primarily motivated by the state of affairs in the tourism industry in my country. The growing importance of tourism had a big impact on my decision to pursue research related to Uganda. With the improved political climate, records indicated that tourism industry in Uganda had taken over from coffee production and commerce as the top foreign exchange earner. Yet, being an agricultural country, the main focus of the local government is still the agricultural sector, and therefore the tourism industry is likely to face challenges in developing with limited resources as tourism expands worldwide. Facts such as Uganda having the highest Total Entrepreneurial Activity (TEA) according to the Global Entrepreneurship Monitor (GEM) in 2003, and hosting the Commonwealth Heads of Government Meeting (CHOGM) in 2007, prompted me to raise questions about who was responsible for the successful exploitation of tourism in the country, and how it was managed and maintained. As you can see, it was not difficult to define my broad research area as tourism development planning in Uganda.

Razak, a student from Egypt, illustrates some of his misconceptions and the realities of dissertation supervision from a student perspective.

The relationship with my supervisor

When I started my research journey, I thought I would have all the support from my supervisors. I was brought up and educated in Egypt, in an education system where students are very dependent on their tutors for their learning. I would describe this as a static learning experience, with the knowledge flow coming only from the tutor's side, and based on individual reading. It was a cultural fact that nobody among the students could question the tutor's views, let alone the published material. There was also indirect control over what students learned and what they could not learn, by tutors telling students that one or two key books would be enough for them to succeed. The recipe for success was crystal clear: listen to your tutors carefully, follow their instructions and read the suggested one or two sources. What a change it was when I got here to study my MSc in the UK. I remember my first meeting with my supervisors like yesterday. 'How does your reading from various sources inform your research idea?' asked my supervisors. My immediate reaction was: 'What sources are you referring to? I have this important book, which I thought will be sufficient. I can tell you what it says and you tell me how you think my reading informs the research idea'.

At the beginning, I never thought that I would be expected to be 'that' independent – and, more importantly, I never thought that I would be expected to challenge the views of other people and come up with my own ideas and perspectives, or to introduce a way forward. Undertaking a research project, in particular a master's dissertation, is a lonely process, and success is strongly dependent upon the performance of the researcher. Strong reliance on the supervision team or someone else throughout the process is not a solution. I have learnt the importance of being strong throughout the research process, and to 'stand on my own two feet'. It is, however, always important to have an experienced researcher around who has been through the same process. This is particularly important in terms of receiving mental support, as well as constructive comments about the dynamics of the research process.

The entire research process was an unstructured, 'garbage-can' journey, which involved a great deal of complexity and ambiguity because of the differences between my expectations and the expectations of my supervisor. My relationship with my supervisor was like a 'dynamic game' throughout the research process. Many times during the research process I wished that I had a supervisor who was familiar with my cultural background and could understand my expectations. I even wished that I had a supervisor of the same country of origin. However, thinking about it now, I think it is particularly important to have a supervisor from a different background and to receive advice from people with different areas of expertise, because this brings multi-dimensional and rich insights into the research project. You, however, need to manage the differences between yourself and the supervisor, and to balance your views in such a way that maximum benefit can be obtained. This requires regular meetings with a positive and open manner that can facilitate the communication and understanding between the parties. To sum this up, please try to understand the expectations of the academic world in the country where you do your research, put yourselves into the shoes of your supervisor, and never hesitate to ask them politely to do the same!

Throughout the research process I made a lot of mistakes. Particularly during the early stages of the research process, every researcher feels anxious because he or she hesitates so as not to make mistakes. It is, however, important to know that making mistakes because of naivety is not something researchers should feel anxious or embarrassed about. Everyone makes mistakes, and this is how everyone learns. I had a mixture of different feelings throughout the research process. The most commonly experienced feeling was 'why can't I do it? Is there something wrong with me or with my supervisor?' It is, however, important for a researcher not to underestimate his or her abilities. Trust yourself, and feel confident with what you think and you do. More importantly, consider the strengths and advantages of coming from a particular country and nation and of bringing your national culture into the research process.

Exercise: your preferred approach to research

Different researchers will naturally be inclined towards different methods because of their diverse researcher personalities. As a means of helping you to evaluate your own preferred style, we include here a self-assessment questionnaire for you to complete. Please note that the analysis that follows is only indicative of possible preferences, and should be considered in the light of your own knowledge about yourself. Hopefully this will prompt you to think about the type of research approaches you might prefer to use.

Answer the following questions and record the score that relates to each of your answers.

	Strongly agree	Agree	Disagree	Strongly disagree
I like to work in areas where there are clear, precise answers	1	2	3	4
I am comfortable meeting and talking to new people	4	3	2	1
I like working with numbers	1	2	3	4
I prefer working with words and language rather than numbers	4	3	2	1
I like to reduce issues to clear cause-and-effect relationships	1	2	3	4
I am happy working in areas where there is uncertainty	4	3	2	1
All issues can be looked at objectively and dispassionately	1	2	3	4
I am good at exploring issues with people	4	3	2	1
I enjoy finding questions as much as I enjoy finding answers	4	3	2	1
Homeopathy is unproven rubbish	1	2	3	4

Source: Adapted from Gill and Johnson, 1997

Calculate the total score for your self-assessment, and then check your result against the following interpretations:

The higher your score within the 30–40 band, the more you are suited to exploring different research problems with people by direct interaction and face-to-face discussion.

The lower your score within the 10–20 band, the more you are inclined towards desk research involving reading, contemplation and thinking. If you do choose desk research, you are likely to lean towards more scientific research involving numbers and statistical analysis.

If you have scored between 20 and 30, you are probably more flexible in your preferred approaches to research. If you scored within this band, total your scores for statements 1–6:

- Scores of between 6 and 11 indicate a preference for methods that require less direct interaction and communication with people
- Scores of between 18 and 24 indicate a preference for methods that involve face-to-face communication and interaction with people.

Review questions

1. What are the three principal purposes of hospitality and tourism research?
2. What, in your view are the main triggers for hospitality and tourism research?
3. Outline the eight characteristics of a research project.
4. A colleague wishes to conduct her research in the area of corporate social responsibility. What sources would you recommend in order to generate some research ideas and select a more specific topic within this area?
5. You are interested in undertaking research on Internet applications in small rural hotels. How would you filter your research ideas to come up with a viable research topic?
6. Using the questions in Box 1.4, try to develop a rationale for the topic of search-engine optimization in the tourism industry.

References

Botterill, D. (2003). *Linking Teaching and Research Workshop*, University of Wales Institute, Cardiff (UWIC). Available at http://www.hlst.heacademy.ac.uk/projects/linking_staff.pdf (accessed 12 May 2006).

Boyer, E. L. (1990). *Scholarship Reconsidered: Priorities of the Professoriate*. Princeton, NJ: The Carnegie Foundation for the Advancement of Teaching.

Brander Brown, J. and Atkinson, H. (2001). Budgeting in the information age: a fresh approach. *International Journal of Contemporary Hospitality Management*, 13(3), 136–143.

Brew, A. (1999). 'Research and Scholarship as Models for University Teaching'. Paper presented at the Conference of the European Association for Research in Education. Gothenburg, Sweden, August.

Burgess, C. and Bryant, K. (2001). Revenue management – the contribution of the finance function to profitability. *International Journal of Contemporary Hospitality Management*, 13(3), 144–150.

Calof, J. L. and Beamish, P. W. (1994). The right attitude for international success. *Business Quarterly*, Autumn, 105–110.

Chakravarthy, S. B. and Perlmutter, V. H. (1985). Strategic planning for a global business. *Columbia Journal of World Business*, 10(2), 3–10.

Chapman, M. (1992). Fieldwork, language and locality in Europe, from the North. In: J. Pina-Cabral and J. Campbell (eds), *Europe Observed*. London: Macmillan, pp. 39–55.

Clark, M., Riley, M., Wood, R. C. and Wilkie, E. (1998). *Researching and Writing Dissertations in Hospitality and Tourism*. London: International Thomson Business Press.

Cooper, C., Shephard, R. and Westlake, J. (1996). *Educating the Educators in Tourism: a manual of tourism and hospitality education*. Madrid: The World Tourism Organization.

Doyle, A. C. (1887; 2001 edition). *A Study in Scarlet*. Harmondsworth: Penguin.

Gill, J. and Johnson, P. (1997). *Research Methods for Managers*. London: Paul Chapman Publishing Ltd.

Glesne, C. and Peshkin, A. (1991). *Becoming Qualitative Researchers: An Introduction*. New York, NY: Longman Publishing Group.

HEA – HLST (Higher Education Academy – Hospitality, Leisure, Sport and Tourism) (2006). *Linking Teaching and Research*, Resource Guide. Available at http://www.hlst.ltsn.ac.uk/Resources/linking.pdf (accessed 10 June 2006).

Healey, M., Jordan, F., Pell, B. and Short, C. (2003). 'The Student Experience of Research and Consultancy in a New University'. Paper presented at SEDA/SRHE Conference on The Scholarship of Academic and Staff Development: Research, Evaluation and Changing Practice. University of Bristol, April.

Hofstede, G. (1993). Cultural constraints in management theories. *The Academy of Management Executive*, 7(1), 81–94.

Kim, H. J., Gursoy, D. and Lee, S. (2006). The impact of the 2002 World Cup on South Korea: comparisons of pre- and post-games. *Journal of Tourism Management*, 27(1), 86–96.

Kolb, D. A. (1984). *Experiential Learning: Experience as the Source of Learning and Development*. Englewood Cliffs, NJ: Prentice Hall.

Krakhmal V. (2006). Customer profitability in a hotel context. In: P. Harris and M. Mongiello (eds), *Accounting and Financial Management: Developments in the International Hospitality Industry*. Oxford: Butterworth-Heinemann, pp. 188–210.

Kuhn, S. T. (1962). *The Structure of Scientific Revolutions*. Chicago, IL: University of Chicago Press.

Leedy, P. and Ormrod, J. (2005). *Practical Research: Planning and Design*, 8th edn. Upper Saddle River, NJ: Pearson Education International.

Lewis, A. and Smith, D. (1993). Defining higher order thinking. *Theory into Practice*, 32(3), 131–137.

Lubbe, S. (2004). From postgrad to professional: useful tips for choosing and executing a doctoral thesis. *Electronic Journal of Business Research Methods*, 2(2), 129–134.

Miller, G. (2001). Corporate responsibility in the UK tourism industry. *Tourism Management*, 22(6), 589–598.

Proust, M. (1923). *The Captive*, Vol. 5 of *Remembrance of Things Past*. Translated from the French by C. K. Scott Moncrieff. Available at http://gutenberg.net.au/ebooks03/0300501.txt (accessed 25 June 2006).

Roper, A., Brookes, M., Price, L. and Hampton, A. (1997). Towards an understanding of centricity: profiling international hotel groups. *Progress in Tourism and Hospitality Research*, 3(3), 199–211.

Saunders, M., Lewis, P. and Thornhill, A. (2007). *Research Methods for Business Students*. London: Prentice Hall Financial Times.

Seaton, A. V. (1996). From thanatopsis to thanatourism: guided by the dark. *International Journal of Heritage Studies*, 2, 234–244.

Seaton, A. V. (1999). War and thanatourism: Waterloo 1815–1914. *Annals of Tourism Research*, 26, 130–159.

Seaton, A. V. (2002). Thanatourism's final frontiers? Visits to cemeteries, churchyards and funerary sites as sacred and secular pilgrimage. *Tourism Recreation Research*, 27, 73–82.

Spradley, J. (1979). *The Ethnographic Interview*. Toronto: Holt, Rinehart and Winston.

Taylor, S. and Edgar, D. (1996). Hospitality research: the Emperor's new clothes? *International Journal of Hospitality Management*, 15(3), 211–227.

Tribe, J. (2004). The 4Ps of research: Practice, Policy, Principles and Positioning (editorial). *Journal of Hospitality, Leisure, Sport and Tourism Education*, 3(1), 1–4.

Tung, R. L. (2005). Perspectives – new era, new realities: musings on a new research agenda . . . from an old timer. *Asia Pacific Journal of Management*, 22(2), 143–157.

Tung, R. L. (2006). North American research agenda and methodologies: past imperfect, future – limitless possibilities. *Asian Business and Management*, 5(1), 23–35.

Welch, C., Marschan-Piekkari, R., Penttinen, H. and Tahvanainen, M. (2002). Corporate elites as informants in qualitative international business research. *International Business Review*, 11(5), 611–628.

Williams, C. L. and Heikes, E. J. (1993). The importance of researcher's gender in the in-depth interview: evidence from two case studies of male nurses. *Gender and Society*, 7(2), 280–291.

Chapter 2
Developing academic reading skills

To read without reflecting is like eating without digesting.

(Edmund Burke, Irish political philosopher; 1729–1797)

Academics (and also sometimes practitioners in the field of hospitality and tourism management) produce articles and research notes with the intention of informing those interested in largely intellectual, but sometimes practical, problems or debates about new work in these areas. They also introduce new perspectives on received knowledge that contribute either to the solving of a particular problem or to a furtherance of the debate. Such scholarly writing is what constitutes academic papers (Brown, 2006), and academic reading is the essence of one of the most crucial elements in research: the enrichment of the 'body of knowledge'.

Why academic reading?

Reading is the most critical part of the learning process. Although reading often appears to students to be the most boring and daunting of tasks, we all know that the benefits outweigh the pain. You can expand your vision by developing a number of intellectual and analytical thinking skills through coming into contact with views and opinions that you may have been unaware of. Your ideas for your research project, in particular, will come mainly from your reading. Innovative concepts originate with the 'spark' of an idea that suggests how apparently disparate entities may connect. Perhaps in your reading you will identify a problem that consumers are experiencing in the hospitality and tourism sectors when they visit a destination, stay in a hotel and/or have their meals in a restaurant. Maybe you will then read about something in another industry – for example, employee training in the car manufacturing industry – and you will tweak it a little and find that it forms a basis for your research into employee training in the catering sector. Wide reading expands your perspectives and helps you to make connections and think innovatively.

Reading is not only a source of new ideas; it is also a way to combine input with existing ideas. For example, in developing a rationale for your hospitality franchising research project, your research might indicate that it is still not known what franchise organizations do when it comes to identifying franchising opportunities and selecting franchise partners in different country markets. Further reading might show that, in particular, there appears to have been hardly any research into the decision-making criteria used in identifying franchise opportunities and selecting franchise partners across different national borders. However, your reading also shows that although franchising literature does not elucidate these issues, joint venture partnership literature explains how prospective partners are selected for a joint venture partnership, and that these methods have not yet been applied to the international franchise context. You can then 'cross-fertilize' the joint venture partnership and franchising literature and evaluate the interplay between franchising and prospective partner recruitment. Here is your 'enrichment of the body of knowledge'! Reading should therefore be seen as an exercise in analytical thinking, as training for challenging ideas and testing frameworks – in other words, for developing the skills required for a successful research journey.

How do you know you have a paper worth reading?

Students who are in the early stages of the research process are under a lot of pressure to do a lot of reading. However, academic reading is not a matter of quantity, but rather of quality. It requires taking an organized approach, and there are skills you need to develop.

It is unrealistic to expect that you can read everything, and you will not be doing justice to yourself if you attempt to, given the pressure of other deadlines and the limited time available. You therefore need to read selectively. This raises a key question: what are the selection criteria or scanning criteria that you can use to decide what you need to take from the text? The answer is to revisit your targets. If you are writing a dissertation, you need to ask yourself again what your research question is. If you are writing an assignment for a hospitality and tourism management module, you need to revisit the learning outcomes of the module and the overall purpose of the assignment. What are you expected to achieve? These should be the lenses through which you select and view your texts, and then underline key words and phrases and make appropriate notes as you read.

How do you know whether a particular academic paper is worth reading until you are well into the reading of it? You can do this by looking at three parts of the article in advance:

1. The abstract, which, according to convention, should tell the reader what the paper is about, what the author did to deal with the topic in question, how the results were ascertained, and what the findings mean in the general or specific scheme of things (Brown, 2006).
2. The introduction, usually the first one or two pages of the paper, which outlines the 'promises' of the author(s) to the readers. These promises are based on three key questions, which the introduction should answer:
   - What, in summary, does the existing research tell us?
   - What, in summary, does the existing research not tell us?
   - Where are the conceptual and/or empirical research gaps in the subject area under investigation? In other words, what are the deficiencies in the existing research, and what are the authors proposing to do in order to fill in these research gaps? What are they promising to achieve through their research aims?
3. The conclusion, which is where the authors of the paper revisit their overall aim and remind themselves of what they promised the reader at the outset of the

paper. Authors make every effort to convince the reader that their paper is worth reading because it generates new ideas and knowledge and contributes further to already existing knowledge. This is where authors answer the 'so what?' and 'what is unique about this research?' questions.

Reading the paper

Knowing the vocabulary associated with hospitality and tourism management is essential, but understanding the conventional layout of an academic paper is also a great help. Academic papers are written according to very concrete conventions, and these conventions are the 'roadmap' for both authors and readers.

The conventional structure of an academic paper is as follows:

- Title
- Abstract
- Introduction (including statement of research problem/aims)
- Background to/context of the research
- Literature review
- Research design
- Findings/discussion of findings
- Conclusions and implications.

Title

The title should give a good indication of what the paper is about. Depending on the journal, the title may either be concise and about eight words long, or it may have a first part followed by a colon and then a longer, more explanatory phrase (Brown, 2006: 109).

Abstract

The title gives an indication of what the paper is about; the abstract has to do far more. A good abstract will help you to decide whether or not the paper is relevant to your (research) needs, and thus whether you should bother to read the rest of it. It highlights the reason(s) for writing the paper, and the aim of the research. The abstract also explains how the overall aim is achieved, and includes the main method(s) used for the research. Here you can see the author's approach to the investigation of the topic. For example, the research might involve 'desk research' incorporating a review of different theories and concepts and synthesizing existing ideas, or it might involve collecting data by using different data collection techniques (which will be discussed in Chapter 6).

It is also expected that the author will report on what was discovered during the course of the work, in terms of analysis, discussion or results. In the conclusion to the abstract, the author should underline what is 'new' about the work. This is to demonstrate who the paper is for, and how it is of value. Depending on the style of the journal, sometimes authors are also asked to state the research outcomes and their implications for practitioners. In such cases we might also expect a short statement of what changes to practice are recommended (or have been implemented) as a result of the paper.

Introduction

This section of the paper is the reader's 'roadmap' or 'route planner'. It is often a sophisticated signpost indicating where you are heading as a reader. The research problem is generally stated, and the aims of the research are listed. The last paragraph of this section will often inform you of what is included in the chapter, and how it is divided into sections.

As already stated, the introduction is the section where the authors 'make a promise'. This part of the paper is like a contract between the authors and the reader. The authors give an assurance that, through prior investigation, they have identified relevant research gaps. Having identified these gaps, they promise that at least some of them will be filled by introducing the context, reviewing the literature, discussing the methodology, sharing and exploring findings and drawing conclusions. It is extremely important that we understand what the authors of the paper are promising to deliver; if not, we will be unable to understand whether the promise has been delivered or not when they finally deliver their conclusions.

The background to/context of the research

The research may concern a country, company, or industry/sector of which you have little or no knowledge. Reading the 'background' section should enable you to have a better grasp of the situation that gave rise to the research, or the 'real world' location into which the research problem might fit. Take the example in Box 2.1: many people might not know where Cyprus is, or they may know only that it is a warm and sunny island! This might be adequate when making up your mind about where to spend your next holiday; however, it is not enough to understand the political dimensions of tourism planning and development on the island. Altinay and Bowen (2006) therefore introduce some background information about the island, including geography, history and tourism, and its contribution to the economies of North and South Cyprus. The authors' intention is to position the 'research' within a real-world context for you.

The literature review

Reading the abstract and the introduction should give you an overall idea regarding the content of the paper. This, however, should not stop you having a quick look at the other sections of the paper, such as the literature review. There are circumstances where the literature review may be relevant even if the paper in question does not have direct relevance to your own research. For example, if you are undertaking research about customer satisfaction in the hospitality and tourism industry, it is very likely that customer loyalty papers will review the literature on customer satisfaction. Similarly, if your research concerns service quality, it is very likely that customer-satisfaction related papers will include mention of service quality. It is therefore very important that you, as a researcher, do some detective work and consider every possibility whilst doing your reading and looking at how to connect ideas and concepts.

Let's put this another way: if you were an architect and we asked you to help us build a house in an earthquake zone – for example in San Francisco, Istanbul or Athens – what would be your major concern, and how would you deal with it? The answer is simple. If you were building a house in an earthquake zone, you would need to make sure that the foundations of the house were strong and solid. This is

Box 2.1	Analysing the introduction to a paper

Altinay and Bowen's (2006) paper, entitled *Politics and Tourism Interface: The Case of Cyprus*, is about tourism planning in a potentially federal Cyprus. It may serve as an illustration for you to judge whether the authors did their homework well.

In the introduction, the authors offer a summary of the existing research into this subject. Having reviewed the extant literature, they argue that previous research focuses on the difficulties of tourism planning and development arising from the political power struggle between different stakeholder groups in a single destination. Then, as a second step, they identify the deficiencies in the existing research. They argue that limited research exists regarding the political power struggle between stakeholder groups of different nationalities in a single destination. Such is the case in Cyprus – the focus of their work. More specifically, they argue that there is no research to date that investigates the possible power struggle between Turkish-Cypriot and Greek-Cypriot tourism stakeholder groups in the case of a federal solution – with important implications for tourism planning and development. Finally, the authors propose to remedy the deficiencies in existing knowledge and present their 'promise' by setting out as the purpose of their paper the investigation of the potential influence of politics and nationalism on tourism planning and development in the event of a United Republic of Cyprus with a federal constitution.

It is important to note in the introduction of this paper the 'roadmap' offered to the reader. In the last paragraph of the introduction, the authors state that first the paper will review existing literature on political federation and tourism, the role of politics on tourism planning, and the influence of nationalism on tourism. Secondly, based on their primary research, the paper will detail and analyse the effects of federation, the distribution of power, and the role of different nationality-based tourism stakeholder groups in tourism planning and development. Finally, the paper will evaluate and project future likely scenarios.

how authors think of their dissertations and academic papers. The house can be a metaphor for a dissertation/academic paper, and the foundations a metaphor for the literature review. Just as you cannot conceive of a house without foundations, you should not be considering a dissertation without a sound and well-developed literature review.

The literature review, if well written, is a critical appraisal of issues and factors, ideas and opinions, and the results of research that others have undertaken in the same area. A good literature review is not just a description of previous work; it also appraises, compares and contrasts it with other relevant work, and with the authors' own work. This is the section that will provide you with references which, if followed up, will widen your knowledge and stimulate independent thought (Brown, 2006: 110). It will broaden your knowledge of the area of interest, and do so in a critical manner, so that you have what you need to form your own viewpoint. The authors will have taken ideas, opinions, or models from others authors in related fields and incorporated these into the research, and a well-written paper will high-light the commonalities and differences found between them.

Box 2.2 illustrates analysis of the literature review, again looking at the paper by Altinay and Bowen (2006).

Box 2.2	Analysing the literature review

In their paper, Altinay and Bowen (2006) review three conceptual areas: federation, tourism planning, and nationalism. The authors consider, compare and evaluate a number of ideas from different authors in these areas. If you were to undertake research on federation, tourism planning, and nationalism, these sections of the paper would provide you with references that, if followed up, would widen your knowledge and stimulate your thinking.

For example, when discussing the views of different authors regarding the tourism planning process, Altinay and Bowen maintain that tourism planning is a pluralistic process in which people should have equal access to economic and political resources. They then relate their review of different authors' ideas to their own research, and argue that the idea of a pluralistic process is especially relevant in their study of the interface of tourism and politics in Cyprus because it strikes at the core of the debate (and struggle) between the Turkish-Cypriot and Greek-Cypriot viewpoints regarding the distribution of economic and political resources.

While reading the literature review, you will need to identify the authors' way of thinking – how they develop and support their argumentation. One way of doing this is to draw a 'sketch' of the ideas and arguments in the literature review by continuously asking 'why?' questions and identifying the linkages between different themes in the literature review. In evaluating the relevance of the literature review, you will need to assess whether your reading of this section will enable you to answer your research questions and achieve your research objectives. You can classify the arguments presented in a literature review according to whether they confirm or contradict your own arguments. In any case, studying the paper will almost certainly have been worthwhile, since it will have stimulated your thinking and broadened your perspectives in some way.

Research design

A good paper will include a section that discusses how the research was carried out. This is sometimes called the methodology or research-design section. A good research-design section can teach you a great deal. It might (and some say that it should) describe both the authors' research strategy (case study, ethnography, survey etc.) and their research methods – who the population is; who makes up the sample, how the sample was chosen from the population and why; who the data were collected from and why they were collected like that; how the data were interpreted or analysed and why those methods were chosen; and what was discovered.

More importantly, the research-design section provides the authors' justification for the chosen research design and methods for a particular topic. For example, if your research is about the impacts of crises on tourism destinations or the crisis recovery strategies of a particular destination, such as China, the research-design sections of articles about crisis management can be good research-design sources and give you ideas about methods for your own research that you might not have considered before reading the papers. A good research-design section will enable you to go out and undertake the research yourself, should you wish to do so.

When you are reading this section, you should expect to see the following points discussed:

- The research approach and/or strategy, and why these were appropriate for the investigation of the chosen topic
- Data collection techniques and their appropriateness for the chosen topic and the research setting
- The sample and the sampling strategy/technique – i.e. how the appropriate people have been chosen to help you to answer your research questions by their contributions (usually either by becoming an informant/respondent or by being observed)
- Analysis and presentation of findings (how the authors made sense of the findings and presented them in such a way that they managed to answer their research questions).

Findings

The findings may appear in two ways – either they are presented (often in the order of importance) and then in a further section discussed in detail in the light of the literature review; or a single finding is presented and immediately discussed in the light of the literature review, before the next finding is presented (Brown, 2006). When you are looking at the findings of an academic paper or dissertation, you need to ask yourselves the following questions:

- Do these findings confirm the existing literature (extant knowledge)? If the answer is yes, what are the similarities between these findings and previously published work in the field?
- Do these findings dis-confirm the existing literature (extant knowledge)? If yes, what are the dissimilarities between these findings and previously published work in the field?
- Do these findings go further than the existing literature (extant knowledge)? In other words, what is unique about these findings? Do they say anything that has not been said before? Do they provide a new angle or angles on specific phenomena? For example, a set of findings might provide new insights into relationship marketing from the employee perspective, as opposed to previous studies which have investigated relationship marketing solely from the customer perspective. Alternatively, the findings might provide interesting or even unique context-specific insights relating to a particular country or sector (airlines, hotels, pubs, restaurants, etc.). Similarly, the findings might provide new insights into tourism planning and the development of a destination. They might concern a country that has not yet been explored, or offer unique insights into a subject as highly specific as the emotional labour of airline crew in the airline industry.

You should bear in mind that there is no single manner or method of presentation of research findings. One form or method may be more appropriate than others for particular purposes and in particular situations. Regardless of the approach taken, researchers aim to develop themes and highlight patterns grounded in the data in a way that can be clearly understood by the readers of their papers.

We believe that, regardless of the approach to research, findings should be structured in such a way that they read like a story. However, we also know that findings are often presented in tables full of numbers – in what some people might term a 'scary' format. In such papers, the authors have assumed that the reader has the ability to read and interpret what the 'numbers' are indicating. Although they may appear intimidating, the numbers will tell you how similar things are, or how different; how they can be connected or grouped together, or in what ways they are distinct or separate (Brown, 2006: 111). If you do not want to disadvantage yourself, you need to put in the effort to understand what the numbers/tables are telling you. How will you know whether these findings have any relevance to your research, or relate to your work, if you ignore them?

Conclusions, recommendations for practitioners and further research

The last section of the paper should draw the threads of the paper's argument together, combining the aims (pointing out how they have been achieved), the findings and what has been discussed in the literature section in order to present a coherent finale (Brown, 2006: 111). The authors do not try to 'reinvent the wheel' here; all they do is deliver the promise given in the introduction section of the paper and make a 'minor' contribution to the body of knowledge on the subject. Some authors summarize the overall findings of the paper in the conclusions; however, such a summary does not address the fundamental 'so what?' question. Rather, it tends to result in repetition. This section should be more than a summary, and should synthesize the overall arguments presented in the paper, highlight meanings, and emphasize contributions to the field.

According to Easterby-Smith and colleagues (1991: 141), the contribution to knowledge that a piece of academic research may make to the field of management can take three principal forms:

> *as new knowledge about the world of management, as new theories and ideas, or as new methods of investigation. Ideally, it should contain some element of each, although one form may be dominant.*

These principles can also be applied to hospitality and tourism management academic papers. When writing an academic paper, authors are expected to include each of the elements mentioned above – and when you read a paper you should try to isolate all three. For example, a research paper might provide new knowledge about crisis management in tourism destinations by introducing a model and framework that could help destinations to signal and detect crises. Using a unique theoretical area (such as complexity theory) to interpret and understand the way in which destinations could signal and detect crisis can help the researcher to contribute to the existing crisis-management theories, which have so far treated crisis management as a rational, linear process. In addition, the researcher may use a research approach/method which has not been used before to investigate the crisis-management strategies of destinations. When reading a conclusion, you should therefore expect to find a full and proper answer to the 'so what?' question, since this is where the authors offer a summary of these basic elements.

In addition, and depending on the journal, hospitality and tourism papers often add policy implications section, providing advice to practitioners. This is the section in which user engagement and the benefits of the research for the practitioners (such as tourism managers, hospitality managers, tourism policy-makers and government representatives) are discussed. For example, a paper might introduce a set of criteria for franchisors that could be used to select partners in markets in different countries. As another example, a paper might give recommendations to hospitality managers about the training needs of employees.

Again depending on the journal, hospitality and tourism researchers are often encouraged to add a section or paragraph outlining areas for further research, and providing advice to researchers regarding any research gaps identified through their research. You might find this section useful when it comes to identifying gaps for your research and formulating your research questions. In simpler terms, what the authors of most papers do is say: 'this is what we have done and what we have found, but there are areas that need further investigation. Researchers who are interested in these areas can take them as research ideas and investigate them further'. So if you are undertaking research from scratch and looking for new research ideas, it is advisable to visit the last sections of the papers written in your topic areas.

Extracting value from your reading

Academic reading is different from other types of reading, and it is useful to develop strategies that will help you to identify and remember the most important information. You do not have to analyse every single word, if you know what you are looking for. In fact, reading with some specific points in mind will help to improve your understanding of the paper.

Find the claim

One of the keys to finding your way through specialized and often dense texts is to remember that somewhere early in the text authors need to tell the reader how their study contributes something original to the subject in question. It may be a correction of some past misunderstanding; it may be the inclusion of some consideration or variable that previous researchers have missed; it may be the application of a theory or concept in a new way or in a location where it has not previously been employed. Make it your first goal to find that claim. Once you discover that claim, you will be better able to understand the author's choices, and to evaluate the effectiveness of the argument. While trying to identify these subtle rhetorical statements, use the following questions to guide you:

- What question does the author pose? This might be implied rather than stated explicitly, so you may be looking for something not directly expressed in the text.
- What is the primary argument made by the author? Where do you first find this argument? Why is this argument significant?

Assess the strength/validity of the argument

Again, you will need to use your reading skills to uncover the nuances of the argument and to evaluate the paper's effectiveness in making claims and engaging with other positions. For example, notice how the authors introduce evidence in support of their claim. Do they simply say, 'Many researchers have argued unconvincingly that optimum service quality contributes to customer satisfaction', or do they engage with arguments of specific scholars with their own perspectives and interpretations of the subject area? It is important to note that authors are normally expected to describe the different positions and perspectives of researchers regarding a particular topic. So be aware of the relative effectiveness or ineffectiveness of the author's approach – according, of course, to the scope of the argument. When trying to identify the way in which the authors develop a case, use the following questions to help you sort out the building blocks of their argument.

1. Evidence:
   - What evidence do the authors offer in support of their position? (Identify all the evidence you find.)
   - What is the nature of each piece of supporting evidence – for example, is it based on empirical research, common knowledge or anecdote?
   - How convincing is the evidence – for example, does the research design adequately address the question posed? Are ethical considerations adequately explored and assessed? Have you read or heard anything on this subject that confirms or challenges the evidence?
2. Counter-arguments:
   - What arguments made in opposition to the authors' views were described?
   - Were these arguments persuasively refuted?
   - What evidence was used in the refutation?
3. Effectiveness:
   - What were the strengths of the article?
   - Was it difficult to read and understand? If so, why? If not, why not?
   - Were the ideas presented in an order that made sense?
   - Were the ideas grouped together into distinct paragraphs?
   - Did the authors begin the piece or the paragraph by introducing a new argument and starting the reader off in the right direction?
   - Did the authors end the piece or paragraph with a conclusion that summed up the point they wanted to make?
   - Was the authors' attitude clear – were they, for example, describing, suggesting or criticizing something?
   - Who was the intended audience?
   - Did you get a clear idea about the context (country, company) in which the research was carried out? Did all the material seem relevant to the points made?

In a sense, reading the paper – absorbing the words and the 'message' – is the easy bit. However, included in the notion of reading an academic paper is the element of evaluation – deciding on the paper's relevance to your research and its overall impact (Brown, 2006). When reading an academic paper, you have to bear in mind that you have to determine your intention – whether it is to gain knowledge, to confirm a suspicion, to add 'evidence' to an argument you are drawing up elsewhere, etc. – and the value you extract will depend on the degree to which your purpose has been fulfilled. For example, if you are in the early stages of your research process and your intention is to gain basic knowledge and develop an introductory understanding of the concepts, the introduction to the paper is the place where authors define concepts and highlight their importance for different parties or groups. Again, if you are writing a dissertation and/or assignment regarding customer satisfaction, it is most likely that you will find the definition of customer satisfaction and its importance for organizations in the introduction to the paper.

Using the same example, if you want to add evidence to an argument for your own literature review, the literature review section of a paper and the conclusions may help you to fulfil your purpose. For example, if you would like to confirm your suspicions concerning Japanese customers' satisfaction in restaurants, the literature review section of the relevant paper and/or its conclusions may well provide you with this confirmation.

A high-quality tourism and hospitality management paper adds to the body of knowledge and helps to develop new insights about the management of hospitality and tourism organizations or destinations. It has strong theoretical foundations, with appropriate examples and use of evidence to illustrate the arguments. It draws substantiated conclusions that give serious consideration to the 'so what?' question. Of course, as a reader, you will be the final judge of 'quality'. One day you might read a badly written paper with a wonderful idea that expands your horizons or alters your perspective; another day you may read a paper that is elegantly written but is merely reinventing the wheel and offers almost no value to the reader.

If you have skim-read a paper by focusing on the abstract, introduction, some parts of the literature review and the conclusions, and if you have understood what the author intended you to understand, then you have not wasted your time. An important step to achieve this is to familiarize yourself with the academic language. Expanding your understanding of academic language should be a top priority for all students, especially for those whom English is not their first language. You therefore need to read extensively, and also to learn how to keep effective records of your reading.

SQ3R: a technique for effective academic reading

One way of approaching a reading task is to use a technique suggested by Robinson (1970), termed SQ3R. This technique enables you actively to elaborate on material that you read, whether an article, a conference paper or a book chapter. It consists of five steps: Survey, Question, Read, Record and Review.

1. *Survey* (this should take you no more than a minute). Scan the title, headings, figures and conclusion. See what the headings are – both major and subheadings; hierarchical structures are usually easy for our minds to understand – check for introductory and concluding paragraphs. Do not be tempted to read the paper properly yet, but try to identify three or four major ideas in it.
2. *Question* (this should take you no more than thirty seconds): Ask yourself what this paper is about: 'What is the research question/problem this paper is trying to answer/solve?' Repeat this process with each subsection of the paper, turning each heading into a question. You can read the first and last paragraphs and skim-read some of the other paragraphs. Were your predictions correct? By now, you should have a broad idea of the structure of the paper and its different parts.

3. *Read* (this may take some time). Read one section at a time, trying to find the answer to the question implied by the heading. This is called 'active reading', and requires a degree of concentration. Always remind yourself why you are reading this paper. Is it directly about your research topic, or simply related to it? Are you looking for background information, or detailed information? Do you simply wish to know what the author's views are on the topic? If you are looking for specific information, read only the parts where you think you will find what you want. By now, you should have a good idea of the paper's content and its usefulness to your research.

4. *Record* (this should take you no more than five minutes). Make notes, using a highlighter, or by writing in the margins of the paper definitions or key phrases that sum up the main points of the paper, and answering the question you asked in steps 2 and 3. Use – as far as possible – your own words, but it is also advisable to start becoming accustomed to using some more academic language.

5. *Review* (this should take you no more than five minutes): After going through steps 2–4 for each section of the paper, you should have a number of highlighted phrases and margin notes that outline its contents. Test yourself by trying to recall them. If you cannot recall key points, you will have to re-visit the relevant sections. At the end of this step, you can ask the following questions: How do these points fit with what you already think and know? Do they confirm your views, add to them, or come into conflict with them? Do you agree or disagree with the authors?

Academic reading from an international student's perspective

Most students experience a great deal of confusion when trying to decipher the conventions of academic writing and the expectations of their supervisors with regard to their research project. This confusion, often described as 'an institutional practice of mystery' (Lillis, 1999, 2001), is even more pronounced for international students, who face the challenge of reading in a language that is not their mother tongue. This is a challenge that must be overcome in the early stages of the research, as it affects not only students' understanding of the theories and concepts related to the topic they are researching but also their writing at all stages of their research.

Bourdieu (1984) suggests that this confusion is due to the fact that many international students have not had the language, literacy and learning experiences required in certain higher institutions, and do not have the 'cultural capital' needed to succeed quickly and easily in a new academic domain. If you are an international student, you therefore have to adopt strategies and effective practices in this area if you are to feel comfortable in the domain and accumulate the 'capital' necessary to bring you a high return for your research efforts.

The first step in that direction is to understand reading as a dialogue in which you listen to what the authors say and then respond. This can be accomplished through a set of four activities (Luke, 2000), in each of which you can apply a different strategy:

1. Code-breaking
2. Participating in the text
3. Using the text for your own purposes
4. Analysing or critiquing the text.

In code-breaking, you are listening to what the author says and trying to understand the content of the text by decoding words into meanings and using various features of the text – such as headings, sub-headings and paragraphs – as well as its overall structure to make sense of its content. Here, you may use what Flavell (1979) calls 'cognitive strategies', which involve adjusting your speed of reading as the language of the text becomes more or less difficult, guessing the meaning of unknown words (remember, you do not have to understand the whole text word-by-word), and perhaps re-reading sentences or paragraphs to gain greater understanding. When coming across new words, concepts or jargon, it may be helpful to associate them with visual images and 'store' them in your memory, or to connect them with sounds (perhaps similar words in your own language), motion or other sensory activities.

While code-breaking is in essence a 'listening' activity, you really start connecting with your reading when you engage in a dialogue with the authors and begin creating new meanings in your head, explaining phenomena and asking the authors questions. Here you use more 'metacognitive strategies' (Grabe, 1991) focusing on certain parts of the text, developing a purpose in your reading (for example, 'I am going to use this idea in my research'), making notes and highlighting words or sentences for future use.

You are becoming a text-user when you identify which elements or parts of your reading you are going to employ for your own purposes. However, you should be careful to use the texts you are reading to support your own writing rather than allowing the authors to dominate your project. In the latter situation, you are running the risk of 'plagiarizing' (in other words, stealing other peoples' ideas).

Finally, you should also become a text analyst by listening to what the authors say with some scepticism, by standing back and questioning them and trying to identify bias, whether personal or methodological. You do not have to accept their views fully or to align yourself with them. The fact that something is written in a journal or a book does not necessarily mean that it is 100 per cent correct. Some of you may find this activity difficult, especially if you come from a background where you have been trained not to criticize or review readings but rather to accept and understand them by memorizing (this is the case in many Mediterranean and Asian educational systems). One way of overcoming this difficulty is to form a 'reading club' with colleagues conducting research in similar areas, where you can discuss jointly your understanding of the texts you are reading. By exposing yourself to a wider range of interpretations and seeing that there is more than one way of looking at a problem, you will both liberate your thinking and develop your critical skills. At the same time, by engaging in such a discourse with your colleagues you will develop your linguistic capability. An additional strategy you are strongly encouraged to engage with is the use of annotated bibliographies (see Chapter 3), which will also help you to develop your critical and reflective skills.

Finally, most higher-education institutions offer special support courses for their international students to develop their academic reading skills. In these courses students normally work individually, in pairs, or in groups, reading extracts from various academic sources and other forms of printed texts (such as newspapers and journals). In attending such a course you will learn (and be expected to demonstrate) the ability to understand, interpret, analyse, summarize and paraphrase these texts. Normally these courses also cover relevant micro-skills, such as note-taking, anticipating main ideas from headings, skimming for main ideas and scanning for specific information, as well as grammar and vocabulary practice.

Summary

- Academic reading allows creative solutions to research problems, and can further your knowledge regarding different subject areas. It helps you to develop analytical thinking skills, and trains you to challenges ideas and test frameworks – all skills you need to develop as managers of the future.
- It is important to understand the key components of an academic paper before you actually start to read it. Every academic paper has a conventional layout, as described in this chapter.
- It is important to assess the relevance of an academic paper before you start to read it in its entirety. You can do this by evaluating its abstract, introduction and conclusions with respect to your research question or learning outcomes.
- Academic reading involves finding claims in the paper, assessing its strengths and validity, and extracting value from it.
- Academic language may be a barrier, particularly if the language of the text is not your first language. However, continual practice will develop your skills, and academic reading will gradually get easier until it ceases to be a chore, developing into something positively enjoyable.

Exercise: reading

Read the following case study, using the SQ3R technique presented in this chapter.

Case study: Bob's success story – an innovator, not a manager of the *status quo*

Background
This is the story of Bob, an exceptional General Manager who managed to introduce and implement a new idea at the International Chain Hotel. Bob gained his hotel management degree and MBA at Oxford Brookes University. He then worked in different positions for different organizations, including General Manager for the Travel Inn chain in Nottingham and London, and Assistant Manager for the Whitbread restaurant division. Prior to becoming General Manager at Manchester Airport International Chain Hotel, he worked as an assistant manager for Whitbread budget hotels.

The idea was to outsource the management of the existing restaurant and offer a dining experience to reflect the changes in taste and needs of the contemporary business and leisure customers of the International Chain Hotel. Bob was an ambitious risk-taker with a proven record of success. He thought that there would be no obstacle he couldn't overcome when he first came up with the outsourcing idea. In fact, he conducted a market study and verified that customers wanted a different dining experience. Customer expectations were continually changing, and there was an obvious need to adapt the products, services and status of the existing restaurant to meet their expectations of a quality dining experience. Given that these expectations involved creative and adventurous cuisine in tasteful but contemporary surroundings, what was there to prevent Bob from introducing and implementing the idea of closing the existing restaurant, which used to operate as a traditional fine dining restaurant offering full silver service to both lunch and dinner customers? The restaurant offered high-quality food, but the operation was labour-intensive and the style of decoration outdated.

Bob was a strong believer in change, and in this case change was inevitable. He was confident because he had a good track record of running operations profitably, a wealth of accumulated experience in hotel and restaurant operations, and a wide range of proven skills in management, leadership, communication and negotiation. Bob thought that everything would go smoothly and swiftly. However, after a while he realized that he had to work extremely hard, using all his negotiation and communication skills, to bring to realization the opening of this new restaurant whilst at the same time remaining accountable to the other initiatives of the organization. Bob knew that his success in the restaurant project would be measured against the overall success of the entire property, including not only the restaurant but also the hotel operation. The success of the project, for which he developed a deep personal commitment, therefore involved a great deal of personal risk.

Barriers for the idea implementation
The first dilemma he faced was to bring the expectations of the International Chain management into alignment with the perceived market, and convince the senior decision-makers about the feasibility of this new idea. Bob had to operate within the established framework of organizational decision-making, in which simply saying 'this is a financially viable idea' would not be enough to get approval. Bob stated:

> *Usually if you go to the International Chain board and ask for a £6m investment, they have to have some confidence in you from the historical point of view. This is an individual. Has he been good or bad in the past? A lot of it is about individuals, in terms of their track records. In addition, you have to be able to, from the commercial view, make things stand up – financial returns in particular – and you have to be able to present them in a way that people understand and believe in. You have to communicate some sort of vision of how it is going to work. You have to be really convincing!*

Bob was confident that, as General Manager of a property in this specific location, he could play the role of 'educator' in the organization. In this capacity, he could make the other people in the organization realize and understand the issues about the local business environment in which his hotel property operated, and thus obtain their full support and approval. Bob was like a 'hinge' between the market and the organization:

> *International Chain has very traditional thinking. They have quite fixed views about what International Chain hotels should be in terms of*

restaurants. There are a lot of good fine-dining restaurants. What they do is very good. Quite often they serve traditional meals. But things had changed a lot. You cannot interest people in fine dining.

Bob's view about International Chain is that it is 'conservative' in its culture. In the company, the relative merits of projects are strictly evaluated and assessed by the different disciplines. Moreover, as Bob stated:

in the company the same details of the deal are reviewed at each level ... I have to go through three or four times with the directors what I would do in in terms of the overall project and in terms of Players {the name of the restaurant}. You have to get a lot of other people convinced because it is new and it is high risk and perhaps not what they are used to.

He tended to operate by assuming risks on a personal level, although his intention was always to take calculated risks on behalf of International Chain:

I had to go and convince company people to give me a huge amount of money. In terms of the restaurant, we had to invest about half a million for refurbishing the kitchen. If I got that wrong personally, I would not be around for very long. From the company point of view, there was some risk as well. It was the biggest single investment with no profit share. There was risk for both parties {Bob and the company}.

Strategic decisions
Bob had to make a number of strategic decisions. His idea of outsourcing the management of restaurant operations would mean a 'commercial marriage' between International Chain and a restaurant operator. This relationship would last for many years, and any mistakes or misunderstandings in the early days of the relationship could prove costly to both parties. Identifying a suitable partner was fundamental to the success of the entire concept, and Bob had to follow a 'live action' philosophy in the market. Bob gained a 'feeling' or 'intuition' about the suitability of the potential partner through close interaction. This took place during a range of activities, including presentations given directly at the International Chain by the potential partner as well as escorted visits to his other restaurants. International Chain needed a partner who could identify opportunities by bringing his activities into alignment with the organization's plans and resources. The new partner needed to have his own strengths and capabilities in terms of knowing the ways of doing business 'locally' and adding local flavour to the organization's attempts to operate the restaurant successfully. The potential partner explained his suitability for the partnership as follows:

Bob, the General Manager, sent down the executives of International Chain to my restaurant to check up the place. I told them that most of my business is local, south of Manchester – it is quite a wealthy area around here. I think that they were trying to attract people from around here to go into the hotel. They needed someone local, someone well established to help them to achieve this. I offered to transfer my business concept. When they asked me what I wanted to do, I said that I got local knowledge and in addition, I had a very long friendship with the owner of a successful sports promotion company. I knew that International Chain has golf courses and a particular interest in the corporate market. This friend of mine asked me one day if I would allow him to be a shareholder and invest in my company, should I make a deal with International Chain. The answer was 'of course, yes' because he (as owner of a sports promotional company) looked after sportsmen and in particular golfers. They were internationally famous.

Bob was also of the opinion that the partner they would choose should have already established and expanded a network of productive contacts including customers closely involved with individual and institutional investors:

Our potential partner had a good customer base locally. He had a good level of followers and was well-established, well-known locally and the reputation of his restaurant was good. If he went down to Bristol and opened a restaurant in Bristol, it would not have the same followers. He would not have the same success as he is having here. When International Chain brings a local restaurant operator in Bristol, then it will be another local brand.

It was also important at this initial stage that Bob tried to get the potential partner to understand what the International Chain's expectations were. Bob's strategy appeared to be one of informing and educating the potential partner about International Chain's practices, and at the same time diagnosing the expectations the partner had from his own perspective:

We actually went out and asked a lot of questions about his restaurants. By asking those questions, we could understand what was in his mind. And it came out from there.

As Bob indicated, 'there was a huge educational process' involved in informing the potential partner about the organization and its attributes, and discussing mutual benefits. Bob illustrated this by referring to an informal meeting he had with the potential partner:

I had a dinner with the potential investor. I explained to him what I saw as the potential benefits. Firstly, I explained to him how we as an organization do business. Why we approach it in a certain fashion. We agreed that the synergy was on the local level. From our point of view, the people coming to the potential partner's restaurants were local and they could be ideal members of our leisure club. So we discussed how we could make those people who had experienced the potential partner's restaurant join our leisure club.

Collaboration between Bob and other senior decision-makers was very important in this education process. Such an approach, it was believed, would also build up the partner's trust regarding the capabilities of the company. With regard to collaboration with people from other areas of the organization, Bob stated that the key resource he had at his disposal was the team he could bring to the table in order to meet the partner's concerns and needs. The importance given to this collaboration was clear from Bob's statements:

> *I managed to get two or three people, then more people to come and have a look at it and the risk in their mind started to diminish because they could actually see this restaurant operating and what was going on up and down. My boss, the Managing Director, came to look at it. Once he had been there, everything from there on became very easy. Then it was all about negotiating the deal.*

Collaboration between Bob and senior decision-makers, such as the Regional Director and the Operational Director, was also central in the overall process. Bob thought it was important to get other people involved in the process by bringing the senior decision-making team and the potential partner together. Many formal and informal meetings took place between both parties. Several important issues, such as the reason for undertaking the project, the market segment that was being targeted, and demand characteristics and trends, were discussed during these meetings. The overall purpose of these meetings was to evaluate the possible impacts of the project on International Chain's position in the market, and the extent to which it would give the hotel a competitive advantage. In addition, the interactions that took place between Bob, the senior decision-makers and the potential partner had to do with the assessment of variables regarding the character, reliability, commitment to and expertise of the potential partner in the restaurant business. Much of the face-to-face communication between the potential partner, Bob and his senior colleagues appeared to be linked to the mutual desire to form a solid basis for a successful business match.

However, these frequent meetings between Bob, the potential partner and senior decision-makers not only slowed down the decision-making process, but also ended up lowering the motivation and, at times, frustrating the partner. Although a centralized, tight decision-making approach aimed to preserve the system's integrity and protect the brand reputation, at the same time such a management approach resulted in discouraging an innovative, opportunity-seeking, entrepreneurial partner from the potential partnership. He reflected upon his negotiation experience with Bob and International Chain as follows:

> *When it got to the lawyers, it became complicated and delayed the process for six months. We could have opened the restaurant six months earlier. The documents were sent backwards and forwards. The most difficult part was the negotiation. It was just a prolonged, very frustrating period of time. To the extent where both sides said that this is not going to work.*

Bob's personal relationship with the potential partner helped a lot in terms of managing this growing tension:

I had many different meetings with the partner and assured him that we would work this through as quickly as we could, apologizing for this messing around. We built a good relationship. We had a good working relationship. Everything is about the development of a good relationship, which means that we both know that it is going to be a success. If I had gone to him and said 'this is not my problem' – that would have gone very sour very quickly.

These long and stressful meetings eventually bore fruit, and Bob managed to get the approval of the senior team for his idea. An important hurdle had been well managed, and the support for Bob's new project was gaining momentum in the organization. He was passionate about the idea and the support he was receiving was proving him right. However, there was still a long way to go. It was a great achievement for him to get the approval of senior decision-makers at International Chain, but it was not these people who would turn this business idea into reality. The existing restaurant had its employees, systems and processes, and its own way of operating. Introducing a new concept and a new way of operating would mean challenging the *status quo* and overcoming resistance to change by employees of the restaurant, who would ultimately be instrumental in delivering the 'quality dining experience'. Bob recalls those difficult days, and wishes that he had thought more about the need to change attitudes rather than just introducing the new concept:

In terms of employees, it was a cultural issue. We were closing one restaurant and moving into another restaurant. I thought it was quite simple, but I completely underestimated the kind of culture shock we had because most people had been working in the restaurant for so long. Morale overnight was not very good. The new challenge was to keep them engaged and help them to see the overall picture.

Bob had to be innovative and seek creative solutions to the problems and needs of the employees. He used strategies of communication and participation to explain how the changes would be beneficial and practical for both the organization and the employees. Bob stated:

It is important that you believe in your ideas. Then, it is all about explaining the reasons behind the thinking. And as things move on, I started to involve some of them in decisions to be made. So, trying to get their involvement and believing in some of their concerns were extremely important.

In addition, Bob had to act like a seller and communicate the special strengths and benefits of the new restaurant – such as its quality and outlook – in order to create tangible and memorable images:

It was important for the employees to see the new restaurant completed. Once they saw it, they were extremely pleased with the outcome. Perhaps, their resentment diminished as well now that they had got their restaurant looking fantastic and there was no point in going and working somewhere else. I started to regain their enthusiasm and motivation.

Successful closure
Overall, it was a long and frustrating process for Bob. It took him eighteen months to open the new restaurant with his concept of outsourcing its management. The employees' attitudes towards change improved as their involvement and understanding increased. The restaurant is now more profitable than ever before. Bob knew that he would not have succeeded if he had seen himself as a manager of an operational *status quo* and had not acted as an innovator and an agent of change. Bob is now being praised by many people, including customers, employees and senior decision-makers, for this success story:

Now a lot of those very same people who were most concerned about what I was doing are coming back to me and saying 'thanks for what you have done'.

Acknowledgement: The authors would like to thank Mike Rimmington for providing the raw data for the above story.

Review questions

1. Why is it important to do academic reading?
2. Find an academic paper from the *International Journal of Hospitality Management,* the *Journal of Tourism Management,* or the *Annals of Tourism Research* relevant to your research for your essay or for your dissertation. Identify the different sections of the paper according to the conventional layout.
3. Summarize the main arguments of the paper by reading its abstract, introduction and conclusions.
4. How do the different sections of the paper add value to your research?

References

Altinay, L. and Bowen, D. (2006). Politics and tourism interface: the case of Cyprus. *Annals of Tourism Research*, 33(4), 939–956.

Bourdieu, P. (1984). *Distinction: A Social Critique of the Judgment of Taste*. London: Routledge.

Brown, B. R. (2006). *Doing Your Dissertation in Business and Management: The Reality of Researching and Writing*. London: Sage Publications.

Easterby-Smith, M., Thorpe, R. and Lowe, A. (1991). *Management Research: An Introduction*. London: Sage Publications.

Flavell, J. (1979). Metacognition and cognitive monitoring: a new era of cognitive-development inquiry. *American Psychologist*, 34, 906–911.

Grabe, W. (1991). Current developments in second language reading research. *TESOL Quarterly*, 25, 375–406.

Lillis, T. M. (1999). Whose 'common sense'? Essayist literacy and the institutional practice of mystery. In: C. Jones, J. Turner and B. Street (eds), *Students Writing in the University*. Amsterdam: Benjamins, pp. 127–147.

Lillis, T. M. (2001). *Student Writing: Access, Regulation and Desire*. London: Routledge.

Luke, A. (2000). Critical literacy in Australia: a matter of context and standpoint. *Journal of Adolescent and Adult Literacy*, 43(5), 448–461.

Robinson, F. P. (1970). *Effective Study*. New York, NY: Harper and Row.

Chapter 3
Developing literature review skills

The ideas I stand for are not mine. I borrowed them from Socrates. I swiped them from Chesterfield. I stole them from Jesus. And I put them in a book. If you don't like their rules, whose would you use?

(Dale Carnegie, American lecturer and author, 1888–1955)

Having tentatively chosen a topic for your research, you will need now to look in greater depth at what research has been conducted in this area so far, how it was conducted, and what its outcomes were. You can imagine this as entering into a 'dialogue' with all the researchers in this topic. They are your colleagues now. By reading their papers (see Chapter 2), you are looking at their work and asking them questions. What questions of interest to you have already been answered? Were they answered conceptually or empirically? What methods did the authors use in conducting their research? What samples did they use? What questions did they not answer? What further research did they suggest should be undertaken? This 'dialogue with the literature' will reveal the main themes, diverse approaches taken, different ideas and interpretations of findings, possible dilemmas and paradoxes, and debates between various researchers; by engaging in it, you will start getting a 'feel' for where your own ideas fit, how they can be better informed, and towards which areas you should be guiding your research, considering the resources you have available.

Obviously, you cannot possibly read everything that has been written (unless your area of research is highly specialized), but you need to select and use the literature that is most appropriate in order to contextualize and underpin your research. To achieve this, you will need to develop some particular skills – locating the appropriate sources of your literature, systematic literature searches, critical reading, summarizing and documenting, as well as good reference-keeping.

There are several academic publications that may be useful sources for your literature review. Although a search of the wider literature is strongly encouraged, Table 3.1 lists some of the most important hospitality and tourism journals you might use. There are also many area-specific (marketing, human resources, food-service, cultural and heritage) journals, but this list will give you a good starting point.

Locating the sources of your literature

The most obvious source of your literature is your institution's library. Familiarize yourself quickly with the library procedures (borrowing, renewing, returning, reserving, fines, short loans, ID cards, etc.) and opening hours, and the security systems that control access to its electronic resources, such as databases and electronic journals. When undertaking research you will certainly

Table 3.1
Some hospitality and tourism journals

Journal title	Purpose	Audience
Anatolia	An international tourism and hospitality research published semi-annually (summer and winter) in Ankara, Turkey. The journal includes peer-reviewed research papers, case studies, updates on Mediterranean tourism, research notes and reports, thesis/dissertation abstracts, book reviews, and calendar of events.	Researchers, students, practitioners in hospitality and tourism. The journal aims to heighten awareness of the Mediterranean region as a significant player in international tourism.
Annals of Tourism Research	A social sciences journal focusing upon the academic perspectives of tourism. While striving for a balance of theory and application, *Annals* is ultimately dedicated to developing theoretical constructs. Its strategies are to invite and encourage offerings from various disciplines; to serve as a forum through which these may interact; and thus to expand frontiers of knowledge in and contribute to the literature on tourism social science.	Tourism researchers in anthropology, economics, geography, history, management science, politics, psychology, regional planning and sociology.
Asia Pacific Journal of Tourism Research	The official journal of the Asia Pacific Tourism Association, publishes both empirically- and theoretically-based articles which advance and foster tourism education, research and professionalism in the Asia-Pacific region.	Researchers and the professional community.
China Tourism Research	Publishes the latest research on tourism (all articles printed in both Chinese and English) that relates to China and its citizens. It is a print-only (all abstracts available online) journal providing a rich forum for the exchange of fresh information and ideas among academics and practitioners; it fosters and enhances cutting-edge research activities that advance the knowledge of tourism; and discusses the relevance of tourism to Chinese society.	Academics and practitioners.
Cornell Hotel and Restaurant	Publishes articles and case studies that provide applied research theories about important industry trends and	Academics and practitioners involved in the hospitality industry.

(Continued)

Table 3.1
(Continued)

Journal title	Purpose	Audience
Administration Quarterly	timely topics in hospitality, restaurant and tourism management.	
International Journal of Contemporary Hospitality Management	A multidisciplinary journal that publishes papers covering issues relevant to hospitality operations, marketing, finance and personnel. It provides information and ideas for those seeking to raise standards, increase market penetration and improve profitability in organizations across the hospitality industry, from single-unit concerns to large multinationals.	Hospitality managers, educators and researchers.
International Journal of Hospitality Management	Discusses major trends and developments in a variety of disciplines as they apply to the hospitality industry, including related areas such as education and training, human resources management, financial management, national and international legislation.	Researchers and practitioners involved in both the hospitality and tourism industries.
International Journal of Tourism Research	An international platform for debate and dissemination of research findings and discussion of new research areas and techniques. It publishes research papers in any area of tourism, including reviews of literature in the field and empirical papers on tourism issues.	Researchers in various the fields of tourism, such as economics, marketing, sociology and statistics.
Journal of Hospitality and Tourism Research	A multidisciplinary journal featuring conceptual and empirical research, and applied research articles in hospitality and tourism. It is the professional journal of the Council on Hotel, Restaurant, and Institutional Education (CHRIE).	Educators, researchers, and professionals in travel and hospitality.
Journal of Travel Research	A research journal focusing on travel and tourism behaviour, management and development, this offers an international and multidisciplinary perspective on the best tourism development and management practices in (among other areas) tourist behaviour and destination choice, marketing, economics, e-commerce, tourism forecasting, destination development, heritage	Tourism researchers, educators, and professionals.

	tourism, cultural tourism, ecotourism, and attraction development.	Researchers and the professional community.
Scandinavian Journal of Hospitality and Tourism	Covers all types of empirical and conceptual research of issues relevant to Scandinavia, the North Sea and Baltic regions, and associated developments in the regional hospitality and tourism industry.	
Tourism and Hospitality: Planning and Development	The contextual scope for this journal is considerable; planning and development issues extend from the macro- to the micro-level, from global concerns to those associated with the individual organizations and companies, while the conceptual scope encompasses issues and techniques from multivariate forecasting to the more creative endeavours of menu planning and property design/development.	Researchers and practitioners, individuals and organizations interested in both the theoretical and the practical aspects of planning and development.
Tourism Management	The journal takes an interdisciplinary approach and includes planning and policy aspects of international, national and regional tourism, as well as specific management studies.	Academics and researchers, government departments and NTOs, consultants and planners in the tourism, hotel and airline industries.

come across references to items that are not held in your library, so find out whether your library can offer you access to other sources, and where you can locate the references you need. Such items can often be obtained for you via interlibrary loan services that enable students and researchers – usually at a small charge – to borrow items from other libraries in the country and even abroad.

Although the types of software may differ from institution to institution, most libraries offer online public access catalogues (OPAC) to help students search the library using, for example, an author's name, the book or journal title, or a key word. The system returns information about which books or journals are available in the library, shelf-mark information, the type of loan and number of copies available, and whether the copy is in the library or on loan.

Apart from the OPAC system, libraries normally also offer databases of abstracts and indexes in electronic form. These databases provide subject/author access to individual journal articles, full bibliographic details (e.g. author, title, journal name, volume and page numbers), abstracts and a brief summary of content; some of them even include the full text of the article. Examples of databases that hospitality and tourism students will probably use when looking for academic journals, trade journals or business magazines are EBSCOhost, Emerald, IngentaConnect, Sage Premier, ScienceDirect, CAB Direct, etc. Other databases include market research reports, which usually concentrate on particular products or services and provide a wide variety of information about sales, market trends, advertising figures, distribution, brands, the companies involved and customer profiles. Examples of such databases are Mintel, Reuters and Euromonitor. For researchers who want to find particular information about companies, such as analyst's reports from banks, stockbrokers and trade associations, or simply company news, the library may offer specialized databases such as Infotrac and Proquest Newspapers. There are also databases (e.g. FAME – Financial Analysis Made Easy – and Thomson One Banker Analytics) that offer more specific company financial information, such as company accounts and share prices.

Most researchers nowadays use the Worldwide Web as an additional source of information. There are several search engines available, but for research purposes one of the most appropriate is a beta search engine called Google Scholar (http://scholar.google.com), which is still under development. Google Scholar helps researchers to identify relevant research across many disciplines and sources – peer-reviewed papers, theses, books, abstracts and articles from academic publishers, professional societies, preprint repositories, universities and other scholarly organizations (http://scholar.google.com/intl/en/scholar/about.html). You may use a number of other search and meta-search engines for your research, but you need to be very cautious about the quality of information provided. It is important to always be aware of who placed the information there, and why. Make sure that the source of information is reliable and has some authority, that the information is current and that it has passed some kind of quality control.

Defining the initial parameters of a search

A good systematic literature search always starts with the identification of core words (or keywords) that will help you to locate materials in the library or the other sources you are using. These words can be identified using a form of brainstorming that may be triggered by a series of questions as described in Box 3.1.

Box 3.1	Brainstorming keywords

- In one sentence, what is my research topic?
- What are the core words in this topic?
- What are relevant words, synonyms and broader or narrower terms?
- How can I combine them so that they can still make sense?
- Are there any known theories linked with these combinations?
- How can I bring these into the context of what I want to research?
- Are there any different versions (English or American) of these words?

Imagine, for example, that the broad research topic you are considering is: 'How well has dynamic packaging been implemented in the hospitality industry?' The core words here are *dynamic packaging* and *implemented*. If you start broadening the term *dynamic packaging*, the words that come up may, for example, include *pricing, software, innovation*. The word *implemented* may lead you to *implementation, strategy, strategic management*. Combining them, you will have *pricing strategy, innovation implementation*. The latter combination can be linked with *innovation adoption* or *innovation diffusion* or both!

Clearly, there is a choice of theoretical foundations here when looking at strategy implementation, pricing strategy, innovation adoption and diffusion. If you want to contextualize your search, you need to look at the words *hospitality industry – industry* itself is not really useful, as it will list thousands of sources in any search, so focus on *hospitality*. This will lead you to the words *hotel(s)*, *hotel chains*, *hotel organizations*, *accommodation*, *catering*. American articles might use the word *lodgings*. All these must be used in your search to obtain comprehensive results. Remember to include both English and American spellings – for example, *organisation* and *organization*.

At this point, the list of keywords generated should be constructed into search strings. A search string is simply a line of text that consists of a combination of keywords that sum up what you are looking for. In order to construct a research string to enter into a database, you will have to use truncations and Boolean search. This is much less daunting than it sounds. Truncations such as the * or $ symbols may be added at the end of a root word to find every variation of the word – for example, *market** (or *market$*) will find *marketed, marketing, markets, marketed*, etc.; *work$* (or *work**), will retrieve *work, worker, workforce, workplace*, etc. The truncation within a word acts as a wildcard and finds every spelling variation – for example, *colo*r* finds both *colour* and *color*.

Boolean search employs a method of constructing search strings by using the Boolean operators AND, OR and NOT. Boolean operators may be used in either a free text or an index search. The operator AND narrows a search by combining terms, and retrieves every document that contains both of the words specified – for example, innovation AND adoption. The OR operator broadens or widens a search to include documents containing either keyword. The OR search is particularly useful when there are several common synonyms for a concept or variant spellings of a word – for example, hospitality OR lodging. In most databases, OR statements are within brackets if you are using the basic or quick search facilities. Combining search terms with the NOT operator narrows a search by excluding unwanted terms. It is not used very often when constructing a search, but it may be that when you look at the results you will want to cut out one particular aspect which is not of interest. Variations on the basic Boolean operators are also supported by many library databases and Internet search engines. Known as proximity operators, these include ADJACENT, WITH, NEAR, and FOLLOWED BY. ADJACENT and WITH require that the words appear next to each other, NEAR requires that the search terms appear in close proximity, and FOLLOWED BY requires that one term follows another. Remember, however, that it is not wise to construct over-elaborate search strings, as they may return very limited results or even none at all.

With first the basic and then some more complicated search strings, you are now in the position to conduct an initial search. From the results of this search you may choose the most relevant articles and see what their keywords are (these are generally listed after the abstract – see Chapter 2). If you find words that you consider to be important, you may enrich your own list of keywords with them so that your main search will yield even more comprehensive results.

Conducting the main search and filtering the results

The main search of your library's catalogues and databases and/or the Internet will normally give you a rich list of results. As with the initial search, it is advisable to conduct the search by moving progressively from the most basic to the more complex means, so that your results will be filtered first by the search engine (automatic exclusion through the search strings). You will then have to filter them further by using specific inclusion and exclusion criteria. In order to do this, you will need to have specified from the outset the attributes of your results. For example, you may want to select articles that were published after a specific date or year, or articles that refer to a particular geographical region. Some examples of inclusion and exclusion criteria are given in Box 3.2.

This 'manual' filtering can start from a review of the full bibliographical reference list in order to remove duplicate papers and articles that, at a first glance, either match the exclusion criteria or do not match the inclusion criteria set out for the search. At a second, more rigorous, level you should review in detail the abstracts of the remaining articles, applying the same inclusion/exclusion criteria.

The next filter to apply is to evaluate the quality of the papers' content. This can be done by looking at the abstracts and evaluating their relevance to your research topic, the extent to which they seem to contribute to your better understanding/ knowledge of the research area, and the possible impact of their findings. However, if you wish to have a better outcome, much more rigorous criteria should be applied that might also require you to 'skim read' all your results. Pittaway *et al.* (2004), in their 'systematic literature review' methodology, suggest a content evaluation based on five distinct criteria:

1. Theory robustness
2. Implication for practice
3. Research design/methodology
4. Generalizability of findings
5. Extent to which it contributes to your research topic.

You can then organize the articles under review into A, B and C lists. The A list should include only articles that fully meet these five criteria, and the B list those

Box 3.2	Literature search – inclusion/exclusion criteria

Inclusion criterion	Reason
Conceptual or empirical paper	Will my work focus on theory or research, or both?
Working paper	Do I need to include the most current developments?
Sectors investigated	Do I want a broader or a narrower perspective?
Geographic coverage	Will I make cross-country comparisons?
Quantitative/qualitative	Which approach will better inform my work?
Focus	What is my main topic?

Exclusion criterion	Reason
Date of publication	I do not want publications before....
Term A	Term is relevant to my research area but not to my topic
Term B	Term is relevant to my research area but not to my topic
Term C	Term is relevant to my research area but not to my topic

(Source: Adapted from Pittaway *et al.*, 2004)

that appear to have some relevance to the criteria although their contribution to your research topic is not very clear. The C list may include articles of two types: first, the articles that are relevant to your topic but remain highly conceptual and do not really provide you with a basis to develop your research; and second, articles where the contribution to your topic is not very convincing or is weak.

This process can be also used for books, reports, chapters and other sources you may have collected during your search.

Organizing your results

Starting with your A list, you now need to 'process' your results. By this time you will have a much clearer idea about where your research is heading, and reading the sources you have on your list is essential in order to decide on the actual aim of your project – the questions it will try to answer or the problem it will attempt to solve. Chapter 2 provided advice on how to read an academic article; all sources should be read in the same manner, but you will need to be organized in documenting and filing your reading.

The first thing you should do is number the sources on your list and file them by number order in a literature folder. You can then start 'processing' them one by one. Once you have identified the main points of the article (conference paper, chapter or report), make notes in the margins (or in a notebook, or on an index card that can be attached to your source) summarizing in your own words the major arguments of each section. Look for quotations and citations in the paper that you may need to follow up. Highlight those references that detail where these ideas or quotations came from. Make a note of the authors' suggestions for further research. You can do this by hand, or you may wish to use one of the software tools for publishing and managing bibliographies in your computer, such as EndNote, ProCite or Reference Manager.

One way of organizing your 'processed' sources is to develop an annotated bibliography. To do this, you expand your A, B and C lists by adding brief (usually about 150 words) descriptive and evaluative paragraphs – annotations – regarding each source. The purpose of this is to provide details of their relevance, accuracy, and quality. It should therefore be both descriptive and critical. This is the main difference between an annotation and an abstract – the abstract is a pure description of an article, whereas the annotation should comment on the authors' point of view, authority, clarity and appropriateness of expression. There are various approaches to writing an annotated bibliography, so it is useful to consult your research supervisor about any special requirements before undertaking this task. However, the core elements of an annotated bibliography are presented in Box 3.3.

Box 3.3	Core elements of an annotated bibliography

- Full bibliographical citation of the source using the appropriate referencing style
- Keywords
- Concise annotation summarizing the central theme and scope of the source under review
- Evaluation of the authority or background of the author
- A comment on the intended audience
- Comparison or links of this work with another you have cited
- A comment on how useful this work will be for your research topic, and why.

As an example, a student undertaking a research on disaster management in tourism destinations might include the following in an annotated bibliography:

Faulkner, B. (2001). Towards a framework for tourism disaster management. *Tourism Management*, 22(2), 135–147.

Keywords: disasters; crises, hazards; disaster management; recovery

Summary: The author explores the nature of disasters and crises and identifies the differences between the two terms; statistical approach to disasters. He also looks at community responses to disaster situations: disaster responses from sociological view and at individual level; community resilience and factors affecting a community's capacity (Granot, 1995), and single- and double-loop learning approaches (Richardson, 1994); disaster management strategies at community level (Fink, 1986); problems in community disaster response – competition, rivalry, different internal cultures, modus operandi, bureaucratic structures (e.g. Kobe earthquake); two different views of the elements of disaster survival strategies (Turner, 1994). He then focuses on tourism disasters, looking at tourism and disaster characteristics; preparedness (Cassedy, 1991; Drabek, 1995); media coverage, market communication and ingredients of tourism disaster strategies proposed by Cassedy and Drabek. Finally, he proposes a generic tourism disaster management model with twelve components.

Authority: Faulkner is the first scholar to propose a complete tourism disaster management model.

Links: Faulkner and Vikulov (2001).

Comment: This is a good model to be used as a basis for my research.

The annotated bibliography is an important stepping-stone in your research project, as it provides an opportunity to bring together all the literature you have identified in a single document so that it can be evaluated by you and by your supervisor. It will help you to decide whether you have enough and useful literature for you to start building a theoretical argument, and to evaluate whether this argument will be valid and believable. It is also a very useful tool when writing up your project – especially the literature review section.

Another way to organize your literature search results is by constructing a literature map. A literature map is the visual representation of your search results, which helps you see how your search results relate with each other and where your study fits in in relation to the broader literature on the topic. It may have many different forms. Creswell (2003: 39) suggests that it could depict your literature in a hierarchical order, 'with a top-down presentation of the literature ending at the bottom with a proposed study that will extend the literature'. Alternatively, it might have the form of a flow-chart, where the literature unfolds from left to right, with the studies on the right being closer to the 'gap' you are proposing to close. A third model, he suggests, is one composed of circles, 'with each circle representing a body of the literature and the intersection of the circles indicating the place at which future research is needed'. Regardless of its form, the process of constructing a literature map is normally the same (Box 3.4).

Box 3.4	Constructing a literature map

- On the top of your map, write the title of the broad research topic you are investigating.
- Think about which theoretical areas are influential in the development of knowledge and scholarship for your topic. List these under your topic heading as subject headings, placing them in a way that represents their relative connection to each other (the further apart, the less related they are).
- Under each subject heading, add the subject topics that are discussed in your literature. Again their placement should reflect their relative connection.
- Classify each of your sources under the relevant subject topic, based on its core ideas, concepts and narrative focus, by citing the author(s) and the year of publication.
- Indicate the links between subject headings, and between subject headings and subject topics, by using directional arrows.

(Adapted from Yee, 2003).

The literature map will also help you to frame your research boundaries and focus your literature on relevant key topics. However, by including peripheral subject headings and topics in the map, you will get a richer and more holistic picture of your study area. This is very important, especially when the research subject is about issues that span different disciplines. Yee (2003) stresses that any classification of the literature on a map should be considered neither fixed nor definitive, but rather as 'sign posts to assist the mapmaker and the map user to navigate through mass amounts of ideas, concepts and methodologies encountered in the literature' (Yee, 2003: 8).

Figure 3.1 provides an example of a literature map. The researcher here is looking at the development of a destination-level anti-terrorism strategy, and wonders whether the destination management organization can play a role in the development and/or coordination of such a strategy.

The three areas that he has looked at for his literature review are: terrorism, strategy and destination management organizations. Then, asking the questions in the boxes, he has identified the relevant literature that will help him to develop his inquiry further.

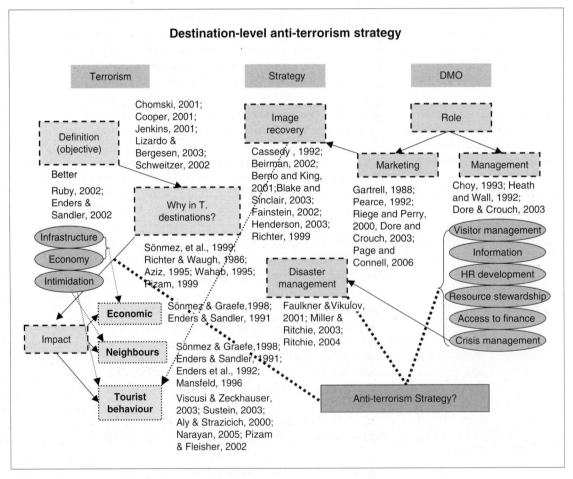

Figure 3.1
Example of a literature map.

Referencing your sources

An important element in organizing your literature search results is the ability to reference your sources appropriately. In fact, whenever you are asked to produce an academic work, such as an essay, report or a dissertation, you will be asked to provide references to support your ideas. Most students do not understand the reasoning behind this, or do not perceive this as important. Referencing is essential for the following reasons:

- It shows that you have worked independently and completed the recommended reading. This is a good indicator of your ability to work independently, and the breadth your reading enhances the credibility of your work.
- It shows that you are playing an active role in engaging in academic debate and positioning your ideas in relation to others'.
- It helps to establish a basis for your claims and arguments, and thus contributes to the credibility of your ideas.
- It will prevent accusations of plagiarism (i.e. stealing other peoples' thoughts, ideas or writings and using them as though they are your own).

When you are writing your academic work you will need to use a number of sources – books, articles, magazines, newspapers, the Internet, lecture notes and others. Every time you use information from a source, you must provide a reference – in other words, cite the authors whose ideas have been mentioned in your work. The details of the cited sources are then gathered together to form a list at the end of your work; this is the reference list.

There are two possible ways of referencing in the text. The first and most commonly used approach is to read a chapter or a paragraph of a book, or various sections from a paper, and then put them on one side and write these ideas in your own words. It is not enough simply to change one or two words of the original text. The second approach is to take a sentence or a short paragraph word by word. This is called *quoting*, and should be done in exceptional circumstances where you cannot paraphrase a sentence and/or where author's views are essential because they are 'unique, thought-provoking and/or innovative'.

There are different referencing styles – for example, Harvard, APA (American Psychological Association) and others. This book will cover the Harvard style. However, if you wish to use other referencing styles, the following websites will provide details:

- The American Psychological Association (APA) referencing system is described at http://apastyle.apa.org/
- The Vancouver style (a 'numbered' style) follows rules established by the International Committee of Medical Journal Editors; details are available at http://www.icmje.org/. It is also known as: Uniform Requirements for Manuscripts Submitted to Biomedical Journals.
- The Modern Language Association (MLA) style is most commonly used when writing papers and citing sources within the liberal arts and humanities. Further details can be found at http://www.mla.org/.

Variations of the Harvard Referencing style are followed by different academic institutions. You may use any of these; they are all 'correct'. This section presents the Harvard version commonly used in hospitality and tourism journals.

Referencing your sources using the Harvard system

The reference is cited by putting the author(s) surname(s) and the year of publication in the text where it is most relevant. Initials are not used except where two authors with the same surname are cited. For example:

> It has been shown that ... (Burgess, 2000)

or

> Burgess (2000) has shown that ...

Where you refer to a specific part of the work, or when using a direct quotation (see below), the page number(s) should be included – for example:

> (Harris, 2000, p. 27)

or

> (Harris, 2000: 27–28).

When citing the works of a number of different sources on a subject, they should be cited in chronological and then alphabetical order – for example:

> (Roper, Doherty and Brookes, 1999; Altinay, 2000; Harris, 2000).

When there are more than two authors for a single source, the first entry may list all the authors but subsequent references are abbreviated – for example:

> (Litteljohn *et al.*, 2007).

In the reference list, though, you must list all the authors – for example:

> Litteljohn, D., Roper, A. and Altinay, L. (2007). Territories still to find – the business of hotel internationalization. *International Journal of Service Industry Management*, 18(2), 169–183.

When referencing more than one work by the same author in the same year, you should distinguish between them by adding a or b to the date – for example:

> (Harris, 2001a, 2001b).

You may be reading a book or article and come across an interesting idea cited by the author. As a general rule, you should track down and read the original reference, because authors do not necessarily interpret the views of others accurately. However, if you cannot do this then you should reference it as follows:

(Leidner, 1993, in Seymour, 2000, p. 161).

Quotations

As stated above, you must use entirely your own words in your written work unless you have a particular reason for quoting others directly. If you use 'direct quotations', placing three to four lines or less within the text, the following style should be used:

Doherty and Stead (1998, p. 142) find that 'equal pay legislation in the UK has had little impact in tackling structural pay inequalities'.

Quotations that are longer than a couple of lines should be distinguished from the rest of the text by indenting them and formatting them in single spacing, while the rest of your text will be in one-and-a-half line or double spacing as below:

regarding intercultural competence. For example:

Many business courses provide education and or training in such management practices as conducting appraisals, team work and leadership, performance management, recruitment and selection and so on, but fewer combine these areas with an equal effort to provide intercultural competence.

(Ledwith and Seymour, 2001: 1292)

Preparing your Bibliography or References

Your list of sources may be entitled 'Bibliography' or 'References'. The former is a full list of all the relevant sources you have used, and can include sources that you have consulted but that are not cited within your text. The 'References' section differs in that it provides information only about the sources cited within your text.

The entries in a Bibliography or Reference section should be arranged alphabetically by the first author's surname. If there is more than one entry for an author, the different entries should be listed in chronological order (by year of publication).

All sources (books, journals, newspapers, websites) should appear in one list in alphabetical order; different types of sources should not be placed in separate sections.

Books

The entry for a book should be structured as in the following examples:

> Burgess, C. (2001). *Guide to Money Matters for Hospitality Managers*. Oxford: Butterworth-Heinemann.
>
> Harris, P. J. and Hazzard, P. A. (1992). *Managerial Accounting in the Hospitality Industry* (5th edn). Cheltenham: Stanley Thornes.

For a particular chapter in an edited book, the entry should be as follows:

> Maher, A. (1997). Labour recruitment and turnover costs in hotels. In: P. Harris (ed.), *Accounting and Finance for the International Hospitality Industry*. Oxford: Butterworth-Heinemann, pp. 73–89.

Journals, magazines and newspapers

The entry should be structured as in the following examples:

> Doherty, L. and Stead, L. (1998). The gap between male and female pay: what does the case of hotel and catering tell us? *The Services Industries Journal*, 18(4), 126–144.
>
> Rimmington, M. and Yuksel, A. (1998). Customer-satisfaction measurement. *Cornell Hotel and Restaurant Administration Quarterly*, 39(6), 60–70.

For newspapers or magazines where there is not a volume number, reference as below:

> Haigh, C. (2001). First steps to recovery. *Caterer and Hotelkeeper*, 23 August, p. 26.

Where no author is identified, the article should be attributed as follows:

> *The Times* (1996). Forte and Granada in take-over battle. *The Times*, 5 February, p. 2.

Conference papers

A similar style should be used for conference papers. For example:

> Brookes, M. (1998). 'Centricity in Corporate Marketing Management in International Hotel Groups'. Paper presented at the Hospitality Sales and Marketing Association International and European Council on Hotel, Restaurant and Institutional Education (HSMAI/EuroCHRIE) Conference. Oslo: Spring.

Thesis or dissertation

A thesis or dissertation should be listed as follows:

> Ciraulo, M. (2002). 'An Investigation into the New Product Development Practice in the Cruise Industry'. Unpublished MSc Dissertation, Oxford Brookes University.

Electronic and other material types

These vary as follows.

1. *Videotape*: for off-air recordings, use the format

> Channel Four (1992). *J'Accuse: Sigmund Freud*. Off-air recording, 10 June. Videotape.

Note that in your text this should be cited as:

> (Channel Four, 1992).

2. *Film*: use the format

> *The Apartment* (1960). Directed by Billy Wilder. 124 mins. United Artists. Videotape.

In your text, this should be cited as:

> (*The Apartment*, 1960)

3. *Websites*: use the format

> Holland, M. (1996). *Harvard System* (online) Poole: Bournemouth University. Available at http://www.bournemouth.ac.uk/service_depts/lis/LIS_Pub/harvardsyst.html (accessed 15 November 2000).

The 'accessed' date indicates when you retrieved the document.

Articulating the research aim

With your literature search conducted and the results organized in lists, an annotated bibliography and a literature map, you are now prepared to articulate the specific research aim. Coming back to the research-painting analogy mentioned in

Chapter 1, you should begin a sketch by asking the question, 'What am I trying to accomplish with my study?' Wolcott (1994) suggests that you must learn to 'think backward' – in other words, to move mentally into a future state – in order to gain a sense of how your finished painting will look like. Then, from the perspective of that future position, you can start thinking about the colours you need, how you will mix them and the brushes you will use. That futuristic view not only develops depth of focus regarding your research topic, but also determines, by extension, the appropriate methodology for data collection, analysis and interpretation for your study. For example, Fredline and colleagues, looking at the impact of events on the enhancement of tourism development in a region, realized that although destination managers had very specific tools to measure the economic impacts, they relied on residents' perceptions to provide a broad estimate of the social impacts of an event. The gap was quite evident, but they did not state the aim of their study as being to 'identify how we can measure the social impact of an event on the tourism development in a region'. Rather, they imagined their completed 'painting' and stated their aim as being 'to test and validate an instrument that can be used to compare the social impacts of a variety of events and ultimately to inform knowledge in the area of social impact assessment in tourism more generally' (Fredline *et al.*, 2003: 23).

As suggested above, the literature map can help you to illustrate the 'gaps' in the literature in a fairly effective way. However, when articulating your research aim you should ensure that you do not include every gap that can be identified via your literature map. Silverman (2005) maintains that a 'kitchen sink approach is a recipe for disaster', arguing that broad research questions will usually result at the study not achieving any depth. He emphasizes that 'your aim should be to say a lot about a little (problem)' rather than 'a little about a lot'. For example, Mossberg (1995) wanted to evaluate the service encounter between tour leaders and tourists participating in charter tours. She articulated her research aim as being 'to study and to enhance the understanding of service encounters in connection with charter tours and their effects on customer satisfaction'. However, as this appeared to be a quite broad aim, she continued by narrowing it down into two particular aspects: (a) 'to investigate what factors determine tourist satisfaction with the service encounter', and (b) 'to investigate how important the tour leader's performance during the service encounter was in the overall perception of the tour' (Mossberg, 1995: 437).

The international dimension of literature review

A significant problem with literature review in student research projects in hospitality and tourism education revolves around what can be called the ethnocentric–polycentric distinction (Adler, 1983).

Students taking an ethnocentric approach in their research project take concepts, ideas and findings of research conducted in one culture and replicate them in another culture. Their basic assumption is that ideas and solutions to a research problem in one context can provide a plausible solution to the same or a similar research problem in another context. Normally the literature review they use is predominantly Anglo-American, given that a large part of the published literature originates from researchers from UK and US institutions in Anglo-American contexts. By contrast, a polycentric approach to a hospitality and tourism literature review accepts that universalism is unlikely, and that diversity of hospitality and tourism is better captured by a thorough review of a more international literature.

Experience has shown that a large number of research projects largely exhibit a ethnocentric bias, because the reviewed literature is not generally international. The mistake that many researchers make is to assume that management approaches and solutions to problems developed in one culture or nation can be equally appropriate and applicable in other nations. However, conducting research in different national contexts aims at examining potential differences and similarities in hospitality and tourism among nations, as well as between organizations and their members in these national settings. For example, a student looking at tourism entrepreneurship in China and using only the existing Anglo-American literature on entrepreneurship while omitting the relevant Chinese or even Asia-Pacific literature will obviously develop an Anglo-American model of entrepreneurship as his or her conceptual framework. As a consequence, any developments in Chinese tourism entrepreneurship will be viewed in terms of their conformity with the Anglo-American model of entrepreneurship – and thus this research project, rather than looking at Chinese tourism entrepreneurship (as intended), may instead reinforce the domination of Anglo-American conceptions. Yet these Anglo-American notions are culturally bound and may consequently have limited applicability to the Chinese situation. Therefore, it follows that, in taking this approach, the key research question the student is seeking to answer will not be whether a Chinese model of tourism entrepreneurship is emerging, but rather: 'To what extent are Anglo-American notions of tourism entrepreneurship emerging in China?'

Arguably, looking at one type of literature is not wrong; however, in such an international industry, researchers ought to have a more pluralistic perspective and to look at the wider international literature. Obviously, taking a more international perspective in your research will largely depend on the topic you are researching and the context of your research, as well as the extent to which this topic has already been researched in different international contexts. On the other hand, if there is a wide range of perspectives employed in the research of your topic, you have a better chance to explore and comprehend it through both inter- and intra-societal comparison and analysis, thus moving the 'body of knowledge' towards a more global understanding of hospitality and tourism management. When you take a more 'inclusive' approach to your literature review on a particular concept, topic or thematic area, you will be more able to appreciate the intangible, subtle, socio-cultural and other forces that underlie policies, practices and phenomena in the international hospitality and tourism industry. You will be able to form a more rounded insight regarding your topic: just as when appreciating a work of art, the total experience is of much greater value than the parts that compose it.

While an ethnocentric bias remains a feature of the published literature within the field of hospitality and tourism, this is no longer as widespread as in the past. The main journals in the field (such as the *Annals of Tourism Research*, the *International Journal of Hospitality Management*, *Tourism Management*, *Cornell Quarterly*, etc.) are increasingly publishing studies with an international dimension, written by multicultural, multinational teams of researchers. These studies may be seen as alternatives to those encapsulated by ethnocentrism, and, rather than favouring any one type of approach to hospitality and tourism research questions, they suggest that there is a multiplicity of approaches.

Summary

- There are several types of sources for a literature review, ranging from your institution's library to electronic databases to which your institution may subscribe, and the Worldwide Web. External sources of literature may be trade publications, as well as reports and statistics published by trade associations, chambers of commerce, governmental agencies and companies in the sector.
- The first step in every literature search is the identification of relevant keywords that capture the content and the context of the topic under investigation. The list of keywords you generate may be constructed into search strings that sum up what you are looking for. In order to construct a search string to enter into a database, you will need to use truncations and Boolean search.
- The literature search findings need to be filtered by using specific inclusion and exclusion criteria. In order to achieve this you will need to have specified from the outset of your search the attributes of your results. An initial filter method is a review of the full bibliographical reference in order to remove papers and articles that do not match your criteria. A second, more rigorous, review of abstracts, by re-applying the same inclusion/exclusion criteria, will provide a further filter.
- A systematic literature review is the content evaluation of your literature search findings based on five distinct criteria: theory robustness, implication for practice, research design/methodology, generalizability of findings, and extent to which it contributes to your research topic.
- An essential step in your project is to document, organize and file your literature review by using a literature folder and producing an annotated bibliography. The purpose of the annotated bibliography is to inform (remind) you of the relevance, accuracy and quality of the sources cited.
- A literature map is a method of presenting your search results visually. It will help you to see how your search results relate to each other, and where your study fits in relation to the broader literature on the topic. The literature map can also help you illustrate the 'gaps' in the extant literature.
- Of the identified gaps, you should focus on one and articulate your research question accordingly. Broad research questions usually result in the study not achieving any depth. Your aim should be to say a lot about one problem, rather than a little about many.
- Depending on the research topic and context, it is advisable to take a polycentric rather than an ethnocentric approach to your literature review. A polycentric (more internationally inclusive) approach will help you to appreciate the intangible, subtle, socio-cultural and other forces that underlie policies, practices and phenomena in the international hospitality and tourism industry.

Student experiences

Mary, a Singaporean student, reflects on her experience of carrying out a literature review, showing the extent of the complexity and ambiguity of the research process. Her professional approach to the literature review also shows us the importance of determination – a discipline required in making your research endeavour a successful one.

Are you about to start your literature review?

Are you the type who picks out your favourite food from a plateful and eats, or one who leaves the favourite to the last to savour? I happen to belong to the first type. Old habits cannot die hard in the case of research. I learned the hard way that researching a topic does not allow you to live the life you want it to be. I started to research my subject area with a general review of the literature, moving on to data collection and even venturing into basic analysis in the first year of my study. I returned to read and refine the literature, on average three times per year (I am entering my fourth year of research). Each time I finished re-writing the literature, I sank into either a minor or a major depression. That was caused by doing what I do not enjoy, and I really wanted to pick out that 'food' last. I enjoy data collection and analysis more, and therefore literature review became a big obligation and misery for me in my research journey. Having said that, in the process of writing up and submitting the first draft, the biggest realization was that I needed to adjust my principle in life. That is, to review and write a critical literature before I ventured too far into official extensive data collection and evaluations. In a subjective way, I have to say that literature review is an important path to lead you to the main road of research – especially for new researchers like you and I. We shall take it from here that that you have a subject area and a working title in mind. Let's get back to basics – a literature review.

In the beginning, you will love it because you discover endless new knowledge, you may pursue relentlessly more authors who are related to the area of your research, or who appear in a bibliography in an article you read. You may also dislike reviewing and avoid it like a communicable disease, like me. The truth is, you might get diverted in your path, get lost and not be able to find your road to your research if you do not conduct a comprehensive literature review. This is an important research process that took my supervisors three long gruelling years to drill into my thick skull. Literature review is important because it provides you with the essential knowledge to know what is going on in the particular area you are researching. You need to know what has been said, why the authors said that and when they said that, and how they came to say that, in order to be able to identify a gap in your research area and to contribute to the body of knowledge. So, back to the basic questions: what, why, when and how? These are the basic questions to start with, yet these basic questions could bring questions themselves. What does that mean? It sounds confusing, and it is. Who says what, and why do they say it? Knowing A says something, you also need to know who says what in arguing against what A says. Simultaneously, you need to know how C, D or E argued for or against A's or B's propositions. It is like a ball of messy thread, and you need to be patient and keep a clear mind to weave the gist of argument into a neat spider's web. Knowing who says what and who counteracts their argument helps you to find out what has been studied, discussed and concluded, or left in the open for debate. This provides you with an opportunity to find a gap and conduct a further study that you can call your own. Knowing who says what is also important because different authors will provide different views about what other authors think, therefore providing you with several insightful perspectives and provoking you to think. Also, authors will normally point out other authors' strengths and weaknesses in their studies, including such things as methodology used, definitions and terms, sample used, sample size and period studied. All these provide a comprehensive knowledge of that particular area of study and guide you through your own critical thinking and writing. To know who says what and why they say that.

There are many questions you may throw up yourself: Can it be the different backgrounds in training amongst authors which lead to their different conclusions and opinions? For instance, authors whose backgrounds are in finance, economics, marketing or human resource management will emphasize different elements in their research design, data collection, interpretation and conclusion, because each discipline is different. One way to find out the background of these authors is to look at their biographies in the organizations they work in, which could be universities and/or commercial organizations or government bodies. This information can be retrieved easily with the advancement of information technology and this thing called the Internet that we can hardly live without today. Knowing the authors' backgrounds could enhance the understanding of the subject being reviewed and increase the credibility of the literature you have reviewed, as well as reinforce the importance of the gap you have identified to research. Knowing how authors come to such conclusions or inconclusive debates, you can ask yourself, can it be linked to how this study was conducted? Can it be the different research methodology they used? Can it be the different research methods they applied to gain results? Can it be the different time period used for the studies? Can it be the sample or sample size which was different? Can it be the definitions of terms used that were different? Can it be a matter of different geographical locations used to study the same organization? As a new researcher, it is imperative to understand the above, as this knowledge provides you with a good opportunity to learn about different research methods and their strengths and weaknesses, and, in turn, to write a critical literature review. More importantly, the same method could be used or improvised to enhance knowledge and/or provoke further research.

As a research question, I found 'when' a confusing word to understand. As a new aspiring researcher, I interpreted it as referring directly to the period during which authors conducted their research – or it could also be indicating the period when the research took place. The former is more related to what happened during that period of research, which is linked closely to the political, economic and socio-cultural change in the particular period studied. The latter is more pertinent to what the authors' environment was like during the period that the studies were conducted. Again, this can be linked back to the researchers' background by training, and this can also be related to the background during the period that the authors were studying this subject. For example, was there a frenzy of studies being conducted during that same period on the same subject, and what was the cause for that increased volume of interest? Was there any particular new theory or commercial innovation that took place to provoke such interest among researchers? The point to note here is that knowing the background could provide you with a context for your study.

   Well, the review process might sound logical and easy, but in reality it is more confusing than we expect, at least for me. In the beginning, you might not understand the literature you are reading and you will feel lost and confused. It is okay, and you are normal. It might take a postgraduate student a month to grasp it, or another student three years to get it. So all you need to do is take a break, step back, then return to read the literature or what you have written and sort it out in a fresh mind. It is also important that you have a structured way that you are comfortable with to organize your data. It is imperative to start this from the very beginning – either use a software programme such as endnotes to help you organize your database, or design your own. The latter is more flexible, and you can change the system easily over time because you designed it to be customized to your needs. It does not need state-of-the-art equipment or a sophisticated program, but a Microsoft word program and its folders are enough to handle your customized database. Finally, you need to communicate with your supervisors regularly to share your thoughts and discuss them. However, discussion is not confined to your supervisors only, and you should speak to other researchers and students – this can take place anywhere, in a formal or informal setting. I had a major breakthrough during a ten-minute conversation over coffee with a seasoned researcher and friend. That conversation helped me to reduce a lot (if not all) of a two-and-a-half year period of agonizing stress with my literature review. Going back to our way of living, what do you pick first to eat? It is a subjective question, and each researcher will need to find their own style. Most importantly, never give up. 'Perseverance: The difference between a successful person and others is not in a lack of strength, not a lack of knowledge, but rather in a lack of will'. I hold this quote by an anonymous author to my heart. It pushed me on in my very difficult research journey, and I hope it pushes you on too.

Ina, from Norway, emphasizes the importance of narrowing down your research by identifying the parameters correctly.

A matter of parameters

I began reading academic journals related to hospitality and tourism in order to identify a researchable dissertation topic. This reading exercise often leads to further reading and reveals gaps in the literature, and although I did not find an accurate topic in these journals, they provided me with an area of interest and motivated further research of selected topics. As a second step, discussion with specialists, in most cases professors at the university but also fellow students, was invaluable. They pinpointed areas I had not found or thought about, and through discussion I slowly got closer in the process of formulating a research question. As this should be as specific and narrow as possible, it is crucial to determine whether the topic of interest is feasible in the provided timeframe. Reviewing the literature was one of the most rewarding and useful parts of the process. In my case this formed the basis of the research, and I found it to be a source of ideas as well as information. Close examination of a selected topic should be captivating in the sense that you dig deeper and deeper into the soul of a problem, and identify new ideas for the current project and probably also for further research. Thus it gives the opportunity to enhance subject knowledge, identify research questions and prepare for primary field research.

Existing literature provided theory linked to the tourism industry, as well as detailed insight into the process of tourism planning, which was my topic. Tourism and hospitality is a wide term and includes various components; thus being specific about what part of the industry you want to investigate is imperative for progress and success. The literature review needs to be planned carefully, and I found that selecting themes helped to structure the writing. For my study I used broad themes, such as supply vs demand of tourism products in Lebanon. These are also useful later in the process as a basis for comparison between theory and primary findings. Broad themes like these may often generate keywords valuable in search engines, library catalogues and, on a later stage, for other researchers. Keywords, both separately and linked, are constructive, as they provide concise information about a topic. At this point I will also highlight the problem of definition within the context of hospitality and tourism research. A word like, for instance, 'leisure' may in some settings imply almost the same as the word 'recreation', while in other contexts it may indicate a distinct part of leisure. Thus, being precise about definitions may reduce unexpected problems at a later stage, such as misunderstandings by readers. Tourism and hospitality research is often concentrated on one geographical location, or is a comparison of two areas; thus updated data on these places must be obtained and filtered. It is advisable to divide the literature review in two parts; one general part in which the main problem or idea is elucidated, and one specific part focused on the country or location of research.

Exercise: literature maps

Having identified that limited theoretical and empirical research has been undertaken into the internationalization of hospitality businesses in general and international market entry modes in particular (franchising, direct investment, management contracting and joint venture partnerships), you have decided that your research project will answer the following question:

What are the factors in the business environment that influence the entry mode choices of a multinational hospitality organization, and how do they influence these choices?

You have undertaken a thorough literature review and found the sources listed in Table 3.2.

Create a literature map showing the main themes identified in this literature review, and the relationship between them and the choice of entry mode in a new market.

Table 3.2
Factors influencing international hotels' entry mode to a new market

Influential factors	References	Key findings and/or propositions
Firm-specific factors		
Objective factors (firm size, international experience)	Gomes-Casseres (1989) Erramilli and Rao (1993)	Larger organizations will tend to favour equity modes of involvement. Smaller organizations lacking in the necessary resources and international experience tend to favour non-equity modes of involvement.
	Gatignon and Anderson (1988)	In hotels, the effective scale required to be a global player is so large that hotel organizations are compelled to have recourse to strategic partnerships in the form of joint ventures, franchising and management contracts. In the hotel industry, these alliances have the potential to deliver the desired benefits to be gained from size just as effectively as direct ownership.
	Contractor and Kundu (1998)	Large international hotel chains appear to utilize non-equity modal forms such as franchising and management contracts rather than control-orientated equity forms.
	Johanson and Vahlne (1977); Erramilli and Rao (1993)	The more international experience an organization gains and the greater its degree of globalization (as measured by the ratio of a hotel firm's overseas rooms to its home country rooms), the less likely it is to resort to host country partnerships of any form.
	Chang (1995)	Examining Japanese organizations, it was found that a sequential process was utilized that led to increasing levels of foreign-market commitment congruent with increasing international exposure.
	Contractor and Kundu (1998)	Non-equity modes (franchising and management contracts) being preferred by the less experienced, less globalized international hotel groups.
Subjective factors (perceptions)	Yip (1989)	Obtaining global economies of scale (where this is believed to be important) necessitates high levels of control and ownership of modes of operation.
	Taylor (2000)	Achieving globalization necessitates that organizations form partnerships in host countries to achieve the desired scale of operations. This will tend to favour franchising and management contracts.
	Contractor and Kundu (1998); Taylor (2000)	When senior management perceives that quality concern can only be accommodated through direct ownership, the firm's portfolio of properties moves heavily towards direct ownership with a limited and very reluctant use of non-equity modes of operation in the form of franchising and management contracts.

(Continued)

Table 3.2
(Continued)

Influential factors	References	Key findings and/or propositions
	Zhao (1994); Contractor and Kundu (1998); Taylor (2000)	Recognition by senior management of the nature of codified assets, such as reservation systems and hotel brands, is supportive of a hotel firm's ability to engage in non-equity based arrangements such as franchising and management contracts, as their control is a powerful barrier against opportunism by contractual partners.
Country-specific factors Political and economic risk and level of economic development	Agarwal and Ramaswami (1992); Kim and Hwang (1992); Turnbull (1996); Zhao and Olsen (1997)	Where a high level of country and political risk is perceived, firms will tend to favour those entry modes with a lower level of resource commitment, such as franchising and management contracts.
	Shane (1996)	Where a high degree of uncertainty is associated with these two variables (e.g. a high level of currency volatility), this will tend to favour the use of franchise agreements.
	Agarwal and Ramaswami (1992); Kim and Hwang (1992); Erramilli and Rao (1993)	Where 'demand uncertainty' is high, firms are less amenable to equity-based arrangements for market entry or expansion. Firms use investment modes in high potential markets.
	Contractor and Kundu (1998)	Franchising and management contracts are preferred in high-income countries; equity-based arrangements are preferred where country income levels are lower. Where political and economic risk is perceived to be high, then non-equity-based arrangements such as franchising and management contracts will be favoured.
Cultural distance	Brouthers (2001)	Firms entering culturally distant markets low in investment risk prefer cooperative modes of entry. Conversely, firms entering culturally distant markets high in investment risk prefer wholly owned modes of entry.
	Erramilli and Rao (1993); Kogut and Singh (1998)	The greater the cultural distance, the greater the reliance will be on non-equity-based modes such as franchising and management contracts.
	Kim and Hwang (1992)	Due to the uncertainty inherent in culturally distant markets, firms attempt to minimize their resource commitment and use joint ventures, instead of using more costly wholly owned subsidiaries.
	Anand and Delios (1997)	In culturally distant markets, investing firms prefer joint ventures with a local firm in order to speed up organizational learning through local knowledge and reduce uncertainty.

Review questions

1. What are the four main sources of information for your literature review?
2. If you were investigating the role of tourism stakeholders in the sustainable tourism development of Jamaica, what keywords would you use for your literature search?
3. For the topic described in (2), what search strings would you use in an Internet search engine or an electronic database? How would you use truncations and/or Boolean operators?
4. What inclusion and exclusion criteria would you use for filtering the literature search findings in your research topic?
5. What are the five criteria for a systematic literature review?
6. What is the purpose of A, B and C lists in literature search filtering?
7. Using Box 3.3, write an annotated bibliography for three articles relevant to your research topic.
8. What is a literature map, and how can it help a researcher?

References

Adler, N. J. (1983). A typology of management studies involving culture. *Journal of International Business Studies*, 14(2), 29–47.

Agarwal, S. and Ramaswami, S. (1992). Choice of foreign market entry mode: impact of ownership, location and internalisation factors. *Journal of International Business Studies*, 23(2), 128–151.

Anand, J. and Delios, A. (1997). Location specificity and the transfer of downstream assets to foreign subsidiaries. *Journal of International Business Studies*, 28(3), 579–603.

Brouthers, D. K. (2001). Explaining the national cultural distance paradox. *Journal of International Business Studies*, 32(1), 112–121.

Cassedy, K. (1992). Preparedness in the face of crisis: an examination of crisis management planning in the travel and tourism industry. *World Travel and Tourism Review*, 2, 169–174.

Chang, S. J. (1995). International expansion strategy of Japanese firms: capability building through sequential entry. *Academy of Management Journal*, 38(2), 383–407.

Contractor, F. and Kundu, S. (1998). Modal choice in a world of alliances: analysing organizational forms in the international hotel sector. *Journal of International Business Studies*, 29(2), 325–357.

Creswell, J. W. (2003). *Research Design: Qualitative, Quantitative and Mixed Methods Approaches* (2nd edn). Thousand Oaks, CA: Sage Publications.

Drabek, T. E. (1995). Disaster responses within the tourism industry. *International Journal of Mass Emergencies and Disasters*, 13(1), 7–23.

Erramilli, M. and Rao, C. (1993). Service firms international entry mode choice: a modified transaction–cost analysis approach. *Journal of Marketing*, 57(1), 19–38.

Faulkner, B. (2001). Towards a framework for tourism disaster management. *Tourism Management*, 22(2), 135–147.

Faulkner, B. and Vikulov, K. (2001). Washed out one day, back on track the next: a post mortem of a tourism disaster. *Tourism Management*, 22(4), 331–344.

Fink, S. (1986). *Crisis Management: Planning for the Inevitable*. New York, NY: American Management Association.

Fredline L., Jago L. and Deery M. (2003). The development of a generic scale to measure the social impacts of events. *Event Management*, 8(1), 23–37.

Gatignon, H. and Anderson, E. (1988). The multinational corporation's degree of control over foreign subsidiaries: an empirical test of a transaction cost explanation. *Journal of Law, Economics and Organization*, 4(2), 305–336.

Gomes-Casseres, B. (1989). Joint ventures in the face of global competition. *Sloan Management Review*, 30(3), 17–26.

Granot, H. (1995). Proposed scaling of the communal consequences of disaster. *Disaster Prevention and Management*, 4(3), 5–13.

Johanson, J. and Vahlne, J. E. (1977). The internationalisation process of the firm – a model of knowledge development and increasing market commitments. *Journal of International Business Studies*, 8(2), 23–32.

Kim, W. and Hwang, P. (1992). Global strategy and multinationals' entry mode choice. *Journal of International Business Studies*, 23(1), 29–53.

Kogut, B. and Singh, H. (1988). The effect of national culture on the choice of entry mode. *Journal of International Business Studies*, 19(4), 411–432.

Mossberg L. L (1995). Tour leaders and their importance in charter tours. *Tourism Management*, 16(6), 437–445.

Pittaway, L., Robertson, M., Munir, K., Denyer, D. and Neely, A. (2004). Networking and innovation: a systematic review of the evidence. *International Journal of Management Reviews*, 5–6, 137–168.

Richardson, B. (1994). Crisis management and management strategy – time to 'loop to loop'? *Disaster Prevention and Management*, 3(3), 59–80.

Shane, S. A. (1996). Explaining why franchise companies expand overseas. *Journal of Business Venturing*, 11(2), 73–88.

Silverman, D. (2005). *Doing Qualitative Research: A Practical Handbook* (2nd edn). London: Sage Publications.

Taylor, S. (2000). Hotels. In: C. Lashley and A. Morrison (eds), *Franchising Hospitality Services*. Oxford: Butterworth Heinemann, pp. 170–191.

Turner, B. (1994). Causes of disaster: sloppy management. *British Journal of Management*, 5, 215–219.

Turnbull, D. (1996). 'The Influence of Political Risk Events on the Investment Decisions of Multinational Hotel Companies in Caribbean Hotel Projects'. Unpublished Doctoral dissertation, Virginia Polytechnic Institute and State University, Blacksburg, Virginia.

Wolcott, H. F. (1994). *Transforming Qualitative Data: Description, Analysis, and Interpretation*. Thousand Oaks, CA: Sage Publications.

Yee, J. S. R. (2003). *Dynamic Literature Mapping: Typography in Screen-Based Media* (online). Centre for Design Research, School of Design, Northumbria University. Available at http://www.designdictator.com/eadpaper.pdf (accessed 26 June 2006).

Yip, G. S. (1989). Global strategy … in a world of nations? *Sloan Management Review*, Fall, 29–41.

Zhao, J. L. (1994). 'The Antecedent Factors and Entry Mode Choice of Multinational Lodging Firms: The Case of Growth Strategies into New International Markets'. Unpublished doctoral dissertation, Virgin Polytechnic Institute and State University, Blacksburg, Virginia.

Zhao, J. L. and Olsen, M. D. (1997). The antecedent factors influencing entry mode choices of multinational lodging firms. *International Journal of Hospitality Management*, 16(1), 79–98.

Chapter 4
Research philosophies, approaches and strategies

All you need is the plan, the road map, and the courage to press on to your destination.
(Earl Nightingale, US motivational writer and author, 1921–1989)

There is a belief, held by many, that 'research' is associated with activities that are remote from daily life and usually take place in a laboratory, carried out by scientists. This belief is partly correct in that research is the study of problems through the use of scientific methods and principles. However, there is a growing number of people outside laboratories (such as managers, consultants, academics and students) who carry out research in order to produce and disseminate knowledge relevant to the business world. In essence, the difference between these two groups is in their research philosophies, approaches and strategies – their perception of how the knowledge can be created and constructed in a rigorous and meaningful way in order to answer a research problem. Your decision regarding these issues is therefore the cornerstone for your study, because it will determine the way you will construct knowledge in your work – i.e. how you will conduct the research.

Research philosophies: positivism and phenomenology

According to Easterby-Smith and colleagues (1999), there are three main reasons why this whole mental exercise regarding the research philosophy you should follow in your study is important:

1. It can help you to choose the research methods that you will use – in other words, to decide on your overall research strategy. This includes the type of evidence gathered and its origin, the way in which the collected evidence will be analysed and interpreted, and how it will help to answer your research questions.
2. Knowledge of research philosophy will enable and assist you to evaluate different research methods and avoid inappropriate use and unnecessary work by identifying the limitations of particular approaches at an early stage of your study.
3. It may help you to be creative and innovative by either choosing or adapting research methods that are, as yet, outside your experience.

There are two main research philosophies: positivism and phenomenology. Positivism promotes a more objective interpretation of reality, using hard data from surveys and experiments, while phenomenology (or interpretivism) is concerned with methods that examine people and their social behaviour (Gill and Johnson, 1997). Positivism has been more commonly associated with scientific research, while phenomenology has its roots in the social sciences (Veal, 2006). Some of the differences between these philosophies are outlined in Box 4.1.

Box 4.1	Key features of positivist and phenomenological viewpoints	
Key areas	**Positivism**	**Phenomenology**
Basic beliefs	• The world is external and objective • The observer is independent • Science is value-free	• The world is socially constructed and subjective • The researcher is part of what is observed • Science is driven by human interests and motives
Method of research	• Focus on facts • Look for causality and fundamental laws • Reduce phenomena to simplest elements • Formulate hypotheses and test them	• Focus on meanings • Try to understand what is happening • Look at the totality of each situation • Develop ideas through induction from data
Research design	• Structured, formal and specific detailed plans	• Evolving and flexible
Involvement of the researcher	• The researcher remains distanced from the material being researched • Short-term contact	• The researcher gets involved with the phenomena being researched • Long-term contact; emphasis on trust and empathy
Preferred methods	• Operationalization of concepts so that they can be measured	• Use of multiple methods to establish different views of phenomena
Sampling	• Large samples	• Small samples investigated in depth or over time
Data collection methods	• Experiments, surveys, structured interviews and observation	• Observation, documentation, open-ended and semi-structured interviews
Research instruments	• Questionnaires, scales, test scores and experimentation	• Researcher
Strengths	• Provides wide coverage of the range of situations	• Ability to look at change processes over time

Key areas	Positivism	Phenomenology
	• Greater opportunity for researcher to retain control of research process • Clarity about what is to be investigated, therefore data collection can be fast and economical • Helps to generalize previous research findings and test previously developed hypotheses	• Greater understanding of people's meanings • Adjustment to new issues and ideas as they emerge • Contributes to the evolution of new theories • Provides a way of gathering data which is natural rather than artificial
Weaknesses	• Methods tend to be rather inflexible and artificial • Not effective in understanding processes or the significance that people attach to actions • Not very helpful in generating theories	• Data collection takes a great deal of time and resources • Difficulty of analysis of data • Harder for the researcher to control the research process • Reliability problem with findings

(Adapted from Denzin and Lincoln, 1994; Easterby-Smith *et al.*, 1999; Wood, 1999)

As a positivist researcher, you take the stance of a natural scientist. You remain distanced from the object that you study; you focus on facts and formulate hypotheses to test them against empirical evidence (a hypothesis is a proposition that is based on a review of the theory about how something might work or behave – an explanation which may or may not be supported by the empirical evidence, i.e. the data you collect). The choice of what you study and how you will study it is determined by objective criteria rather than your beliefs and interests. You, as a researcher, are independent from the object of your study, which exists in isolation from the outside world, and you use a structured methodology (quantitative measurement through questionnaires and experiments) with the aim of collecting quantifiable data from large samples. Your findings lead to laws or law-like generalizations similar to those in the physical and natural sciences. This approach enables your to control the research process, but allows you almost no flexibility or manoeuvring ability in the methodology that you choose (Easterby-Smith *et al.*, 1999; Saunders *et al.*, 2007).

As a phenomenological/interpretive researcher, you study phenomena. You seek insight into these phenomena by reference to the participants in the phenomena in the widest sense. Participants provide the starting point, and through them you try to understand and interpret what is occurring and why. You formulate hypotheses using meanings that arise from your own preconceptions, and test them against empirical evidence. The research appears to be less formal, less structured, and a more flexible methodology enables you to produce ideas from the collected data. This philosophy can often lead to multiple methods of data collection being used on much smaller sample sizes, enabling you to comprehend the research topic better (Easterby-Smith *et al.*,

1999; Saunders *et al.*, 2007). The methods deployed under the phenomenological philosophy range from the more unstructured qualitative techniques of focus groups and participant observation, through interviews, toward the more artistic methods of content analysis, hermeneutics and literary criticism. All of these are useful techniques for developing insights into the areas in which theory is limited or does not exist.

In reality, it is not possible to identify a researcher who supports only one view. Although these two research philosophies are often seen as opposing and polarized views, they are frequently used in conjunction with one another, as the differences between them are not clear cut (Easterby-Smith *et al.*, 1999; Wood, 1999). Positivist and phenomenological philosophies should be seen as the two ends of a continuum, and you may find yourself moving between the two during the different stages of the same research process. Normally, the reality of what is being investigated is considerably more complex in its totality than either positivist or phenomenological philosophies can capture. Combining the strengths of both philosophies may therefore enhance the rigour and systemization of your study, while retaining the ability to investigate phenomena in better depth. In fact, there is a strong suggestion within the research community that research philosophies are complementary, and should therefore be mixed in research of many kinds. The underlying assumption is that the weaknesses in each philosophy will be compensated by the counter-balancing strengths the other.

Each research philosophy has its advantages and disadvantages and, more importantly, they can be complementary. When it comes to which research philosophy to adopt and when, it is important to consider several issues:

- The existing knowledge in the researched area (is it a well researched area, or are there many research gaps?)
- The research question (am I testing existing knowledge, or am I exploring new knowledge?)
- The researcher's skills (am I good at designing questionnaires and analysing them, or am I better at direct interaction with people and exploring their phenomenal world?)
- Time and available resources (would my time and other resources allow me only to test ideas, or do I have enough time and resources to allow exploration?).

Depending on these factors, you may choose either one or both philosophies for your research project.

Research approaches: deduction and induction

The philosophy is all about how you will construct knowledge in your project, so another important decision is whether you will construct it at the beginning of your project or in the end. You may want to start by reviewing the relevant literature, developing a theory and hypotheses – i.e. constructing the knowledge – and then designing your study in a way that tests (corroborates or refutes) these hypotheses; alternatively, you may decide to use the literature to design your research in such a way that analysis of the collected data will help you develop the theory – i.e. construct the knowledge. The decision is directly connected to two research approaches: deduction and induction.

Deduction is 'the human process of going from one thing to another, i.e., of moving from the known to the unknown' (Spangler, 1986: 101). By taking a deductive approach, you use what you know and move to what you cannot see directly – you have a clear theoretical position prior to the collection of data. In deductive reasoning, the conclusion is drawn first and the research is all about proving it to be correct or incorrect.

A deductive approach in your research will help you to better describe and explain the pattern of relationships and interactions between the variables you are looking at. Robson (2002) lists five sequential stages that researchers adopting a deductive approach need to follow:

1. Develop a hypothesis or hypotheses
2. Express these hypotheses in operational terms (showing how they will be measured)
3. Test the hypothesis (through an experiment, a survey or some other kind of empirical inquiry)
4. Examine the specific outcome of the inquiry (corroborate the hypotheses or refute them)
5. If necessary, modify the theory in the light of the findings.

Induction, on the other hand, is 'a process whereby from sensible singulars, perceived by the senses, one arrives at universal concepts and principles held by the intellect' (Johnson-Laird and Byrne, 1991: 16). In this definition, 'sensible singulars, perceived by the senses' are the observations of a researcher who draws a conclusion from one or more particular pieces of evidence. It is the evidence that leads the researcher to the conclusion – not the other way round.

An inductive approach has both advantages and disadvantages, which need to be taken into consideration when deciding which approach to adopt.

1. Advantages:
   - It helps you make a cause–effect link between particular variables and the way in which humans interpret these variables in their social world
   - It is flexible in that it helps you to identify alternative theories on the research topic and permits changes of the research emphasis as the research progresses
   - It helps you explain why a particular phenomenon is taking place
   - It acknowledges that you are a part of the research process
   - It allows research of topics that may have very little existing literature to support them
   - It uses empirical evidence as the beginning of the reasoning process and can be easily applied.

2. Disadvantages:
   - It is more effective with a small sample, so there is a limit to the sample size
   - It is generally more time consuming, as ideas are generated over a much longer period of data collection and analysis
   - The risk of the research yielding no useful data patterns and theories is higher than with deductive research.

As with research philosophies, it is worth mentioning that many studies stand somewhere on an inductive–deductive continuum. The deductive (theory-driven) approach can be used alongside the inductively-oriented approach in a study. Saunders *et al.* (2007) argue that what really matters in selecting a research approach is how appropriate it is for the particular research questions and objectives. For example, if you are particularly interested in understanding why something is happening rather than just describing what is happening, it may be more appropriate to adopt the inductive approach. If you decide to adopt an inductive research approach, you will not force the data to fit a pre-determined framework and it may be easier to make discoveries. Utilizing exploratory research by talking to experts in the subject provides an opportunity to investigate issues without structuring them within the framework of prior definitions. The inductive research approach can therefore help to generate new theoretical insights into a topic.

Case example

Altinay and Altinay's (2006) study aimed to explain the relationship between the small-firm growth of ethnic minority businesses in the catering sector and the socio-cultural networks of entrepreneurs. In the study, the purpose was to operationalize the concepts and propose a relationship between two specific variables: growth and informal networks (co-ethnic capital, co-ethnic labour, co-ethnic information and co-ethnic market). This study deduced a number of hypotheses based on previous research, and these were developed and stated as follows.

- H1: Business growth is positively related to funds raised from informal networks at business start-up.
- H2: Recruitment of co-ethnic labour and business growth are positively associated.
- H3: Information and advice from informal networks is positively associated with growth.
- H4: There is a negative relationship between business growth and reliance on co-ethnic markets.

It is important to note that the relationships and the direction (positive or negative) of the relationships between the variables are determined based on the literature review. This again shows that the deductive approach is a theory-driven approach. These hypotheses were then tested through questionnaire research, and the findings of the study supported some of the hypotheses.

In the example provided in the case example above (Altinay and Altinay, 2006), you can see that the researchers might have adopted an inductive research approach had they been looking at a knowledge gap with regard to the relationship between small-firm growth and the informal networks. The researchers could have chosen an inductive approach for the following reasons:

- The existing literature did not give much detailed information about informal networks and their influence on growth. Utilizing an exploratory and inductive approach could provide an opportunity to explore all those issues and fill the knowledge gap.
- An inductive research approach could provide a relatively open mind to look at how informal networks influence small-firms' growth by preventing the research from becoming structured by prior definitions. This is particularly important in terms of preventing bias from limiting the findings and identifying themes that might evolve from the empirical data obtained in the field.

Quantitative versus qualitative research

The research philosophies and approaches we have seen are directly linked with the methods that are used to collect data in a research project. The positivist philosophy is usually associated with deduction and quantitative research. Quantitative research aims to determine how one thing (a variable) affects another in a population, by quantifying the relationships between variables (the things you measure). To quantify the relationships between these variables, researchers use statistical methods such as relative frequencies, difference between means, correlation coefficients, etc. There are two main research designs within this category: descriptive and experimental. In a descriptive study, the primary goal is to assess a sample at one specific point in time without attempting to change its behaviour or the conditions in which it exists (i.e. you measure things as they are). In an experimental study, your primary goal is to test hypotheses under conditions that you impose on the sample. In such a research design, you take measurements, change the conditions, take the measurements again and then compare them in order to draw conclusions. The conclusions drawn from this kind of research design tend to be generalized.

The phenomenological philosophy is usually associated with induction and qualitative research. Qualitative research aims to develop an understanding of the context in which phenomena and behaviours take place. It focuses mainly on experiences and emotions and is designed to be probing in nature, thus encouraging informants to introduce concepts of importance from their perspective, rather than adhering to areas that have been pre-determined by the researcher. Qualitative data are usually in a text form, and offer a richer, more in-depth representation of people's experiences, attitudes and beliefs. Due to the personal and contextual dimensions of these data, conclusions drawn from such research designs cannot be generalized.

The main differences between the two approaches are summarized in Box 4.2.

Box 4.2	Quantitative vs qualitative research

Quantitative	Qualitative
Objective	There are issues about 'objectivity'
Deductive	Inductive
Generalizable	Not generalizable
Numbers	Words

They are both systematic approaches to research.

Many researchers favour the use of just one of the two methodologies (either quantitative or qualitative), and a number of their arguments, such as time constraints and the need to limit the scope of a study, are valid. However, a combination of the two offers you the best of both worlds, and if you think that a mixed methodology is appropriate then do not hesitate to adopt it.

Case examples

In their study of hotel housekeeping work in Cardiff (UK), Powell and Watson (2006) used multiple sources to generate both quantitative and qualitative data. Their study drew on questionnaire responses from sixty-four room attendants (which led to the generation of quantitative data) along with twenty hours of recorded responses recorded during individual interviews held in private with six room attendants and four head-housekeepers (which led to the generation of qualitative data). It was thought that data collection by using questionnaires was a practical and efficient way of gaining data from a large number of people, but that this was less effective at discovering the meanings and the motives that form the basis of social action. Therefore, they combined quantitative and qualitative approaches by using both interviews and questionnaires. The questionnaire produced answers only to those questions asked, whereas the free-flowing interviews focused on sensitive issues, allowing room attendants and head-housekeepers to speak freely from their own viewpoint, and as a result yielded wide-ranging and unexpected issues.

In another study designed to discover employment and labour market practices in the Australian hospitality industry, Davidson and colleagues used both quantitative and qualitative sets of empirical data from luxury hotels (Davidson *et al.*, 2006). The research had two phases, which complemented one another. The quantitative phase comprised an employee relations survey that sought data on operational employee and management demographics, wage levels, gender, acquiring skills, and working conditions, while the qualitative phase involved interviewing fourteen hotel human resource managers. The interviews focused on accountability systems for managing labour turnover, covering broader HRM practices, and provided data that supplemented the insights derived from the survey data collected.

O'Connor and Frew (2004) also combined both qualitative and quantitative approaches through a Delphi study to explore expert opinion on how an electronic channel of distribution might best be evaluated. The use of qualitative research and the Delphi technique (where a panel of experts is chosen to give their opinions on the subject under investigation; they then answer questions provided by the facilitator, and are normally given at least one opportunity to re-evaluate their answers based upon examination of the group response) acted as a foundation for an informed quantitative investigation of the key evaluation factors of electronic channels of distribution.

It is important to note that those researchers combining qualitative and quantitative methods use qualitative methods at a preliminary stage to determine the depth of an issue, followed by quantitative methods such as surveys to investigate the breadth of a phenomenon.

Research strategies

A research strategy is a general plan of action that will give direction to your research, enabling you to conduct it in a systematic manner. There are quite a few different research strategies you may consider for your research; some of them are clearly linked to the deductive approach and others to the inductive approach. However, you need to remember that what is important is not the label attached to each strategy, but its appropriateness in helping you achieve your research objectives – given any constraints you may have. The strategies considered here are:

- Case study
- Grounded theory
- Ethnography
- Action research
- Survey research
- Experimentation.

Case study

The case study has been a popular research strategy among hospitality researchers investigating a number of subject areas in the context of hospitality and tourism firms or tourism destinations. Robson (2002: 178) defines a case study as 'a strategy for doing research which involves an empirical investigation of a particular contemporary phenomenon within its real life context using multiple sources of evidence'. In your study, you can choose one or more hospitality or tourism firms as a case study (or studies) to investigate your topic – say, for example, employee motivation and its influence on service quality. On the other hand, if you are looking at political instability and its impacts on the tourism industry, you will choose a country or a destination for your case. A case study strategy will allow you to generate new knowledge about the topic when the existing knowledge is inadequate and incomplete (Otley and Berry, 1994). It will also allow you to explore the real-life complexities of managing the organizations and destinations.

In order to build your case study, your research will need to generate more than one type of data. Normally, a case study of a company would be developed with the help of company documents and archival records (brochures, reports, meeting minutes, memos, etc.), interviews with key informants, observation of operations, meetings, etc., and company artefacts. Using multiple sources of evidence will increase the reliability and validity of your data and, consequently, your study.

Case example

Haktanir and Harris (2005), in their work to explore performance measurement practices in the hospitality industry, use the case of an independent 392-room 5-star resort hotel in Northern Cyprus. The case was built using a multiple data collection approach over a nine-week period. The researchers, in order to obtain detailed information concerning the performance measurement practices, conducted semi-structured interviews with employees, managers and the regional executive. At the same time, in order to understand the decision-making mechanism and the performance measures utilized, they collected and analysed financial statements and other departmental reports. Finally, they undertook an observation of the hotel's operations, as this was felt to be critical for understanding the procedures and systems of the business, and for scrutinizing the data.

There is a longstanding debate as to whether multiple-case research (Yin, 1994) is superior to a single-case study (Pettigrew *et al.*, 1992), in terms of increasing the rigour of the research. Eisenhardt (1989) states that the concern is not whether two cases are better than one or four better than three; the appropriate number of cases depends upon how much is known and how much new information is likely to be learned from incremental cases.

Case example

In her study on how marketing decisions are made by European tour operators, Roper (2005) looked at the extent of marketing standardization/adaptation across and within the Nordic region, and the centric profile of the European tour operators in terms of marketing decision-making. The researcher took a multiple-case study approach in order to elicit patterns common to cases and theory, and selected three tour-operating firms operating in the Nordic region but listed on stock exchanges outside the Nordic countries. She collected data from a range of sources – secondary sources; semi-structured and telephone interviews with executives from the three firms at local and regional level, and document analysis.

Nevertheless, according to Yin (1994), a single-case study is an appropriate design under several circumstances. One rationale for a single case is when it represents the critical case in testing a well-formulated theory – for example, if your organization is the only organization implementing total quality management. A second rationale for a single case is when the case represents an extreme or unique case – for example, if your case-study organization is the most international hotel group in the world.

Another rationale for selecting a single-case rather than a multiple-case design is that the investigator has access to a situation previously inaccessible to scientific observation.

Grounded theory

Grounded theory is a qualitative type of research that generates theory from observation. The resulting theory is 'grounded' in the observable experiences (their categories, their properties and the relationships between them), but the researchers add their own insight into why those experiences exist – i.e., go beyond just 'what is' to suggest 'why' it is (Strauss and Corbin, 1990). The basic idea behind this research strategy is that the researcher goes into the field with an open mind and no presumed relationships, and generates knowledge about the relationships between the variables from the raw data collected from the fieldwork (Glaser and Strauss, 1967). Although an open mind is a basic assumption of grounded theory, a more pragmatic approach would be to begin the research process with a preliminary review of the literature to identify the gaps within the extant literature and clarify the research focus before entering the field (Strauss and Corbin, 1990). A more thorough literature review and the development of the research framework can take place after the fieldwork has been done. This will help the researcher to interpret the findings in light of this literature review and the resultant conceptual framework.

The grounded theory strategy advocates the use of multiple data sources to examine the same phenomenon from different angles. Glaser and Strauss (1967: 65) state that:

> *In Grounded Theory Study, neither one kind of data on a category nor technique for data collection is necessarily appropriate. Different kinds of data give the analyst different views or vantage points from which to understand a category and to develop its properties; these different views we have called slices of data.*

Similarly, Strauss and Corbin (1990: 5) indicate that:

> *data collection procedures involve interviews and observations as well as such other sources as government documents, video tapes, newspapers, letters and books – anything that may shed light on the questions under study. Each of these sources can be coded in the same way.*

As the resultant theory emerges, researchers have to enter and exit the field on a regular basis in order for them to be able to carry out data collection and analysis simultaneously.

Case example

Decrop and Snelders (2003) proposed a new typology of vacation decision-making where vacationers' socio-psychological processes and decision styles are combined. The researchers observed the vacation decision-making process of twenty-five Belgian households. The participants were initially interviewed in February about their vacation plans, their expectations of and motivations for their holidays, then again in April. Twenty of them were interviewed for a third time in June, because their decision-making process had not been completed in April. The analysis and interpretation of the interview transcripts and field (observation) notes were based on the grounded theory approach. The grounded theory strategy followed by the researchers included the concurrent collection and analysis of data in order to enhance their theoretical sensitivity. From this analysis emerged certain categories, patterns and propositions, which were permanently called into question by the researchers. Through the analysis of data at three levels (i.e. open, axial and selective coding), from the most descriptive to the most interpretative, the researchers developed a new typology with six types of vacationers – habitual, rational, hedonic, opportunistic, constrained and adaptable.

It is worth noting that it is difficult for an inexperienced researcher to follow a grounded theory strategy. This is because the researcher does not start with the theory and explain or prove it; instead he or she has to be 'open' to all the theories that may emerge when studying a phenomenon. Therefore, an inexperienced researcher following a grounded theory strategy might struggle with the staggering volume of data and either suffocate under all the data or leap to early conclusions.

Ethnography

Ethnography is an ideal strategy for developing a holistic understanding of a society, community, group or organization from an insider's perspective, by living with members over an extended period of time (Spradley, 1979, 1980). This strategy is popular among anthropologists and people carrying out cultural studies. It is a time-consuming qualitative strategy, and uses multiple methodologies to arrive at a theoretically comprehensive understanding of a group or culture. The objective here is detailed exploration of group activity, which requires the researcher's immersion and ideally participation in the group under study. The researcher often has to live with the group in order to learn their language, culture, traditions and way of living. An analogy can be made with Edward Zwick's film *The Last Samurai*. In this film, Captain Nathan Algren is captured by and lives with the samurai for an extended period, and learns about their traditions and code of honour. Had he not been a military officer, he could have been a good 'ethnographer' and written what Geertz (1973) calls a 'thick description' of Samurai culture and ethics. Ethnography is the preferred research strategy among many researchers in the tourism field, especially those investigating the behaviours of tourists from a cultural perspective.

Case example

Muzaini's (2006) research adopted ethnography as a strategy and drew data from observation, supplemented by interviews, in order to explore particular aspects of the backpacker culture within Southeast Asia. Moore's (1985) ethnographic research investigated the popularity of Los Angeles with Japanese tourists, answering the research question: 'What do Japanese tourists seek in Los Angeles?' These two studies examine the worlds of two groups – backpackers visiting South Asia and Japanese tourists visiting Los Angeles – based on observation of the informants' behaviours and on interviews with them. Their research took place over an extended period of time, until researchers were able to interpret what backpackers and Japanese tourists do, how they behave and what they value in their lives.

Action research

Action research is a strategy in which the researcher joins the organization under study for a period of time and, with his or her findings, helps the organization to solve the problems it is facing. This research strategy has the potential to have a significant impact on reducing the knowledge gap between academia and industry, while simultaneously offering something beneficial to the tourism and hospitality organizations. Waser and Johns (2003: 376) state that:

> *Action research is especially suited to service industries such as the hospitality industry, where guest satisfaction is dependent upon organizational culture. Action research might make it possible to describe, and at the same time to change the cultural status quo, to the benefit of both the guest and the organization.*

Action research suggests a closer engagement with the research problem, owing to the fact that the researcher is actively involved in the research environment. Results are continuously fed back, and the research problem receives systematic reconsideration and solutions. In other words, the researcher and the research project are oriented towards bringing about change in an organization, often involving informants in the process of investigation. This is particularly important in today's knowledge-driven world, where partnerships between industry and universities have become increasingly important.

A common characteristic of action research and ethnography is that the researcher 'becomes one of the group', even if this is for a shorter time in action research than in ethnography. The findings of the study are used by the group itself to develop a solution that is often far more effective than one developed by outsiders, since the members of the group know the problem and alternative solutions best. Moreover, when the researcher provides the group with a systematic approach to problem-solving as well as with basic theories on the problem under study, all the participants profit in the form of mental growth, and in some cases a learning attitude can be created which persists for a long time after the project has finished (Waser and Johns, 2003).

Case example

In her study of work–life balance initiatives for women, Doherty (2004) reported on an action research project conducted in the UK hospitality industry to explore the effectiveness of work–life balance initiatives in helping women progress to senior management. Whilst the researcher was the coordinator of the project, the client and the research subjects were involved in shaping the research questions and methods, in meetings and in focus groups. The research involved building case studies of best practice of work–life balance in a number of pre-selected hospitality organizations. Data were collected through semi-structured interviews with nine human resource managers and four general managers/owners, and with fourteen employees who had benefited from work–life balance arrangements. Eight strong cases were developed, and these were supported with evidence taken from a further three organizations. The initial results of the research were published in an 88-page glossy publication entitled *Creating a Work–Life Balance: A Good Practice Guide for the Hospitality Industry* (Department of Trade and Industry, 2001), which was intended for the research participants themselves and to stimulate discussion and change within a wide range of hospitality organizations. The findings from the eight good-practice cases were then further analysed and discussed in the article.

Survey research

Survey research is another popular strategy among hospitality and tourism researchers. In this strategy, closely associated with the deductive approach, the researcher selects a sample of informants from a population and administers a standardized questionnaire to them. Tourism and hospitality researchers interested in explaining the attitudes, behaviours and perceptions of consumers, managers, employees and local residents adopt a survey strategy to collect data from and draw inferences for these groups.

There are two main types of surveys; descriptive and the analytic. Descriptive surveys are concerned with particular characteristics of a specific population, and are used to gather information largely on what people do and think. Thus, you might use this type of survey to find out what tourists think about a destination, what attractions they intend to visit, and which leisure activities they will undertake during their stay. The emphasis here is placed on the representative sample of the population under study.

Analytic surveys are used to answer research questions or test hypotheses by taking the logic into the field – for example, to understand the relationship between service quality, customer loyalty and restaurant profitability. The emphasis here is placed more on the variables under study (e.g. service quality, customer loyalty, etc.). A review of the literature is of utmost importance in the design of the survey.

For more about questionnaires, questionnaire design and issues related to validity and reliability, see Chapter 6.

Case example

In order to measure the effect of human resource management (HRM) on performance in the hotel industry in Barbados, Alleyne *et al.* (2006) used a quantitative survey covering forty-six out of a population of seventy-five hotels. The researchers invited all seventy-five hotels to participate, and sent the questionnaires by post to an HR manager, a general manager or a deputy general manager of each. They telephoned three times to remind non-respondents to complete the questionnaire; when this did not work, additional copies of the questionnaire and a reminder letter were faxed, emailed, delivered or posted to the respondent, followed by several final follow-up telephone calls. The questionnaire was analytic, and included variables such as human resource management practices, business strategy, human resource outcomes, performance outcomes, etc.

Experimentation

Experimentation is a strategy that is more popular among natural scientists and social scientists, and is aiming at testing for cause and effect. In this strategy the researcher directly manipulates one or more independent variables in order to observe their effect on another variable – the dependent variable. This research strategy, explanatory in nature, is firmly rooted in the deductive approach, and requires a thorough definition of research hypotheses, selection of samples of individuals from known populations, and allocation of samples to different experimental conditions, usually in research labs. The typical experimental design involves three steps that will lead the researcher to the acceptance or rejection of the hypothesis:

1. Measurement of the dependent variable
2. Exposure of the dependent variable to the independent variable
3. Re-measurement of the dependent variable.

Case examples

After looking at different studies showing that odours have an effect on human behaviour and on consumer's behaviour, Gueguen and Petr (2006) carried out an experiment in a restaurant, diffusing lemon and lavender aromas and seeing what effect these had on customers' length of stay. The control was a no-aroma condition. Results showed that lavender, but not lemon, increased the length of stay of customers and the amount they purchased. The hypothesis that lavender produces a relaxing effect is offered to explain the results.

In another experimental study, Gueguen and Jacob (2005) investigated the effect of touch on tipping in France. The experiment was carried out in a French bar. A waitress either briefly touched the forearm of a patron while asking what he or she wanted to drink, or didn't make physical contact. Results showed that touch increases tipping behaviour, although tipping to a waitress in a bar is unusual in France.

As you can see from our examples, researchers following this research strategy manipulated one or more of the variables and measured the change to a small number of variables whilst controlling the others.

The international dimension in choosing a methodology

Those of you who have worked in an international context will have been amazed at how differently people from other cultures behave. This is particularly pertinent in international business in the hospitality and tourism industry, because of its 'global' nature. If we move to another country and make decisions based on how we work in our own home country, we will make some bad decisions. It is important to understand that customers, employees and managers in our home country are not the same as those in other countries. For example, there are remarkable differences between the way business is conducted in countries such as UK, Spain, France and Italy. In Spain, you sit at the table and can do business in two hours at breakfast, lunch or dinner meetings. The philosophy of life is very different from that in the UK. A UK businessman might not be willing to sit with a couple of investors in a restaurant; he would be likely to say 'ok, let's meet at the office and continue'. In Spain, Italy or other Mediterranean countries, business is more about meeting people and slowly building up relationships and trust, whereas in the UK it is more focused. There is less socialising and more concern about sorting out the business issue in question as soon as possible. These are just few examples showing why it is critical to understand other cultures you may be doing business with – whether you are on vacation in a foreign country, or negotiating an important deal for your hospitality and tourism firm.

Similarly, when you are doing research, you need to consider both your cultural background and that of the context (country, society) in which you carry out your research activities. If we consider Hofstede's (1991) four dimensions, namely power distance, individualism, masculinity and uncertainty avoidance, this will give us a good framework to help us to understand the likely impacts of a culture on our research strategy or approach.

Power distance is the extent to which the less powerful members of organizations and institutions accept and expect that power is distributed unequally. This represents inequality (more versus less), but defined from below rather than from above. This implies that in some societies the hierarchical structure and sense of superiority are embedded in people's perceptions of each other. It is therefore very likely that those researchers coming from high power distance societies will find it difficult to have direct face-to-face interaction with people in the industry, particularly with those in senior positions. These researchers would prefer to choose the positivist tradition and perhaps use a survey strategy rather than following a phenomenological philosophy that requires close interaction with informants. Doing research in a high power distance society might also require adapting your approach, as informants might not be willing to have direct interaction with those researchers whom they perceive to be superior.

Collectivism versus individualism is the degree to which individuals are integrated into groups. If a country has a high individualism score, this indicates that individuality and individual rights are dominant. Individuals in these societies tend to have relationships with larger numbers of people, but the relationships are weak. A low individualism score points to a society that is more collectivist in nature. In these countries, the ties between individuals are very strong and the family is given more weight; the members of such societies lean towards collective responsibility. If you as a researcher come from a collectivist society, you might want to be more integrated with the society you are in and place more emphasis on trust and empathy. In this case, a phenomenological research philosophy and an inductively-driven research strategy might be more appropriate. In the case of representing the characteristics of an individualistic society where independent attitude is well regarded and the individuals remain distanced from the larger community, a positivist research philosophy might yield better results. It is important to note that in an individualistic society it might take a long time or even be impossible to gain access to informants, as developing relationships and building trust can be more complicated than in collectivist societies. It is therefore advisable to consider adopting a phenomenological research philosophy in a collectivist society, and a positivist research philosophy in an individualistic country.

Masculinity versus femininity refers to the distribution of roles between the genders in a society. This dimension pertains to the degree to which societies reinforce (or do not reinforce) the traditional masculine work role model of male achievement, control and power. High masculinity in a country indicates that a country experiences a higher degree of gender differentiation. In such cultures, males tend to dominate a significant portion of the society and power structure. In contrast, in a low-masculinity country, the society has a lower level of differentiation and inequity between genders. In these cultures, females are treated equally to males in all aspects of society. This masculinity versus femininity dimension has implications for researchers of different sexes (male and female). It might be argued that those male researchers from a high-masculinity society would not be willing to have direct face-to-face interaction with female informants, and would therefore prefer to follow methods and strategies informed by the positivist tradition and remain distanced from the female informants. Those female researchers conducting research in a masculine society might also consider adopting a positivist tradition, since in high-masculinity societies their power and authority as researchers might be questioned by those men dominating the senior positions of hospitality and tourism organizations.

Uncertainty avoidance deals with a society's tolerance to uncertainty and ambiguity. It indicates to what extent a culture programmes its members to feel either uncomfortable or comfortable in unstructured situations. Uncertainty-avoiding cultures try to minimize the possibility of such situations by strict laws and rules. The opposite, uncertainty-accepting cultures, try to have as few rules as possible. In terms of research, it is important to note that every research process has a certain degree of ambiguity and uncertainty. Researchers have questions in their minds for which they seek answers at the outset of the research. Therefore, they are impatient to find the answers and to reach early conclusions in order to get rid of the research uncertainty. If you as a researcher come from a high uncertainty-avoidance society and cannot tolerate uncertainty for long, it is advised that you follow a more structured, positivist and deductive approach for research. However, if you believe that you can follow an unstructured research journey and tolerate uncertainty, you can adopt a phenomenological research philosophy with a more inductively-driven research strategy. Such an 'adventurous' journey can help you to develop risk-taking, exploration and intuitive skills. In countries where uncertainty avoidance is high, it might be difficult for researchers to follow a phenomenological research philosophy and inductively-driven strategies because people may question the rationale behind the research and the possible consequences of contributing to the research project. They might seek explicit explanations for the value of research before providing support.

Summary

- Identifying your research philosophy and/or research approach helps you to clarify what kind of evidence (qualitative or quantitative) will be gathered, how (interviews, questionnaires, observations) and from where (individuals, organizations, laboratories). It also helps you to clarify how the collected data will be analysed.
- Researchers and research projects stand between the opposing ends of the positivist–phenomenological and/or inductive–deductive continuum at different stages of the research process. It is important to understand how you and your research projects will be influenced by these philosophies and approaches at different stages of the research process.
- Different research strategies suit to different research purposes, and therefore it is important that you consider your overall research aim, as well as the advantages and the disadvantages of each strategy, before choosing your strategy.
- The case study, survey and action research are the most popular research strategies in the hospitality and tourism industries, as they help to bridge the gap between the theory and management practice.

Exercise: research philosophies, approaches and strategies

- Lucy was trying to establish whether consumers choose hotels on the basis of brands or product attributes. She selected a sample of consumers who were asked individually to describe how they would choose a hotel from a fictitious list provided. Was Lucy's research qualitative or quantitative?

- Sven is exploring consumers' experiences of long-haul holidays. He decides to take a long-haul holiday himself to collect data while enjoying himself watching others on holiday. Is his research inductive, deductive, qualitative or quantitative?
- Yueh-Hsin was researching the literature on strategy implementation in the context of the hospitality industry, and found that much had been written on factors that influence the strategy implementation process. From the analysis and evaluation of this literature, she was able to propose a framework that incorporates the main factors. Was her research inductive or deductive?
- Boris was interested in the salary level differences between men and women in hotels. He hypothesized that the income gap is due to differences in education and whether people are employed part-time or full-time. He gathered data from the national census on income and employment, and used multiple-regression analysis to test this hypothesis. Interestingly, he found that gaps in income were not wholly explained by his hypothesis, and suggested that forms of pay discrimination exist. Was this research inductive, deductive, qualitative or quantitative?
- Saskia has taken a vacation job with a hotel company. The company is in the process of opening its first hotel in a new city. Saskia has been asked to join the pre-opening sales and marketing team to help launch the new hotel into the marketplace. As the company knows that she is doing a Master's degree, they have asked her to report back on her experience of the hotel opening and to suggest how the company could improve its practice in this area. She decides to gather data from her daily experiences and from a range of sources. What research strategy has Saskia adopted – action research, ethnography, experimentation or grounded theory?

Review questions

1. What are the basic beliefs underpinning positivist and phenomenological research philosophies?
2. With which data collection techniques is the phenomenological research philosophy associated?
3. With which data collection techniques is the positivist research philosophy associated?
4. Review your research question(s) and objectives for your study. How appropriate would it be to follow an inductive research approach? Explain the relationship between your research question(s) and objectives, and the use of the inductive research approach.
5. What are the most popular research strategies pursued by hospitality and tourism researchers, and why?
6. Would every research philosophy, approach and/or strategy suit every researcher? If not, how do cultural differences influence a researcher's choice?

References

Alleyne, P., Doherty, L. and Greenidge, D. (2006). Human resource management and performance in the Barbados hotel industry. *International Journal of Hospitality Management*, 25(4), 623–646.

Altinay, L. and Altinay, E. (2006). Determinants of ethnic minority entrepreneurial growth in the catering sector. *The Service Industries Journal*, 26(2), 203–221.

Davidson, M., Guilding, C. and Timo, N. (2006). Employment, flexibility, and labour market practices of domestic and MNC chain luxury hotels in Australia: where has accountability gone? *International Journal of Hospitality Management*, 25(2), 193–210.

Decrop, A. and Snelders, D. (2005). Grounded typology of vacation decision-making. *Tourism Management*, 26(2), 121–132.

Denzin, N. K. and Lincoln, Y. (1994). *Handbook of Qualitative Research*, London: Sage Publications.

Department of Trade and Industry (2001). *Creating a Work–Life Balance: A Good Practice Guide for the Hospitality Industry*. London: DTI.

Doherty, L. (2004). Work–life balance initiatives: implications for women. *Employee Relations*, 26(4), 433–452.

Easterby-Smith, M., Thorpe, R., and Lowe, A. (1999). *Management Research: An Introduction*. London: Sage Publications.

Eisenhardt, K. M. (1989). Building theories from case study research. *Academy of Management Review*, 14(4), 532–550.

Geertz, C. (1973). *The Interpretation of Cultures*. New York, NY: Basic Books.

Gill, J. and Johnson, P. (1997). *Research Methods for Managers* (2nd edn). London: Paul Chapman Publishing.

Glaser, B. G. and Strauss, A. L. (1967). *The Discovery of Grounded Theory*. Chicago, IL: Aldine Publishing.

Gueguen, N. and Jacob, C. (2006). The effect of touch on tipping: an evaluation in a French bar. *International Journal of Hospitality Management*, 24(2), 295–299.

Gueguen, N. and Petr, C. (2006). Odours and consumer behaviour in a restaurant. *International Journal of Hospitality Management*, 25(2), 335–339.

Haktanir, M. and Harris, P. (2005). Performance measurement practice in an independent hotel context: a case study approach. *International Journal of Contemporary Hospitality Management*, 17(1), 39–50.

Hofstede, G. (1991). *Cultures and Organizations: Software of Mind*. London: McGraw Hill.

Johnson-Laird, P. N. and Byrne, R. M. J. (1991). *Deduction*. Hove: Lawrence Erlbaum.

Moore, R. (1985). Los Angeles: an anthropological inquiry of Japanese tourists. *Annals of Tourism Research*, 12(4), 619–644.

Muzaini, H. (2006). Backpacking Southeast Asia: strategies of 'looking local'. *Annals of Tourism Research*, 33(1), 144–161.

O'Connor, P. and Frew, A. (2004). An evaluation methodology for hotel electronic channels of distribution. *International Journal of Hospitality Management*, 23(2), 179–199.

Otley, D. T. and Berry, A. J. (1994). Case study research in management accounting and control. *Management Accounting Research*, 5(1), 45–65.

Pettigrew, A., Ferlie, E. and McKee, L. (1992). *Shaping Strategic Change*. London: Sage Publications.

Powell, H. P. and Watson, D. (2006). The hotel room attendant at work. *International Journal of Hospitality Management*, 25(2), 297–312.

Robson, C. (2002). *Real World Research* (2nd edn). Oxford: Blackwell.

Roper, A. (2005). Marketing standardisation: tour operators in the Nordic region. *European Journal of Marketing*, 39(5/6), 514–527.

Saunders, M., Lewis, P. and Thornhill, A. (2007). *Research Methods for Business Students*. London: Prentice Hall Financial Times.

Spangler, M. M. (1986). *Logic: An Aristotelian Approach*. Lanham, MD: University Press of America.

Spradley, J. P. (1979). *The Ethnographic Interview*. New York, NY: Holt, Rinehart and Winston.

Spradley, J. P. (1980). *Participant Observation*. Forth Worth: Harcourt Brace.

Strauss, A. L. and Corbin, J. (1990). *The Basics of Qualitative Research: Grounded Theory Procedures and Techniques*. Newbury Park, CA: Sage Publications.

Veal, A. J. (2006). *Research Methods for Leisure and Tourism* (3rd edn). London: Pitman Publishing.

Waser H. and Johns N. (2003). An evaluation of action research as a vehicle for individual and organizational development in the hotel industry. *International Journal of Hospitality Management*, 22(4), 373–393.

Wood, R. (1999). Traditional and alternative research philosophies. In B. Brotherton (ed.), *The Handbook of Contemporary Hospitality Management Research*. New York, NY: John Wiley & Sons Ltd, pp. 3–18.

Yin, K. R. (1994). *Case Study Research: Design and Methods*. London: Sage Publications.

Chapter 5
Sampling

People are pretty much alike. It's only that our differences are more susceptible to definition than our similarities.

(Linda Ellerbee, broadcast journalist, 1944–)

When undertaking any research, it is essential that you obtain data from people that are as representative as possible of the group you are studying. Even with the perfect questionnaire or interview guide (if such a thing exists), your data will only be regarded as useful when your respondents are representative of such a population. For this reason, a clear understanding of the principles of sampling is essential in order to conduct any type of research, whether quantitative and qualitative. Imagine a researcher investigating how tourism policies are developed for a destination or a country. This researcher obviously needs expert opinion, and most probably the views of those who develop policies. Even if the researcher develops an excellent questionnaire or interview guide, appropriate responses will not be acquired if the people interviewed are local people and/or visiting tourists. These respondents will probably not have any idea about how policies are developed.

What is sampling?

Sampling is the process by which researchers select a representative subset or part of the total population that can be studied for their topic so that they will be able to draw conclusions regarding the entire population. These conclusions and any generalizations the researcher makes are only as good as the sample they are based on. The obvious advantage of sampling is that the smaller number of elements (e.g. people, organizations) to be studied makes the research more manageable and time-efficient, less costly, and potentially more accurate (since it is easier to maintain control over a smaller number of elements). For example, if your research is looking at how consumers in the People's Republic of China make their travel decisions, it is clearly impossible to send out 1.3 billion questionnaires in order to cover the entire population. You will need to select a sample of people that is, as far as possible, representative of the entire population of China. This, of course, is quite a challenge. All samples deviate from the true nature of the overall population by a certain amount, owing to chance variations in the selection of the sample's few elements from the population's many possible elements. This is called sampling error, and can be reduced by selecting a large sample and using efficient sampling design.

A large sample alone does not guarantee that the conclusions from your study will hold for the entire population you are studying – in other words, it does not guarantee the external validity of your study. A classic example of a large-sample study which produced a totally wrong outcome was the *Literary Digest* poll held before the 1936 US presidential elections (Squire, 1988). In this study, a sample of two million ballots was analysed and the results predicted a landslide victory for Landon over Roosevelt (55 per cent to 41 per cent). The actual result was Roosevelt 61 per cent and Landon 37 per cent – i.e. there was a 20 per cent error in predicting Roosevelt's vote. The reason for this error was that the sample had been selected from from telephone directories and lists of car owners. At that time, only wealthier people had telephones and/or drove cars, and most of these were Landon voters. In 1936, the majority of the US population was without cars or telephones, and most of these voted for Roosevelt – giving him the largest presidential victory in history. This large error in prediction is a perfect example of the possible consequences of poor sampling design.

Efficient sampling design starts with defining a target population properly. Reverting to the above example, perhaps it is too ambitious to target the entire population of China. However, focusing on Chinese business travellers seems more realistic. Since it is not practical to approach every Chinese business traveller for this study, the second step is to define an accessible population. The accessible population is a subset of the target population that reflects specific characteristics of the target population and is accessible for study.

Therefore, in the Chinese business travellers' example, it is essential to define the target population before a sample of participants can be defined. For example, will all Chinese business travellers be included? Is the question to be limited to Chinese business travellers travelling outside China, to those who fly business class, to those who use international hotel chains, etc? This narrowing and refining of the research question is particularly helpful, as you will be able to define the target as well as accessible populations and directly influence the external validity of the conclusions to be drawn from your study.

Box 5.1	Sampling guidelines	
	Considerations	**Example**
Target population	General characteristics Particular characteristics	Chinese business travellers Male, aged 25–45 years
Accessible population	Geographic/time constraints	Business travellers flying from Shanghai Pudong International Airport Travellers flying in May and June 2008
Inclusion criteria	Specific criteria by which participants will be selected for the study	Using business-class lounges
Exclusion criteria	Factors that will affect data collection	Frustrated delayed travellers Non-English speaking
	Ethical issues	Non-consent to recording the interview

Once you have defined the specific characteristics of the accessible population, it is important for you to consider the geographic and time constraints that you and your potential participants will have to contend with. Will your study require more than one location? If so, where are you going to access the participants? If the research is to be conducted in several cities in China, how will you deal with transportation? In the case of the Chinese business travellers' study, you may decide that you cannot really travel in several cities but can only conduct your research in Shanghai. This leads to the next step of your sampling design, which involves establishing certain inclusion and exclusion criteria for the accessible population (see Box 5.1).

There are two main categories of sampling methods: probability and non-probability. Within the sampling guidelines described above, you can employ a variety of sampling methods, either individually or in combination. The following section outlines these sampling methods.

Probability sampling

When trying to define a representative subset of the population you wish to study, the first important problem in your selection is selection bias. Selection bias arises when certain members of the population under study are under- or over-represented relative to others. It can easily occur, as you have seen in the example of the *Literary Digest* poll above, where some members of the population were less likely to be included than others. It results in distorted (erroneous) findings that cannot be generalized for the entire population under study. In order to avoid selection bias in your study, it is important for to guarantee that each member of your target population has an equal opportunity for selection. In order to achieve this, your participants must be selected at random – in other words, the selection of your sample must be based on the principle of randomization or chance, and your sampling method must be probability sampling (also referred to as representative sampling). When choosing to use a probability sample, your aim should be to minimize the sampling error of the estimates for the most important variables in your study, and at the same time to minimize the time and cost of conducting the study. For example, if you want to find the effect that the application of a revenue management system has on guest satisfaction in a given hotel, you will have to interview these guests. However, in a year this hotel hosts about 10 000 guests, and you may decide that, considering the expense and time involved, you are only able to interview 50. This means that you need to interview 1 in every 200 guests, provided that each guest has an equal chance of being picked up for an interview. There are several different ways of selecting a probability sample, but here we discuss four of them: simple random sampling, systematic sampling, stratified sampling and clustering sampling.

Simple random sampling

One of the best-known probability sampling techniques, this is, despite its name, neither simple nor random (in the sense of accidental or unsystematic). According to this sampling technique, all members of the population under study have the same chance (probability) of being selected. To select a simple random sample, you need a table of random numbers (statistics books include such tables; computer statistical packages, such as SPSS, are also able to generate random numbers). An example of such a table of random numbers is provided in Box 5.2.

Box 5.2	Table of random numbers

39634	62349	74088	65564	16379	19713	39153	69459	17986	24537
14595	35050	40469	27478	44526	67331	93365	54526	22356	93208
30734	71571	83722	79712	25775	65178	07763	82928	31131	30196
64628	89126	91254	24090	25752	03091	39411	73146	06089	15630
42831	95113	43511	42082	15140	34733	68076	18292	69486	80468
80583	70361	41047	26792	78466	03395	17635	09697	82447	31405
00209	90404	99457	72570	42194	49043	24330	14939	09865	45906
05409	20830	01911	60767	55248	79253	12317	84120	77772	50103
95836	22530	91785	80210	34361	52228	33869	94332	83868	61672
65358	70469	87149	89509	72176	18103	55169	79954	72002	20582

(Source: University of Minnesota Morris, available at
http://www.mrs.umn.edu/~sungurea/ introstat/public/instruction/ranbox/
randomnumbersII.html)

Suppose that the hotel has decided to provide you with the contact details of 1000 of its hotel guests for your study on the impact of revenue management practice on hotel guest satisfaction (i.e. the accessible population is 1000 guests). From this accessible population you have decided randomly to select 100 guests to be interviewed for the study. The first step is to assign a number from 1 to 1000 to each member of the accessible population. The next step is to choose a starting number in the table. You can start at any point on the table and move in any direction to choose the numbers required for the sample size. Decide on a pattern of movement through the table and then stick to it – for example, numbers from every third column and every second row. If a number comes up twice or a number is selected which is larger than population number, simply ignore it.

Assume that the number selected is 40469 (column 3, row 2), and that you have decided to use the last three digits to determine which members of the population will be selected for your sample. Here, the last three digits are 469, and therefore the guest 469 will be the first guest to be selected for your study. The next guests would be numbers 178, 089, 361, etc., until the entire sample of 100 guests has been selected.

Case example

Chi and Qu (2004) used a simple random sampling approach to survey 500 members of the Oklahoma Restaurant Association (in USA) in order to measure the attitudes of foodservice employers toward hiring persons with disabilities, and to assess the effects of these attitudes on employers' hiring practices.

Systematic sampling

Systematic random sampling is a method frequently chosen for its simplicity because it is a periodic process involving the selection of every *n*th member of the targeted population. For example, an airline wishing to assess the effectiveness of its check-in procedures may offer a questionnaire every eighth passenger that checks in for a specific flight – i.e. the eighth, sixteenth, twenty-fourth, thirty-second passenger, etc. This method is usually carried out by selecting the first subject randomly and then choosing every *n*th passenger who arrives at the counter for check-in. The number *n* is called the sampling fraction, and is determined by dividing the target population size by the required sample size – for example, if there are 200 passengers on the specific flight and the airline wants a 25 per cent systematic sample (i.e. a sample of 50 passengers), the sampling fraction is one-eighth (i.e. the airline will select one passenger out of every eight in the population). With the sampling fraction of one-eighth, the starting point must be within the first eight passengers that check in. The advantage of this sampling method is its relative simplicity and the fact that no specific frame is needed (although inclusion/exclusion criteria can also be applied).

Case example

Poon and Low (2005) used a systematic sampling approach in their study of factors measuring different satisfaction levels between Asian and Western travellers during their stay in hotels in Malaysia. They interviewed every tenth traveller passing through the security checkpoint at the departure hall of Kuala Lumpur International Airport, reaching a total of 200 interviewees.

Stratified sampling

Stratified sampling is a method by which the population is divided into homogeneous, mutually exclusive groups called 'strata' – by, for example, age, gender or market segment – and independent samples are then selected from each stratum. For example, if a hotel wants to introduce a new restaurant concept, then it is useful to define 'market segment' as the stratification criterion for its focus groups because this often relates to hotel guests' preference for particular hotel characteristics. This kind of stratification permits comparison between the attitudes of the different market segments (business transient, leisure transient, tour group, conference delegate, etc.) towards the new restaurant concept. If the market-mix for this hotel is 40 per cent business transients, 20 per cent leisure transients, 10 per cent tour groups and 30 per cent conference and associations, then a focus group of twenty guests should consist of eight business guests, four leisure guests, two tour group guests and six conference guests, all selected from the hotel's guest list using simple random and systematic sampling techniques.

Cluster sampling

Cluster sampling is a method you can use to allow random sampling while limiting the time and costs that would otherwise be required to study either a very large

Case example

Felsenstein and Fleischer (2003) used a slightly different stratified sampling approach in their study of festivals in Israel and their contribution to local economic growth. At the Kfar Blum Chamber Music Festival, they distributed survey questionnaires randomly to patrons in the concert halls. As most of the performances required the purchase of tickets but a minority did not, they employed stratified sampling that divided the population into ticket-purchasing and non-ticket-purchasing strata. Questionnaires were distributed to all patrons at ticketed performances, and to every twentieth visitor to a non-ticketed performance. Similarly, in the 'Alternative Theatre' Festival in Acre, questionnaires were distributed to patrons at the end of performances, and to visitors to the street market who were not ticket purchasers.

population or one that is geographically diverse. Here, you have to divide the population into mutually exclusive subsets, and then select a random sample of the subsets. If you study all the members in the selected clusters, the procedure is called one-stage cluster sampling. If, on the other hand, you probabilistically select a sample of participants from the selected subsets, the procedure is called two-stage cluster sampling. An example of how this might be used is as follows.

Suppose that you are studying the spending patterns of tourists in a tourism destination. In order to obtain as many participants as possible and to eliminate any potential bias inherent in selecting participants from one specific hotel, you may wish to select tourists from all of the hotels and other types of tourist accommodation within the tourism destination. However, this would be very costly and time-consuming. Therefore, you decide to use a one- or two-stage cluster approach to sampling. First, you identify each hotel and other tourist accommodation that meets your inclusion criteria. Second, you use one of the selection methods described above to randomly select a portion of these accommodation facilities. You may include all the tourists staying in the randomly selected facilities (one-stage clustering), or randomly select tourists staying in each of the randomly selected facilities (two-stage clustering). The important element in this process is that each of the facilities and each of the tourists staying in them have an equal opportunity to be chosen, with no researcher or accommodation facility bias.

Case example

McKercher and Chan (2005), in their study of special interest tourism, undertaken in the departure lounge area of the Hong Kong International Airport, used a multi-stage cluster sampling to ensure that their sample approximated a random sample of visitors from six source markets (North America, Europe, Australia, the People's Republic of China, Chinese Taipei, and Singapore/Malaysia). Their respondents were pleasure, business, and VFR (visiting friends and relatives) tourists, but had to satisfy three additional criteria before being incorporated into the study: they had to be non-residents of Hong Kong, non-transit passengers, and residents of one of the target source markets.

Non-probability sampling

In the real world of hospitality and tourism research, probability sampling is often quite difficult to achieve. Time, cost and ethical considerations are the most common obstacles for researchers in making the necessary arrangements and securing access to, for example, hotel guests or cruise-line passengers in order to test a hypothesis. Therefore you may have to use a different set of sampling techniques, classified under the category of non-probability sampling. Non-probability sampling is defined as 'sampling where it is not possible to specify the probability that any person or other unit on which the survey is based will be included in the sample' (Smith, 1983); it is frequently used in qualitative studies (Robson, 2002), providing researchers with the opportunity to 'select samples purposively' and enabling them to reach 'difficult-to-identify members' of the population (Saunders *et al.*, 2003: 178). With non-probability sampling it is unlikely that valid inferences can be made regarding the entire population, as the sample selected is not representative (all members of the population do not have an equal chance of being selected). Five non-probability sampling techniques have evolved: convenience sampling, judgmental sampling, quota sampling, snowball sampling and self-selection sampling. These sampling techniques are useful when the population is so widely dispersed that cluster sampling will not be efficient. If your study is not so much interested in working out what proportion of population gives a particular response but rather in exploring the idea of the range of responses on ideas that people have, then non-probability sampling is the most appropriate route for you to follow.

Convenience sampling

With convenience sampling (sometimes referred to as haphazard or accidental sampling), participants are selected because of their convenient accessibility. The trade-offs made for the ease of this technique are the non-representative nature of the sample, and the bias that is likely to be introduced into it. If, for instance, you intend to interview tourists in a given tourism destination, you may approach them in some of the major attractions in this destination. Of course, you will visit several different types of attractions (theme parks, historic sites, museums, etc.), and perhaps try to go at different times of the day and/or week to reduce bias, but in effect, the interviews that you conduct will be determined by convenience and not by randomness. Your sample will largely consist of leisure travellers, and business and conference travellers will probably be underrepresented. Moreover, if the interviews are conducted in English, then non-English speaking tourists will be excluded.

Case example

Huang (2006), in his attempt to develop an optimal e-commerce strategic model for the leisure farm industry in Taiwan, used convenience sampling because his survey required respondents with e-commerce business model experience. In addition to this characteristic, his sample originated from the Taiwan Farmers Management Association, and participants had to be directly responsible for e-commerce or sales affairs and to have already built up a website.

Judgmental sampling

Judgmental sampling (also called purposive or expert sampling) is another form of convenience sampling where participants are handpicked from the accessible population. This type of sampling technique is appropriate if the population to be studied is difficult to locate, or if some members are thought to be more appropriate (knowledgeable, experienced, etc.) for the study than others. For example, if your study is about meeting-planners' needs related to conference/convention facilities, you might find that planners are relatively few and also far too busy to talk to you. Selecting just a few of them (perhaps the most prominent) will be far more effective than trying to develop a list of the entire population of meeting-planners in order randomly to select a subset of them. The underlying assumption here is that you will select participants that are representative of the entire population, but how objective can this selection be? This technique is very much subject to the researcher's preconceptions, and the sample selection can be very biased.

Case example

Morrison and Teixeira (2004) used judgemental sampling in their study of small tourism business performance in Glasgow. Their sampling frame was constructed from the 2002 Greater Glasgow and Clyde Valley Area Tourist Board's *Directory of Tourist Accommodation*, with a total population of sixty-six. The authors 'handpicked' twenty-two hotels that they felt best fitted their research, using a series of criteria such as size of operation (between four and fifty bedrooms), being independently owned and not part of a corporate group, and having a city centre location.

Quota sampling

Quota sampling is a technique used to ensure equal representation of participants in each layer of a stratified sample grouping. The population under study is first divided into mutually exclusive subsets, just as in stratified sampling, and judgment is then used to select the participants from each stratum, based on a specified proportion. It is this second step that makes this a non-probability technique. For example, for a research project investigating the growth of Turkish and Chinese entrepreneurs in London, a quota needs to be used to ensure that the sample for research includes representation of Turkish and Chinese entrepreneurs, and of firms in different sectors – including retailing, wholesales, catering and manufacturing.

For example, assuming that, based on previous ethnic minorities research, you know that 60 per cent of Turkish and Chinese entrepreneurs are in retailing, 20 per cent are wholesalers, 15 per cent are in catering and 5 per cent are in manufacturing. You also know that 80 per cent are based in North London, 10 per cent in central London and 10 per cent in other areas of London. A total of 100 Turkish entrepreneurs are to be interviewed. The number of interviews might therefore be determined based on the proportion of each of the characteristics in the population – so once sixty retailers have been interviewed, this category will no longer be pursued, and only those who belong in the other categories will be interviewed until their quotas are filled. The main weakness of quota sampling is that it does not meet the basic requirement of randomness. Some Turkish entrepreneurs in our example may have no chance of selection, or the chance of their selection is unknown. Therefore, the sample may be biased.

Case example

Van Zyl and Botha (2003), in their attempt to determine the motivational factors that push and pull the local residents of Potchefstroom (in South Africa) to attend and participate in the Aardklop National Arts Festival, the festival activities they enjoy most, and also the situational inhibitors discouraging them from attending it, used quota sampling for selecting local residents to participate in their study. They used a map of Potchefstroom to identify all of its residential areas, and then randomly selected households from each area. The quota sample contained an equal number of participants from the high- and lower-socioeconomic areas, and equal numbers of men and women in three age groups (the authors used screening questions to exclude candidates who did not fit the criteria).

Snowball sampling

Snowball (or chain referral) sampling is a technique used to identify potential participants when appropriate candidates for the study are hard to locate. It involves using referrals from initial participants. For example, in a study of the airline sector crisis management planning, you have identified and interviewed the Director of Security of Heathrow's Terminal 1. After the interview, you ask this person to identify other persons involved in airline crisis management, who can themselves be interviewed, and so on. Snowball samples cannot be considered random, because there is no way of knowing the precise size of the population that can participate in the study. The problem with this technique is that the sample can be highly biased, because the nature of the technique itself reduces the likelihood that the sample will represent a good cross-section of the entire population.

Case example

Kibicho (2005), in his research into the relationship between tourism and the sex trade in Kenya's coastal region, conducted interviews with commercial sex workers in seven resort areas (Shimoni, Diani-Ukunda, Mombasa Island, Bamburi-Kisauni, Mtwapa, Watamu and Malindi). Due to the lack of a predetermined sampling frame, he employed snowball sampling, where each person interviewed was asked to nominate others for inclusion in the survey process. This referral methodology resulted in the identification of 580 participants.

Self-selection sampling

Self-selection sampling is a non-probability sampling technique in which individuals identify their wish to participate in the study. Researchers have to make known their need for participants by advertising/publicizing their research through articles, advertisements in magazines and journals, e-mails, letters, postings in newsgroups, etc. It is wise for researchers using this technique to propose clear inclusion and exclusion criteria in order to identify the target population relevant to the research question. One advantage of this technique is that the candidates (accessible population) contact the researcher themselves, which minimizes time spent by the researcher on individuals that are not suitable for the study. Also, participants are more committed to the study, which is always helpful for the researcher. The disadvantage of self-selection is that the voluntary nature of self-selection sampling means that there is always a lack of control over who takes part. Volunteers are not typical of the general population, and this usually causes what is termed a 'self-selection bias'. The volunteers' decision to participate may be correlated with traits that affect the study, making the sample non-representative and/or the findings exaggerated.

Case example

Hwang and Fesenmaier (2004) conducted a study, in North Indiana, USA, on the coverage error of self-selected Internet-based samples within the context of tourism. Bias immediately occurred because the Internet is not universally available to the entire population; also, people could participate using false identities online. The study showed that self-selecting participants are not representative of potential users of tourism websites because of the coverage error embedded in the sampling process. It revealed that self-selecting participants are more likely to be younger and have higher income; also, respondents who live with children at home are more likely to provide personal information than those who do not. Finally, travellers who are familiar with the Internet and use it actively to plan trips have a much higher chance of being included in a self-selecting sample than those who are not.

Sample size

In any type of social research (including hospitality and tourism research) the ideal would be to cover the entire population of interest when undertaking a study; this would make generalization of the findings possible about the population as a whole. However, obstacles such as cost and time constraints, as well as (possibly) low accessibility, make it impossible to study all the members in a targeted population – hence the various sampling methods that were presented above. Yet many research projects run the risk of not achieving their intended aims because researchers are not able to include enough participants in their sample. Therefore, at some point in the research design, you should consider your sample size.

Although in practice sample size is often arbitrary, if you are interested in exploring the behaviour of a given population then the larger the sample you study the more likely it is that your findings will be representative of this population, and the more correct your inferences about the collected data will be. So, what is the right sample size for your research? The simple answer here is, 'it depends' – on the amount of sampling error you are ready to tolerate (the level of precision you wish to achieve), the level of confidence required that your collected data are actually representative of the population, and the kinds of analysis you wish to undertake.

The sampling error, sometimes called level of precision, is the range in which the true value of the population is estimated to be, and is usually expressed in percentage points (e.g. ±5 per cent). Thus, if you find that 60 per cent of hotel guests in a sample strongly agree with the proposed new restaurant concept, with a precision rate of ±5 per cent, then you can conclude that between 55 per cent and 65 per cent of the hotel guests will like the new concept.

The level of confidence (or risk level) is based on the premise that the larger the size of a sample from a population, the closer the average value of the answers obtained by the participants will be to the true population value (Tijms, 2004). Furthermore, the values obtained by these participants will be distributed normally around the true value, with some answers having a higher value and some a lower score than the true population value. In a normal distribution, approximately 95 per cent of the sample answers are within two standard deviations of the true population value (e.g. mean). Usually researchers prefer to work with a 95 per cent confidence level, which means that if the sample were selected 100 times, on at least 95 of these times it would represent the entire population.

The literature offers several 'rules of thumb' regarding sample sizes (see, for example, Morse, 1994; Stutely, 2003; Mertens, 2005), as well as formulas for estimating optimal sample sizes; however, each study should be considered on its own merits. You are the one who should make the decision, always in collaboration with your supervisor.

The problem of non-response

An important element when considering your sampling method is that you secure a high response rate for your study. The response rate is broadly the ratio (usually expressed in a percentage) of the number of participants who have actually taken part in your study divided by the number of people in your sample. A low response rate may have a negative effect on the credibility of your findings, because the sample will be less likely to represent the overall target population. However, regardless of your type of study, whether you are conducting interviews or using self-administered questionnaires, some people who in your sample will refuse to participate or will not return the questionnaire. There is no generally agreed standard for a minimum acceptable response rate. Baruch (1999) found an average response rate of 56 per cent in five leading management journals (the *Academy of Management Journal*, *Human Relations*, the *Journal of Applied Psychology*, *Organizational Behavior and Human Decision Processes*, and the *Journal of International Business Studies*) for the years 1975, 1985 and 1995, with response rates in surveys of top managers being substantially lower (36 per cent) than response rates in surveys of employees (61 per cent). By contrast, Bartholomew and Smith (2006), analysing the response rates of studies on small businesses published in *Entrepreneurship Theory and Practice* and the *Journal of Small Business Management* over the period 1998–2004 revealed an average response rate of 27 per cent. Nevertheless, you will find that most researchers consider an acceptable response rate to be anything from 15 to 20 per cent and above, with 10 per cent being the minimum.

Case example

Nickson *et al.* (2005) used structured questionnaires with employers in the retail and hospitality industries in Glasgow when they were looking at the importance of not only the right attitude of employees in the service sector, but also the right appearance in that they have to 'look good' and 'sound right'. They distributed 1023 postal questionnaires to retail outlets, hotels, and restaurants/bars/cafés in Glasgow, but it rapidly became apparent that forty-four of these businesses were members of groups where the recruitment and selection of staff tended to be conducted by central office, therefore reducing the number of possible responses. A further twenty-nine questionnaires were returned because of wrong or outdated contact details. As a result, the accessible sample for their study was reduced to approximately 950. Eventually, 147 questionnaires were returned. The authors argued that although this was a relatively low response rate, response rates are generally lower in central cities, especially when using a postal method to distribute questionnaires. They asserted that recent survey-based research indicated that business surveys have response rates of 15–20 per cent, and concluded that, although there is no agreed standard for a minimum acceptable response rate, it is important that a minimum 10 per cent response rate be achieved in order to comment on the significance of the findings.

Box 5.3 shows two formulas that you can use in order to calculate your response rate. The term 'Completes' signifies the number of actual participants (completed interviews, usable questionnaires). 'Not qualified' signifies participants who are eventually found not to meet the inclusion criteria, as well as those who would have qualified had their quota group not already been full. 'Not contacted' indicates the candidates who, although included in the sample, could not be reached because they were located too far away, were on holiday, an answering machine repeatedly picked up calls, or the contact details were wrong, etc.

Box 5.3	Response rate formulas

Total response rate = Completes/(Total sample − Not qualified)
Active response rate = Completes/(Total sample − {Not qualified + Not contacted})

Based on these formulas we can say that the total response rate obtained by Nickson *et al.* (2005) was 15.02 per cent, whereas the active response rate was 15.47 per cent. Let us see how we reached these figures.

Total response rate:
The number of completes was 147.
The total sample was 1023 employers, of which 44 were not qualified as they had a central recruitment office.
The total response rate was therefore $147/(1023 − 44) = 147 − 979 = 15.02$ per cent.

Active response rate:
The number of non-contacts was 29.
The active response rate was therefore $147/(1023 - \{44 + 29\}) = 147 - 950 = 15.47$
  per cent.

Of the several techniques that are used for increasing response, the most powerful tool is to use follow-ups or reminders (Jobber and O'Reilly, 1998; Roth and BeVier, 1998; Dillman, 2000; Greer *et al.*, 2000). Various studies indicate that the response rates may vary between 10 and 60 percent without follow-up reminders. These studies indicate that researchers can increase the response with telephone or personal contact follow-ups, financial incentives, and stamped return envelopes. When designing a follow-up procedure, it is important to keep in mind the unique characteristics of the people in your sample. Fox and colleagues (1998) show that postcard follow-up is the most cost-effective method among business samples, with an aggregate gain of 3.5 percent; however, the most successful of all follow-up techniques is the use of telephoned reminders.

Sampling in qualitative research

In quantitative research, sampling is very important for the statistical validity of a study that will enable inferences for the entire population and generalization of the findings. In contrast, qualitative research does not attempt to generalize (Alasuutari, 1995: 156–157) but aims at gaining an in-depth understanding of the topic or phenomenon under study and at extrapolating the findings beyond the material in hand, thus developing theory. In qualitative research, the sampling method must serve the purpose of in-depth understanding and must be selected for the information-rich data that it can yield (no different from the judgmental or purposive sampling described earlier). However, this does not mean that sampling is less important in qualitative research – quite the contrary; it can have a profound effect on the quality of a study. Morse (1991: 127) offers the example of a study where the researcher used random sampling in a qualitative study, and points out that a small, randomly selected sample 'violates both the quantitative principle that requires an adequate sample size in order to ensure representativeness and the qualitative principle of appropriateness that requires purposeful sampling and a "good" informant (i.e. one who is articulate, reflective, and willing to share with the interviewer)'.

Qualitative researchers have developed a number of sampling techniques that have some differences from those described above, but can all be encompassed under the broad term 'purposeful (purposive) sampling' (Patton, 2002). As indicated previously, purposeful sampling focuses on selecting information-rich cases to illuminate the question under study. There are quite a few strategies to do this (see Box 5.4); most of those overlapping with the ones described above are beyond the scope of this book. However, we feel that two qualitative sampling meth ods need some further clarification: theoretical sampling and maximum variation sampling.

Theoretical sampling

Theoretical sampling (theory-based or operational construct sampling) is a method that has it roots in grounded theory (Glaser and Strauss, 1967), whereby the researcher simultaneously collects, codes and analyses the data in order to decide what data to collect next. In other words, the researcher initially starts with purposive sampling by

Box 5.4	Qualitative sampling strategies

- Extreme or deviant case sampling
- Intensity sampling
- Homogeneous samples
- Stratified purposeful sampling
- Snowball or chain sampling
- Confirming and disconfirming cases
- Purposeful random sampling
- Convenience sampling

- Theory-based or operational construct sampling
- Maximum variation sampling
- Typical case sampling
- Critical case sampling
- Criterion sampling
- Opportunistic sampling
- Sampling politically important cases

(Source: Adapted from Patton, 2002)

selecting the sample deemed more appropriate to describe the phenomenon under study at this stage of the research. Then, at a second stage, the researcher moves into theoretical sampling, which involves selecting samples that are more appropriate to understand the theories that emerged from the findings of the first stage. The difference between purposive and theoretical sampling is that the former is determined by a list of variables, whereas the latter is determined by the needs of the emerging theory. The sampling is open to those participants and cases that will provide the greatest opportunity to gather the most relevant data about the research question. Consequently, the size of the sample is not defined from the outset of the investigation, and the sampling process terminates when the researcher feels that enough data have been collected.

Case example

Daengbuppha *et al.* (2006) chose grounded theory as an alternative approach for conceptualizing and modelling the consumer experience at three World Heritage Sites in Thailand (Sukhothai, Ayutthaya and Sri Satchanalai). As they did not start their study with a developed theoretical framework from the literature, or predefined relationships to test, they conducted (prior to data collection) a series of interviews with 'insiders' (managers in local tourism organizations, site administrators, tour guides, travel agents, etc.) to generate an 'inside view' of the sites and the visitors' behaviour. In the first stage of data collection they used a combination of participant/non-participant observation and ethnographic interviews, using a population of both individual visitors and groups selected through convenience sampling. During the process of conducting the interviews, the data were continually analysed and the researchers moved into theoretical sampling according to the themes that were emerging. They contend that it is this process of ongoing and simultaneous data collection, analysis and sampling that allowed concepts and themes to emerge from data and facilitated recognition of the point when data saturation was reached.

Maximum variation sampling

Maximum variation sampling is a type of purposeful sampling that describes 'central themes ... that cut across a great deal of participant ... variation' (Patton, 2002: 53). This sampling technique is trying to achieve accurate representation of the total population, not through equal probabilities but by including a wide range of extremes. The underlying principle here is that by studying very different selection of people, their aggregate answers can be close to the whole population's value. A maximum variation sample, if carefully drawn, can be as representative as a random sample. For example, in seeking the views of hotel guests about the new restaurant concept, you may want to interview guests of different nationalities, professional backgrounds, cultures, work experience and the like. In this way you will record unique or various attitudes towards the new concept, but also identify important common patterns that cut across the diverse clientele that you are interviewing. The technique is appropriate for qualitative studies in which the sample is very small (e.g. less than thirty) or difficult to find.

Case example

Poria (2004) used the maximum variation sampling technique when he studied the distribution of hotel guest satisfaction questionnaires and the biases that employees bring to the process. Wanting to reduce the risk of producing findings that were specific to a certain hotel or specific environment, the researcher collected data from a sample with very different characteristics and backgrounds. He conducted fifty interviews in Israel and in United Kingdom, and his sample included hotel employees from all levels of a hotel hierarchy and with various degree of guest contact. Participants had worked in different countries around the world (e.g. Belgium, Canada, Egypt, United Kingdom, Saudi Arabia, Singapore) and in various types of hotels (business, leisure and family hotels). Poria's study was clearly aiming to capture central themes by selecting a population with diverse characteristics rather than by attempting to achieve representation.

Summary

- Sampling is the process by which researchers select a subset or part of the total population that can be studied for their topic so that they will be able to draw conclusions about the entire population or gain understanding about a phenomenon.
- There are two main categories of sampling methods: probability and non-probability. In probability sampling, the chance (probability) of each candidate being selected from the population is known and it is not zero; in non-probability sampling the chance of selection is not known.
- Randomly selected samples allow generalizations to the entire population. The most direct way to achieve this is to draw units at random in a simple random sample using, for example, a random number table to assign numbers to each person randomly and then select them.

- In a systematic sample, every nth (e.g. fifth, eighth, etc.) person is selected. Systematic samples can, if done properly, maintain the principle of randomness.
- Stratified sampling is used when the population is divided into identifiable groups and then sampling within the groups proceeds. Other more complicated techniques, such as cluster sampling (where first broad clusters of units are selected, then units within that cluster) may also be used.
- Non-probability sampling techniques are frequently used in qualitative studies, providing researchers with the opportunity to select samples purposively and enabling them to reach difficult-to-identify members of the population. Such techniques include convenience sampling, where people are selected because they are conveniently accessible; judgmental or purposive sampling, where people are selected based on a judgment regarding their relevance to the study; quota sampling, where a sample is selected that has the same proportions of key groupings as does the population; snowball sampling, where those initially selected recommend others; and self-selection sampling, where participants volunteer to take part in the study.
- The 'right size' for a sample depends on the level of sampling error you are prepared to tolerate (i.e. the degree of precision you wish to achieve), the level of confidence you need to have that your collected data are actually representative of the population, and the kinds of analysis you wish to undertake.
- There is no generally agreed standard for a minimum acceptable response rate to a questionnaire, but most researchers consider anything above 15 to 20 per cent to be acceptable, with 10 per cent being the minimum.
- Qualitative researchers have developed a number of sampling techniques that have some differences from those described above, but they can all be encompassed under the broad term of purposeful (purposive) sampling. Theoretical sampling is determined by the needs of the emerging theory, and is open to those participants and cases that will provide the greatest opportunity to gather the most relevant data about the research question. Maximum variation sampling is a technique that achieves representation of the total population, not through equal probabilities but by including a wide range of extremes.

Review questions

1. What is the difference between probability and non-probability sampling?
2. What is the meaning of (a) convenience sampling and (b) judgmental sampling?
3. What are the benefits of using simple random sampling?
4. What is a stratified sample? What criteria are used to form strata for stratified sampling?
5. What elements influence the correct sample size?
6. Describe the two-stage cluster sampling procedure. What is the main distinction between cluster sampling an stratified sampling?
7. Which is the most cost-effective and least time-consuming sampling technique? What are its main limitations?
8. How might you select, step by step, (a) a sample of 200 visitors at Madame Tussaud's; and (b) a sample of local and international hotel managers to compare their salaries?
9. What is the difference between theoretical and judgmental (purposive) sampling?
10. In which cases would maximum variation sampling be more appropriate?

References

Alasuutari, P. (1995). *Researching Culture: Qualitative Method and Cultural Studies*. Thousand Oaks, CA: Sage Publications.

Bartholomew, S. and Smith, A. D. (2006). Improving survey response rates from chief executive officers in small firms: the importance of social networks. *Entrepreneurship: Theory and Practice*, 30(1), 83–96.

Baruch, Y. (1999). Response rates in academic studies: a comparative analysis. *Human Relations*, 52(4), 421–438.

Chi, G. C. and Qu, H. (2004). Integrating persons with disabilities into the work force: a study on employment of people with disabilities in the foodservice industry. *International Journal of Hospitality Administration*, 4(4), 59–84.

Daengbuppha, J., Hemmington, N. and Wilkes, K. (2006). Using grounded theory to model visitor experiences at heritage sites: methodological and practical issues. *Qualitative Market Research: An International Journal*, 9(4), 367–388.

Dillman, D. A. (2000). Mail *and Internet Surveys: The Tailored Design Method*, 2nd edn. New York, NY: John Wiley & Sons.

Felsenstein, D. and Fleischer, A. (2003). Local festivals and tourism promotion: the role of public assistance and visitor expenditure. *Journal of Travel Research*, 41, 385–392.

Fox, C. M., Robinson, K. L. and Boardley, D. (1998). Cost-effectiveness of follow-up strategies in improving the response rate of mail surveys. *Industrial Marketing Management*, 27(2), 127–133.

Glaser, B. and Srauss, A. (1967). *The Discovery of Grounded Theory*. Chicago, IL: Aldine Publishing.

Greer, T. V., Chuchinprakam, N. and Seshadri, S. (2000). Likelihood of participating in mail survey research: business respondents' perspective. *Industrial Marketing Management*, 29(2), 97–109.

Huang, L. (2006). Rural tourism revitalization of the leisure farm industry by implementing an e-commerce strategy. *Journal of Vacation Marketing*, 12(3), 232–245.

Hwang, Y. H. and Fesenmaier, D.R. (2004). Coverage error embedded in self-selected Internet-based samples: a case study of Northern Indiana. *Journal of Travel Research*, 42, 297–304.

Jobber, D. and O'Reilly, D. (1998). Industrial mail surveys: a methodological update. *Industrial Marketing Management*, 27(2), 95–107.

Kibicho, W. (2005). Tourism and the sex trade in Kenya's coastal region. *Journal of Sustainable Tourism*, 13(3), 256–280.

McKercher, B. and Chan, A. (2005). How special is special interest tourism? *Journal of Travel Research*, 44, 21–31.

Mertens, D. M. (2005). Research methods in education and psychology: integrating diversity with quantitative and qualitative approaches, 2nd edn. Thousand Oaks, CA: Sage Publications.

Morrison, A. and Teixeira, R. (2004). Small business performance: a tourism sector focus. *Journal of Small Business and Enterprise Development*, 11(2), 166–173.

Morse, J. M. (1991). Strategies for sampling. In: J. M. Morse (ed.), *Qualitative Nursing Research: A Contemporary Dialogue*. Thousand Oaks, CA: Sage Publications, pp. 127–145.

Morse, J. M. (1994). Designing funded qualitative research. In: N. K. Denzin and Y. S. Lincoln (eds), *Handbook of Qualitative Research*. Thousand Oaks, CA: Sage Publications, pp. 220–235.

Nickson, D., Warhurst, C. and Dutton, E. (2005). The importance of attitude and appearance in the service encounter in retail and hospitality. *Managing Service Quality*, 15(2), 195–208.

Patton, M. Q. (2002). *Qualitative Research and Evaluation Methods*, 3rd edn. Thousand Oaks, CA: Sage Publications.

Poon, W. C. and Low, K. L. T. (2005). Are travellers satisfied with Malaysian hotels? *International Journal of Contemporary Hospitality Management*, 17(3), 217–227.

Poria, Y. (2004). Employees' interference with the distribution of guest satisfaction questionnaires. *International Journal of Contemporary Hospitality Management*, 16(5), 321–324.

Robson, C. (2002). *Real World Research*, 2nd edn. Oxford: Blackwell Publishing.

Roth, P. L. and. BeVier C. A. (1998). Response rates in HRM/OB survey research: norms and correlates, 1990–1994. *Journal of Management*, 24(1), 97–117.

Saunders, M. N. K, Lewis, P. and Thornhill, A. (2003). *Research Methods for Business Students*, 3rd edn. Harlow: Financial Times Prentice Hall.

Smith, T. F. M. (1983). On the validity of inferences from non-random samples. *Journal of the Royal Statistical Society*, 146, 394–403.

Squire, P. (1988). Why the 1936 *Literary Digest* poll failed. *Public Opinion Quarterly*, 52(1), 25–33.

Stutely, R. (2003). *The Economist Numbers Guide: The Essentials of Business Numeracy*, 5th edn. London: Profile Books Ltd.

Tijms, H. (2004). *Understanding Probability: Chance Rules in Everyday Life*. Cambridge: Cambridge University Press.

University of Minnesota Morris. *Table of Random Numbers* (online). Available at http://www.mrs.umn.edu/~sungurea/introstat/public/instruction/ranbox/randomnumbersII.html (accessed 22 May 2007).

Van Zyl, C. and Botha, C. (2003). Motivational factors of local residents to attend the Aardklop National Arts Festival. *Event Management*, 8(4), 213–222.

Chapter 6
Data collection techniques

Nothing is to be expected from the workman whose tools are for ever to be sought.
(Samuel Johnson, English poet, critic and writer, 1709–1784)

There is range of data collection techniques available for researchers to allow them fulfil the requirements of their research. One technique may fit the purpose of your research better than another. It is therefore important that you consider the appropriateness of several data collection techniques in relation to the aim and objectives of your research. You should consider the practicalities of different data collection techniques – given the advantages and disadvantages of the various techniques, are your research questions 'researchable' by particular methods? This chapter will explain the advantages and disadvantages of such techniques, in particular interviews, questionnaires, observation and document analysis, and highlight your options depending on your topic.

Interviews

Interviewing is the systematic collection of data through asking questions, then carefully listening to and recording or noting the responses concerning your research topic. This data collection technique provides access to a range of experiences, situations and knowledge, and provides the opportunity to explore issues according to your research purpose. During the interviews, your informants may describe private or sensitive behaviours, or events that happened in the past. They might also provide information regarding the meanings and definitions that people give to events and behaviours. This is particularly useful for understanding how things are done in different contexts and by different groups, such as organizations, communities, senior executives or consumer groups.

Interviews can take place in any location and at any time, with different individuals (hospitality managers, employees, policy-makers, groups of customers, etc.). They may be formal and especially arranged for the purpose, or informal, taking advantage of opportunities to question people about a topic of interest – for example, to explore local meanings in a tribe, to understand customer satisfaction problems, or to describe the attitudes and opinions of local communities towards a recent crisis in a tourism destination.

Although interviews offer many opportunities, there are several difficulties associated with them. First, it may be difficult to secure the interview itself. Access to people may be denied for a number of reasons, including the informants' busy schedule, their reluctance to spend time with 'students', politics in the organization, and sensitivities associated with the confidentiality of information. Also, organizing, preparing for and conducting an interview can often be very time consuming. You should remember that conducting interviews involves first reviewing the relevant literature in order to devise your questions, then piloting your questions, and finally undergoing a time- and energy-consuming period of access negotiation. Generally, you need to start securing necessary permissions for your fieldwork at least three to four months before actually doing it.

Preparation for the interview

Before conducting the interview, you must prepare what is called an 'interview guide' or 'interview schedule'. This interview guide is a list of all the questions, topics and issues that you want to cover during the interview. It may include open questions (which informants can answer with their own words) and closed questions (where answers are limited to a fixed set of responses, usually a 'yes' or 'no'), as well as possible probes and prompts to encourage informants to provide more information or talk more about certain topics. Bearing in mind that open questions aim to encourage informants to define and describe a situation or event, they should start with a 'how', 'why' or 'what' – for example, 'Why did the organization introduce this specific marketing strategy?' or 'How has your corporate strategy changed over the past five years?' A probe is an extra question that encourages informants to elaborate on their responses when you feel that they have more to give (see Box 6.1). It can be used to explore responses that are of particular significance to the research topic. A probe may be worded like an open question, but request a particular focus or direction.

Box 6.1	Probing in an interview

- *The basic probe*: the interviewer repeats a question to get the interviewee back on track; this technique is frequently used when the interviewee is going off tangent.
- *The explanatory probe*: this is used to achieve clearer understanding by completing the incomplete statements of the respondent; the interviewer asks questions such as 'Can you give an example?' or 'Can you explain that?'
- *The focused probe*: this is used to reach particular details of a topic – for example, 'What type of … did you use?'
- *The silent probe*: here, the interviewer maintains silence and waits for the interviewee to break it; this technique is generally used when the interviewee is taking lot of time to respond or is hesitant.
- *Drawing out*: this is used when the interviewee has stopped responding; the interviewer restates or rephrases the last question or topic (e.g. 'So, the question was … What else can you tell me about that?'), which helps the interviewee to start talking again.
- *Giving ideas or suggestions*: here, the interviewer makes suggestions or ideas for the interviewee to think about – for example, 'Have you thought about …?'
- *Mirroring or reflecting*: here, the interviewer repeats what the interviewee has just said but in different words; this helps the interviewee to think about what he or she has just said.

(Source: Adapted from Easterby-Smith *et al.*, 1991.)

The interview guide can be divided into several parts, depending on what you want to achieve in the interview. If you wish to have an introductory stage, your guide should include a short briefing about the aim of the research and the purpose of the interview, which you can use as a reminder when you first contact the informant. Points such as the confidentiality of the interview and permission to use a tape or digital recorder may also be noted here. In addition, you may include some general questions about the informant's background, job roles and experience.

The main body of the interview guide should include questions that you have developed to allow you to structure your knowledge on the topic using the answers of the informant (see Box 6.2). These questions may vary, depending on the purpose of your research, from simple to elaborate.

Box 6.2	Interview guide

Kayat (2002) conducted forty-six interviews with local residents in Langkawi Island, Malaysia, to explain residents' attitudes toward tourism and examine how their evaluation of the impact of tourism influences their attitudes. He used the following interview guide:

Interview questions	Probing questions
1. How long have you lived in Langkawi?	
2. When (what year) did you first realize that you are living in a tourist area? What made you realize this?	
3. From your own experiences and observations, what changes has tourism brought to your life?	
4. From your own experiences and observations, what changes has tourism brought to your community?	
5. How do you feel about these changes?	• Do you consider these changes to be of benefit to you/your community? • Do you consider these changes to have costs to you/your community?
6. What kind of opportunities does tourism offer to the residents?	
7. How do you think you can benefit from tourism?	• Do you think you could benefit more if you had certain resources that you do not have now? • What kind of resources do you think would help you to benefit more from tourism?

8. Do you support tourism in your area?	• Are you in favour of tourism in Langkawi?
9. What do you know about the residents' ability to voice their opinion?	• Do you have any comments about it?
10. How would you like Langkawi to be in the future?	• Have you ever voiced your opinion?

It is obvious that your questions should be linked to the purpose of your research. Therefore, you should be familiar with the relevant literature and link this literature with the intended outcome of each question when you are developing the questions. This process requires some reflection on your literature review areas, and will inevitably take some time. It is unrealistic to sit down and come up with the questions for your interview overnight, and it is extremely unwise to start on your fieldwork interviews without having completed your literature review. Moreover, when designing your interview guide it is useful to write down the possible linkages between the interview questions and the literature. You should also be very explicit in terms of what kind of knowledge an informant's answer will supply regarding your research area. The example in Box 6.3 relates to an investigation of the challenges international hospitality organizations face in their attempt to recruit franchise partners; the researcher also notes the aim of each question next to the question itself.

Box 6.3	Interview questions and aims

1. What was the context of the particular franchise proposal? (aims at finding out how an organization identifies the international expansion opportunities in the market)
2. Who was involved at what time during the franchise process, and how? (aims at finding out the key decision-makers and their roles)
3. How was the proposal initiated? (aims at collecting contextual data about the country or market from which the proposals emerged)
4. Who promoted which aspects of the proposal? (aims at finding out the role of people in identifying franchisee opportunities, and which factors are considered and interpreted by these organizational members whilst promoting the proposal)
5. Who, and which aspects of the proposal, presented obstacles to progress. How? (aims at exploring the internal and external decision-making dynamics, particularly the international challenges faced by the organization)
6. How were these obstacles overcome? (aims at exploring how the organization took decisions with regard to franchise projects)
7. What was the role of the market-based organizational members in overcoming these obstacles, and how did they select the potential franchises? (aims at exploring how the organizational members selected prospective franchise partners, given the international challenges they face in different country markets).

(Source: Altinay, 2006: 115)

In developing your interview guide, make sure that you avoid including long questions. The interviewee may remember only part of the question and respond only to that part. You may also want to avoid double-barrelled questions such as 'what do you think about service quality offered by the hospitality industry compared with five years ago?' Instead, you can break this down into simpler questions:

1. What do you think about current service quality?
2. Can you recall the level of service quality five years ago?
3. How do you feel they compare?

An important issue that must be considered when developing interview questions is the use of complicated theoretical concepts or technical jargon. This should be avoided; it will not help you get the answers you want, and might alienate informants who cannot understand the question. You should not be surprised to hear from fellow students that 'People in the industry know nothing about behavioural and attitudinal loyalty {or emotional labour, database marketing, search engine optimization, etc.}. There was nothing I could do – it was shocking for me to discover that experienced managers knew nothing about my topic.' These students probably went out in the field and asked questions full of complicated terms which were comprehensible to them but not to their informants.

Leading questions should also be avoided, because they will result in biased (influenced, not objective) answers. For example, a question such as 'Why do you like Cyprus?' might make your informant think that they are obliged to like the country. Interviewer bias occurs when the interviewer intentionally or unintentionally sways the responses of those interviewed. Informant bias occurs when the informant responds to the interviewer, but does not tell the truth because he or she does not want the truth known (perhaps the questions are too personal or are seen as threatening).

As all things come to an end, so will your interview. Try to stick to the agreed duration of the interview, and be sensitive to your informant's schedule and time limits. However, it is preferable to 'wind down' the interview rather than ending it abruptly because you run out of time. A well-timed interview will allow you to summarize the major points of the conversation, make sure that you have a good understanding of the informant's views, and ask whether he or she would like to add anything else. By asking this question, you will encourage the informant to talk about issues that may have not been covered during the interview, or to clarify others. You may also ask the informant to recommend some relevant company documents and other key people they feel might be willing to help you in your study. It is a good strategy to ask them if they wish to see the interview transcript before you do anything with it; this shows that you are considerate and gives you the opportunity for yet another contact, should you require clarification of any of the answers you have recorded. The final step is, of course, to thank the informant for helping.

All of these points could be included in your interview guide You do not have to memorize it, but it will provide you with a good structure and a reminder at all points of the interview, so that you will always project the image of a confident, well-prepared and organized researcher. Piloting your interview with one or two people will always help you become more confident about your interview questions and the process itself. During the pilot interview, you might realize that some of your questions are not comprehensible to others, some questions might need to be combined, the wording of the questions might need to be changed, and you might want to add some specific prompt questions.

Interview techniques

There are four main interview techniques: unstructured, structured, semi-structured and focus group interviews.

Unstructured interviews

The unstructured interview is a very flexible way of getting interviewees to reveal their opinions, knowledge and experience. Researchers using this interview technique have three or four broad questions in their interview guide, which encourage informants to provide as much detail as possible about the topic. The main strength of this technique is that it does not impose any restrictions on what can be discussed. The key to using it successfully is thinking carefully about which questions to ask, how to phrase them, and when to use probes and prompts without interrupting the flow and the focus of the conversation.

Using unstructured interviews requires good communication, listening and facilitation skills. You must listen carefully, observe the flow of conversation and be aware of any new or interesting insights in order to be able to probe appropriately. You need to maintain control of the interview throughout, as it is very easy for the informant to 'slip' into irrelevant and unimportant issues. For the more experienced researcher, unstructured interviews may give the flexibility to modify a line of enquiry, follow up interesting responses and explore underlying motives. If you do not have much experience in conducting interviews, this technique may present a few challenges. However, it might be useful as a way of collecting background data in the early stages of your research, when you still have very little knowledge about your research topic, as the responses may guide you to more solid research topics and questions.

Normally, unstructured interviews are used in combination with other data collection techniques, although several papers have been published based on this technique alone.

Case example

In their study in Norfolk Island, an Australian dependency located in the South Pacific Ocean, Prideaux and Crosswell (2006) were aiming to develop a socio-demographic profile of the Australian visitors of the Island, identify the major motivators to travel there, and compare visitor profiles with the perceptions of the Island's tourism industry. They conducted their study in two phases. The first phase involved a series of unstructured interviews with fourteen Island tourism representatives. These interviews were designed to identify the perceptions these representatives had of the visitors to Norfolk Island and upon which they were basing their marketing activities. Another purpose of these unstructured interviews was to gain an understanding of the tourism resources that these informants believed were the main attractions of the Island. The second phase of the research involved a survey (by means of a structured questionnaire) of inbound visitors designed to test the assumptions identified in the unstructured interviews and achieve the other aims of the study (socio-demographic profile of visitors and motivations to visit the Island).

Structured interviews

When you want total control over the topic areas covered during the interview, you can use structured interviews based on a predetermined and standardized set of questions. Researchers who use structured interviews read out each question and then record the response on a standardized schedule, usually with pre-coded answers (Saunders *et al.*, 2007).

There are several advantages to using structured interviews. The detailed and standard interview guides will allow you have more control over the process, compared with unstructured interviews. The interview guide in this case will help you to prioritize questions and keep the conversation focused, especially when the informant is granting you only a short amount of time. Structured interviews also help to boost the response rate and maximize the reliability and validity of data. In addition, the standard format for each interview makes it easier for you to code, analyse and compare the data (for coding and analysis, see Chapters 9 and 10).

Structured interviews are often undertaken after exploratory research, as adherence to a standard guide usually prevents exploration and collection of unexpected but relevant information.

Case example

Taking advantage of the increase in 'wine tourism', the Portuguese tourism authorities developed a number of 'wine routes' in Portugal, each one with its own structure. In order to evaluate the performance of the Bairrada Wine Route (BWR), Correia *et al.* (2004) used structured interviews with the representatives of fourteen key wineries (all members of the BWR). The interviews were structured in six sections: the members' image, culture and style; their wine tourism activity before they joined the BWR; their activity after joining; their evaluation of the cohesion of the BWR; the management of supply and demand by the BWR; and perspectives on the future of the route. The researchers argued that they used this interviewing technique because it 'helped to keep interviewees talking and the interview focused' (Correia *et al.*, 2004: 19). Moreover, they said that structured questions 'enabled easy identification of the similarities and differences' between the informants.

Semi-structured interviews

A semi-structured interview strikes the balance between a broad investigation through using unstructured interviews on one hand, and a very structured explanatory/descriptive approach on the other. This interview technique is used to find out what is happening, seek new insights, identify general patterns and understand the relationship between variables. Researchers using this technique have a list of topics, and have greater freedom in terms of sequencing questions and modifying them according to the flow of conversation.

If you decide to use this interview technique, it is necessary to design a set of questions in advance. However, their order can be modified during the interview, based on your perception of what seems most appropriate in the context and flow of conversation. You can also change the way in which you phrase your questions. In addition, you can provide explanations and omit particular questions – for example, if they seem inappropriate for a particular interviewee. During the exploration, details can be probed concerning all facets of the topic.

Box 6.4 provides an example of semi-structured interview guide for a research project that investigates how new products are developed in the cruise industry. The researcher developed the interview questions based on the key themes in the relevant literature. He designed this interview guide after several sessions with his supervisor, during which the guide was revised several times to ensure that the set of questions would yield information appropriate for the aim of the project. The interview guide was divided in five sections:

1. Background-related questions designed to break the ice between the interviewer and the interviewee and establish trust
2. Product-related questions designed to allow understanding of the nature of the product in the cruise industry
3. New product development-related questions designed to explore the informants' perceptions of 'new products'
4. New product development process-related questions designed to allow understanding of those factors that trigger new product development, and also to identify those individuals responsible for new product development
5. New product development case study-related questions designed to explore the process of new product development in the case study organization.

The questions were open-ended, with some having sub-questions (probes) that allowed deeper investigation of the topic. The set of questions was recorded in a way that gave flexibility to the researcher in altering their sequence. Each section had between two and four questions, starting with general new product development questions and ending with more specific questions regarding the process, key people involved, and how the decisions were made.

Focus group interviews

A focus group consists of a number of informants who are selected purposively and interviewed collectively because they have a common experience, come from a similar background or have a particular expertise in an area. The focus of the discussion is determined according to the characteristics of the informants, and the natural flow of the conversation among the participants quickly generates a lot of information about the research topic. This technique elicits information that paints a portrait of combined perspectives; it enables you to see how everything 'fits together'. Apart from answering your main research question, focus group interviews can also identify ideas for further investigation. Although the degree of flexibility associated with focus group interviews is as high as with semi-structured interviews, the number of questions that can be addressed during the interview is less than in the latter.

Facilitating a group discussion requires good listening skills in order to be able to ask the appropriate questions. Also, using focus group interviews requires careful management of group dynamics so as to stimulate a natural discussion where, in the course of (normally) a two-hour session, informants talk, express their views, laugh, tell personal stories, disagree, interrupt one another, contradict themselves, go back

Box 6.4	Interview guide (semi-structured questions)

Thank you for agreeing to participate in this interview and contributing to my research study. All information will be strictly confidential. This interview will be divided in five sections, under the following headings: Background, Product, New Product Development, New Product Development Process, New Product Development in your organization.

A. Background
1. How long have you worked for this organization?
2. How long in this current post?
3. Could you describe the organizational structure and tell me where your position is within this structure?
4. What are the main responsibilities of your current post?

B. Product
5. How would you describe the typical product in the cruise industry? (up to the manager to decide what a typical product is, but focus on significant products)
6. What is the main product in the cruise industry? (supporting product – service as a part of product – tangible – intangible product)

C. New product development
7. What would you describe as a new product in the cruise industry? Can you give examples? (focus on significant products, not on new knives, etc).
8. What was the last new product your company developed? (most significant – impact on organization – competition)

D. New product development process
9. What influences the decision to develop a new product in this organization? (internally – externally – market research, etc.)
10. Who are the key decision-makers in this organization regarding which new product to develop? (which people were involved in the decision – new product development team, marketing – different functional areas, top management)

E. New product development case study
11. Can you explain to me the process for launching a new product – from the initial decision to develop a new product to its actual launch? (You might like to explain the process of developing and launching the new product you referred to earlier) (special new product development team – what is the influence of XY department in the process – chain of command – time frame – budget allocated – incentives for people involved in the new product development – mission statement for the new product development team – internal e.g. HRM/external e.g. customer-related factors were considered – measure for success – difference of the process to other companies – strategic planning – cost/benefits of a new product.

Thank you for your valuable time and contributions.

(Source: Ciraulo, 2002)

and forth in questions, etc., whilst maintaining the focus of the discussion on the research topic. You will be able to accomplish this balancing act by using (as in the above techniques) a well-designed interview guide that will enable the informants to relax, open up, think deeply and consider alternatives, while at the same time avoiding making the interviewing process mechanical and list-like.

When you are planning research with focus groups, you should not assume that inviting informants from a highly diverse background to the same session would give you the desired results. In most cases this does not work well, as individuals tend to repress their opinions and views in the presence of people with significant differences from them in terms of power, status, job, income, education or other personal characteristics. In order to achieve a cross-section of views from diverse informants you will need to run multiple sessions, to each of which you should try to invite around twenty people with similar characteristics – with the aim of seven to ten turning up (regardless of the incentive, no-shows are very common in this technique).

Case example

Vernon *et al.* (2003) studied the response of micro-businesses (with less than ten employees) to environmental sustainability issues within the context of the tourism industry in southeast Cornwall, situated in the southwest peninsula of the United Kingdom. Towards this end they used five focus groups consisting predominantly of between five and nine micro-business owners from different parts of the district and from a range of tourism sectors (caravan and campsites, holiday parks, guesthouses, hotels, inns and public houses, self-catering accommodation and tourist attractions). In the room where the focus groups were held, as well as the facilitator (interviewer) there was also a note-taker who kept a record of the discussion even if, with permission, the discussions were recorded. The researchers offered refreshments and a light buffet meal to the informants as an incentive for participating, as well as reimbursement of any reasonable out-of-pocket expenses. Two separate focus groups were organized; one for the members of the SUSTAIN Network (a 'green' business organization encouraging improvements in the environmental performance of businesses), who were expected to have significantly different views from those of the other informants, and one for larger businesses (for the same reason), which was eventually cancelled due to the lack of participants.

Remember that you always run the risk that powerful personalities may dominate the entire discussion, while people from some cultural backgrounds may not feel comfortable in focus groups because they are perhaps too 'shy' to express their views or are afraid that they might make a mistake and say something wrong during the conversation. You will need to be very aware that social norms often get in the way and may affect the reliability of the participants' answers. For example, during the session an informant may support another informant by saying, 'Right! I could not agree more' – but this does not mean that this is the informant's final opinion on the matter.

Observation

Compared with other data collection methods, observation provides rich, detailed, context-specific descriptions, which are close to the insider's perspective (Sackmann, 1991). Observation is also used to validate or further explore information obtained in interviews through a process of constant questioning, comparing and contrasting (Schein, 1992). In other words, observation complements other research methods, helps to generate theories and ideas for further research, and helps to validate existing findings.

If you are using observation as a data collection technique, you learn by being present in the research setting, by seeing what people do and how they interact with others, by listening to what they say and asking questions. This data collection technique allows you to gain first-hand experience of the informants' behaviours, and the underlying meanings of their attitudes, relationships and contexts. For example, observation may be used to describe the purchasing behaviours of Japanese travellers during a city tour because it will give you the opportunity to get involved in the daily lives of the subjects under investigation. Observation can also be used to explore sensitive issues in a research context, such as politics in an organization or sensitivities associated with a cultural group. It may, for example, be used to understand how budgeting decisions are taken in hospitality organizations, and to help identify the politically driven interactions among individuals and the emphasis placed on different criteria in allocating budgets to the various departments of the organization. There are two basic methods of observation: participant and non-participant (sometimes referred to as 'unobtrusive').

As a participant observer, you will take part in the situation being studied rather than simply acting as a 'researcher'. For example, Bowen (2002) used participant observation to study the factors that affect consumer satisfaction and dissatisfaction in long-haul inclusive tours by himself taking part, as a customer, in a small-group, soft-adventure, long-haul inclusive tour from the United Kingdom to Malaysia and Singapore. Participant observation increases your opportunities to understand the study context 'from the inside', and you may become a research subject yourself (as a participant). As a non-participant observer, unsurprisingly, you will not take part in the situation being studied, but may well be present in the environment. For instance, Guerrier and Adib (2003) studied tour representatives working in Mallorca, Spain, for a British budget tour operator in their exploration of the paradoxes of delivering emotional labour in a work setting that is so explicitly about delivering fun. One of their data collection techniques was non-participant observation of the reps' work at the desk in hotel lobbies and on excursions and airport duties. Theoretically, non-participant observation limits your impact on the situation under study. The distinction between the two observation techniques, however, is not as clear-cut as it may seem. You can never be sure that as an observer you are participating fully or, on the other hand, that as a non-participant you are not having an impact on the situation being studied.

The choice between participant and non-participant observation is one that you will have to make after taking into consideration the particular circumstances of your research project. In many cases you will have to compromise, depending on the nature of the study environment, your research experience, the nature of the data you wish to collect, and possible ethical issues that may arise.

In terms of the stages of the research process, observation can be used to identify areas for research in the early stages, to clarify your research focus further, or to facilitate access by building trust and identifying key informants. During your research process, you can use observations to validate and cross-check findings from other data collection techniques and from different informants. You may also use this technique to explore the underlying meanings behind the attitudes (identified as a result of a questionnaire or an interview) of informants.

Conducting observation

When undertaking observation, you need to have a systematic approach and concentrate your observation on specific aspects of a situation (the observation objectives). Observation objectives may include people and their roles, activities and behaviours, goals of individuals and what they are trying to achieve, networks and relationships between individuals. What is important is that these objectives are relevant to your research project. You therefore need to make sure that you observe carefully selected issues based on a literature-guided framework highlighting the key themes for observation. This framework can help you to prioritize each aspect in terms of its importance to the research project. It may be useful to create a list of things to pay attention to (an observation guide developed from your literature review) and keep it in your pocket for quick reference. Note, however, that it is very important to be ready to encounter unexpected scenarios during your observation, which may indicate new directions for your research. Box 6.5 provides an example

Box 6.5	Observation guide

1. Describe general employee characteristics, including age, physical appearance, number of employees in the restaurant, etc.
2. Describe general customer characteristics, including age, physical appearance, number of customers in the restaurant, etc.
3. Describe how customers are served by service employees and the communication between them.
4. Level of personal/standardized service:
   - Do service workers smile at the customers very often?
   - What kind of language do they use when they serve customers? Is the language the same among the employees?
   - Describe body language and report on any comments or overhead conversation.
5. Active customers and questioning, level of social respect to service worker:
   - Do customers seem to enjoy being served? Do employees seem to enjoy serving the customers?
   - Describe the interactions between service worker and customers.
6. Inner reflection and imagination:
   - How is inner reflection and imagination encouraged? To what extent? If any, what is customer's reaction?
   - Does it raise any questions, or does it create any sign of appreciation or emotional reactions?
   - Does the service procedure seem to require some emotional interaction? To what extent?

(Source: Deng, 2005)

of an observation guide prepared by a student investigating the provision of emotional labour in restaurants in China. The student observed local employees' behaviours in their work environment, and in particular during service interaction.

In preparing for the observation activity, it is useful to find out as much as you can about the site where you will be observing as a non-participant, or about any activities in which you might participate if you will be a participant observer. You could also visit the site before your formal observation in order to familiarize yourself with it and perhaps make some initial observations.

During observation, make sure that you do not stand out or affect the natural flow of activity. One way to do this is to behave in a way similar to the people around you, so you need to be familiar with such things as local meanings of particular body language (positions and gestures), types of physical and eye contact, and tone of voice. Another important aspect you need to be aware of while observing is that, when taking notes, you separate your objective observations from your interpretations. Your notes should be brief, so that you do not miss out events and behaviours while you are writing them down. Rather than trying to document every detail from your observation (especially quotations), record key words and phrases that will trigger your memory later, when you expand your notes.

As soon as possible after collecting your observation data, you should expand whatever notes you were able to make into a descriptive narrative. If you plan participant observation late in the morning, make sure that you will have time in the evening to expand your notes while events are still fresh in your mind. Include as many details as possible, and write down questions you may have about the situation that need further consideration or follow-up, issues to pursue, new information, etc. Box 6.6 offers an example of expanded observation notes from the study presented above. In these notes, you will notice that there are comments made by the researcher; these helped later, in the analysis process.

Box 6.6	Expanded observation notes

Monday 5 June, 2006, Day 1   Hours 5–8 pm
Location: Jinghaihua Seafood Restaurant

Observation notes
It is a busy day. There are many customers who come for business purposes. There are fifteen VIP rooms and one large eating room in the restaurant. As one of the employees showed, the small tables are all reserved but large the VIP rooms are not popular during the weekends. Thus, the way restaurant is interpreted and communicated leaves the customers free to choose their tables. They can choose whichever table they wish. Normally, service workers check the numbers of guest to arrange the tables for the customers. For example, a six-seat table was recommended for a five-customer group.

I saw many customers spending as short time as possible at the reception desk and choosing the table they want. There are about ten 'Miss Welcome' receptionists standing at the reception desk to take the customers to their tables. The service process they follow is: welcome the customer; check the booking information; check the table notes; arrange proper table for customers; take customer to the table; finally, say good-bye when customers leave.

Observation comment
I can see that this restaurant places emphasis on welcoming customers, which helps a lot to make customers feel at home when they first arrive. This, however, increases pressure on the service worker. As a 'Miss Welcome', she is only escorting the customers to their tables but does not serve them; this requires more teamwork from service workers. Besides, I think the restaurant encourages more of a standardized service, as I observed the 'Miss Welcomes' saying 'welcome' all together at the same time.

Observation notes
I sat at one of the tables in the large eating room. There were young service workers, aged in their twenties and thirties; 60 per cent of them were female. All of the employees were wearing uniforms, but the uniforms of receptionists, team leaders and managers were more distinctive.

Observation comment
This represents standardization.

Observation notes
Chinese Food in the East of China is normally served separately as cold dishes, hot dishes (main course), and fluid dishes. The cold dishes come once customers have finished ordering their food. From where I was sitting, I could see that some customers were not happy with the speed of service. Most of the customers chose to pay cash, and they did not tip employees. Service employees were not polite in the way they used language, and they never smiled.

Observation comment
Service employees did not express their emotions. The speed of the service was well below the expectations of the customers. This had implications for customer satisfaction.

(Source: Deng, 2005)

Questionnaires

Questionnaires are one of the most popular methods of collecting data among hospitality and tourism researchers. Researchers use a pre-determined, structured set of questions to obtain information from a sample of respondents and record it. They are very effective in systematically collecting information from a large number of people, at a low cost, in order to produce summaries and quantitative descriptions. In other words, questionnaires are a particularly useful data collection technique when you know exactly what to ask, need to ask a lot of people and can ask standard questions that everyone will be able to understand and respond to.

Saunders *et al.* (2007) maintain that you can collect different types of data using questionnaires, as follows:

- *Opinions*: the questionnaire can ask how respondents feel about something or what they think or believe is true or false – for example, 'How would you evaluate the service quality in the pool bar?' or 'To what extent do you agree with the statement that British Airways is the best flag carrier in the world?'
- *Behaviours and attitudes*: the questionnaire can ask what respondents do or what their intentions are – for example, 'How often do you fly to long-haul destinations' or 'How many trips do you intend to do by air within the next six months?'
- *Attributes*: the questionnaire can ask about the respondents' characteristics, such as age, gender, education, occupation and income – for example, 'What is your nationality?'

As this is a very structured research technique, when designing a questionnaire you will need to follow various stages in order to ensure the success of your design. The process is not dissimilar to that described in the previous techniques. You always start with the aim and objectives of your study in mind. Box 6.7 gives an overview of these stages.

Box 6.7	The eight stages of questionnaire design

1. Decide on the information required
2. Define the target informants
3. Choose the method(s) of reaching your target respondents
4. Decide on question content
5. Develop the question wording and format
6. Check the length of the questionnaire
7. Pilot the questionnaire
8. Finalize the questionnaire form.

Information required

When you are designing your questionnaire, you need to translate the general topic of interest into specific research aims and then questions. This may seem obvious, but it is not unusual for a questionnaire to fail to address particular topics either because of inadequate preparatory work from the researcher or because of insufficient understanding of the research topic. For example, if you wish to investigate the determinants of airline choice of long-haul travellers between Japan and Europe, you may need first to understand the areas of brand loyalty, service quality and customer satisfaction in order to know what broad questions to ask your informants. Only after determining these broad questions can you break them down into a detailed list of sub-areas, which will be the basis for developing your questionnaire.

Target informants

At the beginning of your study, you need to decide which broad characteristics of the informants will be appropriate to your study. Chapter 5 discusses in more detail how you can make these decisions. In terms of questionnaire administration, you can choose between face-to-face contact (self-administered or researcher-administered), postal contact and online contact. Each method has its own advantages and disadvantages that must be considered, bearing in mind budget and time constraints.

Self-administered questionnaires are completed by the informants themselves. They can be completed quickly, and use fewer resources than researcher-completed questionnaires. The disadvantages are that you cannot be entirely sure who has filled in the questionnaire; that there is no opportunity to clarify a response if it is not clear; and that they can be unsuitable for those who have difficulty in reading or writing, or in understanding the language in which the research is conducted.

Researcher-administered questionnaires take usually the form of telephone questionnaires and structured interviews. The researcher asks the question and records the informant's answer. The advantage of researcher-administered questionnaires is that you have better control over the research process – for example, you make sure that appropriate informants answer your questionnaire, and such questionnaires also offer the opportunity for both interviewer and interviewee to request clarification if necessary. The disadvantages of this approach are that they take longer to complete, and the possibility of interviewer bias is increased.

Question content

In order to make decisions regarding the questions, you will need to divide each broad question (objective) you have identified in the first stage into more specific investigative questions. This is an iterative process that will stop only when you feel that the investigative questions are sufficiently precise. You will then need to identify the variables about which you will need to collect data in order to answer each investigative question and establish how to measure the data for each variable.

If, for example, you were looking at customers' attitudes on the introduction of a non-smoking policy in pubs and restaurants in England, you would probably start your questionnaire with a table similar to that provided in Box 6.8.

Once you have developed your list of investigative questions you will need to re-check it, asking yourself: 'Is this question really necessary for my research?' Often researchers are tempted to ask questions that are not directly related to their research aim and objectives. The result of this non-critical inclusion of questions that are 'interesting' is a very long questionnaire that will tire the informant and often lead to them thinking less carefully about their answers.

Question wording and format

Questionnaire design is a communication exercise, since words often have different meanings for different people. The point here is that you need to elicit the information you want, but in order to achieve this you have to ask the informants questions that they understand. Choosing the right words and keeping technical terminology and jargon to the minimum is a first step in the right direction. The general rule is to keep the questions as simple as possible. To achieve this, follow the advice given in

Box 6.8	Investigative questions, variables and measures	

Investigative questions	Variable(s) required	Detail in which data measured
Do customers feel that they should be able to smoke in the restaurant if they want to as a right? (opinion)	Opinion of customer regarding smoking in restaurant as a right	Feel ... should be allowed, should not be allowed, no strong feelings
Do customers feel that the owner of the pub/ restaurant should provide a smoking room for smokers if smoking is banned? (opinion)	Opinion of customers regarding the provision of a smoking room for smokers	Feel ... very strongly that it should, quite strongly that it should, no strong opinions, quite strongly that it should not, very strongly that it should not
Would customers accept a smoking ban in a restaurant if the majority of people agreed to it? (behaviour)	Likely behaviour of customer regarding the acceptance of a ban	Would ... accept with no preconditions, accept if a smoking room was provided, not accept without additional conditions, would not accept whatever the conditions
Age (attribute), whether or not a smoker (behaviour)	Age of customer; smoker	(Youngest 16, oldest 65) Non-smoker, smokes but not in office, smokes

the 'Interviews' section above – avoid double-barrelled and leading questions, break complex questions down into two or three, etc.

When developing the questionnaire, you also need to consider which question format to use. The format affects the length and type of answer respondents provide; it also affects the amount of time you will require to code the answer, and the complexity of the data analysis. Questionnaire questions can be classified into four types: closed, open-ended, open response-option, and rating/scale questions. The former two were discuss ed briefly in the context of interviews, however, here they are examined at greater length.

Clearly, in most situations a questionnaire will include all four types of question, as some are proven to be more effective in eliciting particular types of answers. When you feel that the informant needs some help to articulate an answer or give an answer in a manner that will help you to better understand the topic, then closed questions should be used. Closed questions provide two or more alternatives from which the respondents select the choice closest to their own thinking; they also include list-type questions where the respondent is offered a list of items, any of which may be selected (see example below).

Please tick ☑ the box in the 'provided' column those services you provided as a housekeeper in this hotel during the past month. If you have not provided a particular service, please leave the box blank.

Service	Provided
Cleaning rooms	☐
Bed-making	☐
Laundry	☐
Other	☐

(Please describe)...

Closed questions also include category-type questions, where only one response can be selected from a given set of categories (see example below).

How often do you visit this Italian Restaurant? Please tick ☑ as appropriate.

☐ First visit

☐ Once a week

☐ Two or more times a week

☐ Less than once a week to fortnightly

☐ Less than fortnightly to once a month

☐ Less often

Closed questions can be very helpful in that they provide the informant with an easy way of answering without having to think too much; moreover, the elicited answers can be easily coded, making the questionnaire analysis pretty straightforward. However, you need to also take into consideration the fact that they limit the informant to responding only within the suggested framework.

Open questions, on the other hand, allow respondents to answer in an unconstrained way, often using as many words as they like. These types of question allow exploration to occur, and enable you to collect rich and detailed data. An example of an open question is shown below.

Please list up to three things you liked about the restaurant:

1. ....
2. ....
3. ....

While open-ended questions are a valuable tool, you should avoid over-using them in a questionnaire. They often result in informant fatigue, and they make coding and analysis of your findings far more complicated.

Open response-option questions overcome the disadvantages of both open and closed questions. An open response-option is a type of question that is both open-ended and includes specific response options as well. You can also include ranking questions, where the respondent is asked to place items in order (see below).

Please number each of the factors listed below in order of importance to you in your choice of a restaurant. Number the most important 1, the next 2 and so on. If a factor has no importance at all, please leave blank.

Factor	Importance
Service quality	[ ]
Staff friendliness	[ ]
Serving size	[ ]
Location	[ ]
Atmosphere	[ ]
Cleanliness	[ ]
Other	[ ]

(Please describe) . . . .

You can also use rating and scale questions to obtain opinion data. The most common form is the scale question, in which you ask your informant how strongly they agree or disagree with a statement or series of statements (Saunders *et al.*, 2007; see below).

For the following statements, please tick ☑ the box that matches your view most closely.

	Agree	Tend to agree	Tend to disagree	Disagree
I feel that employee training has influenced employee satisfaction at work	☐	☐	☐	☐

You can also use numeric rating scale questions. With these questions, it is important that the numbers make sense to the informants. An example is given below.

> For the following statement, please circle (O) the number that matches your view most closely.
>
> This meal was ... Poor value   1   2   3   4   5   Good value
>   for money   for money

Remember that the endpoints of response scales must be anchored with meaningful labels. Always have three things in mind when using this type of question:

1. An odd number of points provides a middle option for informants that either do not know what to answer or have a neutral opinion
2. If it is important for your study to measure extreme opinions, then use a scale with a larger number of points (e.g. 1–7)
3. Scales larger than 7 are usually not very helpful, and researchers often collapse larger scales when it comes to analysing their data.

Length of the questionnaire

The common assumption is that questionnaire length affects the response rate, in the sense that increased length tires informants and pushes more of them over a threshold beyond which they are no longer willing to participate. Although this common assumption does not seem to be well supported in the experimental literature (the few studies that have actually examined the correlation between the length of questionnaires and response rate have yielded confusing results), it is advisable to ensure that the questionnaire is not be too lengthy – although it must be long enough to provide rich and accurate information about the study. For student research projects, we would advise a questionnaire of not much longer than thirty to forty questions spread over six to eight A4 pages.

Piloting the questionnaire

Your questionnaire will not be ready for fieldwork unless you first test (pilot) it with a small number of informants. This piloting is similar to test-driving a car; it will show whether your questionnaire is suitable for your research project in the sense that it will produce the desired outcomes. It also gives you the opportunity to identify possible design or content weaknesses that need improvement:

- The wording of the questions may not convey to the informant the meaning attributed by the researcher
- The questions may not be fully understood by all the types of informants you intend to question

- Additional questions may be needed in order to achieve the research objectives
- Clarification may be required
- The order of the questions may need to be altered
- Some questions may need to be removed
- The instructions to the informants may need further clarification.

In order for your pilot to be effective, you should not confine it to your supervisor and a few of your fellow students. Rather, you should select a small number of people who are broadly representative of the type of informants that you will have in your main study. In the pilot, it is not enough to get responses; you should also ask the informants to comment on the questionnaire itself – whether they had difficulties in understanding the questions, whether you should be asking some additional questions relevant to the research problem, and which questions in particular might pose problems.

The final questionnaire

After your pilot test, your questionnaire should be almost ready for the main study (your fieldwork). All that is left for you to do is to lay out and set up the questionnaire in its final form. You will therefore need to group and sequence the questions into an appropriate order, number them, and insert instructions for the informant at the top of the questionnaire. Even if you have a covering letter to accompany your questionnaire, it is always useful to include these instructions at the top of the questionnaire as well, in case it becomes separated from the letter. Remember that informants always read the questions, but unless their attention is really drawn to the instructions they are likely not to read them. Therefore, make sure that these instructions stand out – perhaps by writing them in a bold or italicized typeface.

With regard to sequencing the questions, it is quite common to start a questionnaire with demographic questions, but it would not be wrong if you were to 'break the mould' by starting with a few questions that engage the informant in the study. Demographic questions are easy to answer, and would be much better at the end of the questionnaire, when informants are getting tired. On the other hand, if you start with some straightforward questions with relatively few categories of response, you will trigger the informant's interest and perhaps increase the response rate in your study.

Normally, you should group questions in sections with a logical sequence. However, it is important not to underestimate the problem of 'positioning bias', where earlier questions are treated differently (often seen as more important) from later ones. One method of overcoming this problem is to list your questions randomly in the questionnaire and state this clearly in the informants' instructions, thus reducing the likelihood that they will treat the first questions as being more important.

Content analysis of documents

Content analysis of documents can be used as a complementary data collection method. Instead of interviewing informants, directly observing or asking someone to fill in a questionnaire for the purposes of your research project, this research technique requires you to analyse published documents produced for other purposes. In simple terms, this data collection technique involves analysing meanings and relationships of certain words or concepts within texts, and making inferences about the messages.

The variety of documents for analysis may include textbooks, book chapters, journal articles, commercial publications, publications about companies and destinations, press releases and company documents (internal memos, reports, etc.). These sources can be used to corroborate and augment evidence, as they cover a long time span and also provide exact names, references and details of events (Yin, 1994 ; May, 1997). The information obtained from the documents may also be compared and contrasted with findings from other sources to determine its validity. Robson (1993) provides a neat summary of the advantages and disadvantages of content analysis.

Advantages:

- It is less time-consuming and costly, compared with other data collection techniques
- It may allow a 'low-cost' form of longitudinal analysis by reviewing a series of documents over a number of years
- It allows you to conduct what can be called 'desk research' without any disruption
- The data are in permanent form, ready, collected for analysis, and hence can be re-analysed, thus allowing reliability checks.

Disadvantages:

- You might have only a limited or partial set of documents
- The analysed documents may have been written for another purpose and thus not be in line with your research focus; they therefore need careful consideration and treatment
- It is very difficult to assess causal relationships by asking why or how questions, as your documents might not answer these questions.

Content analysis can be divided in two broad categories: conceptual and relational. *Conceptual analysis* can be seen as identifying in a text the existence and frequency of concepts, whether in simple words or in phrases. In this type of analysis you choose a concept for examination and then look at the documents you have available for analysis in order to identify the occurrence of terms related to this concept, even if it appears implicitly. You will first need to decide whether you are going to count a concept only once, no matter how many times it appears, or if you will count it each time it occurs. Obviously, explicit terms related to the concept are easy to identify; however, identifying implicit terms and deciding on their connotations may be complicated and highly subjective. In order to limit this subjectivity, you will have to use either a specialized dictionary or some contextual translation rules that will allow you to include the implicit terms consistently throughout the text, in the same way every time. Once identification of all the concepts you are looking for is complete, you will have to examine the data and attempt to draw whatever conclusions and generalizations are possible.

Case example

Su (2004) examined hotel guest comment cards (GCCs) and customer satisfaction management schemes in Taiwan using conceptual analysis to determine the extent to which each hotel's comment card design corresponded to the identified best practice criteria. Using a checklist of thirty-two criteria – developed earlier by Gilbert and Horsnell (1998) – as a framework for comparison, the researcher analysed the GCCs of seventy-six international tourist hotels in Taiwan, trying to identify the existence and the frequency of these criteria in the GCCs. The results of this analysis showed that no single hotel company in this study met all best-practice criteria, and many fell substantially short in terms of overall best practice. For example, the majority of GCCs did not include questions relating to customer motivation, such as purpose of visit and previous stays in this hotel/hotel chain, while very few offered sections relating to specific market segments, tested marketing channel effectiveness, or identified competition. Su concluded from these findings that these questionnaires provide very little information to influence marketing decisions, and limited opportunities for cross-referencing of findings to different market segments.

Relational analysis (also called semantic analysis), like conceptual analysis, begins with the identification of concepts present in a given text or set of texts. However, relational analysis goes further than counting frequencies and existence in the text, and explores relationships between the concepts identified. In other words, in relational analysis the focus is not on individual concepts but on identifying semantic or meaningful relationships between them. The methodology followed here is similar to that above. The difference begins after the identification of the concepts, when you have to analyse the text for the relationships among them. These relationships will need to be identified and evaluated according to their strength, sign (positive/negative) and direction.

- The *strength of relationship* is the characteristic that shows the degree to which two or more concepts are related in the text. In order for you to determine the strength of the relationship between two concepts, you may look at the number of their co-occurrences in the same sentence or paragraph as well as the words that may relate them. For example, the word 'unless' shows a relationship of great strength, whereas the word 'perhaps' shows a weaker relationship.
- The sign of a relationship is the characteristic that shows whether the concepts are positively or negatively related. For example, the concept 'promiscuous customer' is negatively related to the concept 'customer retention' in the same sense as the concept 'loyal customer' is positively related to the latter.
- The *direction of the relationship* is the characteristic that shows the relative positioning of a concept *vis-à-vis* another. There may be several types of directional relationships, with most common being 'A occurs before B', 'B is a consequence of A', 'if A then B', etc. These types of relationship, which normally imply that concept A is a 'prime mover' of B, or *vice versa*, are referred to as unidirectional. Bidirectional relationships occur when the concepts involved have equal influence in the relationship.

These relationships may be represented on a map that you can create yourself, or using a special software design for such analyses (see Chapter 9). Once the relationships have been assigned a value and a sign, it is possible for you to conduct statistical analyses of them – which can include an investigation of correlations, differences or other relationships between the concepts you have chosen to study.

Increasing the credibility of your research

Strauss and Corbin (1990) argue that it is important to evaluate the adequacy of the research process in order to judge the quality of the outcome of the research process. The research process of a project can be evaluated against two research quality criteria: reliability and validity.

Reliability can be defined as the degree to which the data collection method(s) will yield consistent findings, whether similar observations could be made or conclusions reached by other researchers, and whether there is transparency in terms of how much sense was made of the raw data. In other words, how well does it measure, and can the results of a study can be reproduced under a similar methodology? (Saunders *et al.*, 2007).

If a question in your questionnaire or your interview guide can be misinterpreted by informants and consequently answered in different ways, then the reliability of the survey or interview is low. To avoid this problem, you can check the consistency with which a question is answered through the test–retest method, whereby an informant is asked the same question(s) at two different times. If you receive consistent answers, then the results are repeatable and your data collection method is reliable. In a questionnaire, you can ask (in different sections) questions that are similar but phrased differently. If the informant answers them consistently, your questionnaire shows high reliability. However, your data collection method may consistently provide similar results, but not measure what you want it to determine. In this case, you have a reliable but not valid method.

Validity can be defined as the extent to which the data collection method accurately measures what it is intended to measure, and the extent to which the research findings are really about what they profess to be about. In other words, 'do the results say what they are supposed to say?' and 'how truthful are the results?' (Saunders *et al.*, 2007).

You can check the validity of your method by asking a series of questions, starting with your research question, and seeing whether you can actually answer it with the data collection technique you have chosen. If, for example, you are looking at mapping the travelling habits of Brazilian business people and your questions revolve predominantly around long-haul trips (thus favouring answers related to flying), then you will have a problem with the face or content validity of your method. In your pilot, you need to ask your informants whether the questions are clear and easily understood, and whether you need to include additional questions to answer your research objectives. When you have your initial findings, you may want to compare them with those of similar studies and check them for consistency. All these actions will confirm the criterion validity of your method. Consistency of findings may also be checked with the test–retest method or by asking the informant the same question differently in the various stages of the study. If the answers are the same, then your method has high internal validity. The validity of your study also depends on the informants that you choose to approach. If your sample is not representative of the population you want to study and you have missed a certain type of respondent, then your research method does not have the necessary external validity because your findings are likely to be biased and not applicable in a wider sense to the population at large (i.e. not generalizable).

In terms of data collection techniques, it is important to note that each data collection technique – interviews (qualitative) or questionnaires (quantitative) – has something to offer to researchers seeking ways to strengthen the reliability and validity of their study. Different methods use different processes to construct findings, and these processes are valuable in contextualizing data generated in various ways. Mixed research paradigms will help you to make the data collection and analysis more accurate and the inferences more useful because they can represent a plurality of interests, voices and perspectives (Patton, 2002). The underlying assumption is that research is stronger when it mixes research paradigms, because a fuller understanding of human or organizational phenomena is gained.

Summary

- There are different data collection techniques available for researchers, and each data collection technique is more appropriate for different research purposes.
- Interviews are a systematic way of collecting data through asking questions and carefully listening and recording data. This data collection technique gives you the opportunity to explore issues with your informants in depth.
- Observation involves observing and interacting with your informants and the research setting, asking questions and seeking answers for your research questions. It gives you the opportunity to get close to the phenomenal worlds of the informants.
- Questionnaires are a popular data collection technique among hospitality and tourism researchers investigating consumer behaviour and customer satisfaction. They are effective in collecting information from a large number of people.
- Content analysis of documents is a cost-effective way of collecting data. It involves reviewing and analysing the contents of documents, and drawing inferences from the analysis.
- Research instruments should normally be developed based on the review of the literature. Your research questions should be in line with the themes identified in the literature.
- It is important to increase the rigor of your research by improving the validity and reliability of your research.

Review questions

1. Evaluate the advantages and disadvantages of each data collection technique presented in this chapter with regard to your research topic.
2. What role does the literature review play in developing an interview schedule?
3. How can you develop an observation guide, and what role does it play in recording your observations?
4. What are the steps you need to go through when designing a questionnaire?
5. What is the difference between conceptual analysis and relational analysis?
6. How can you increase the credibility of your research?

Annex: Hospitality and tourism studies using different data collection techniques

Authors	Data collection technique	Aim of the study	Justification for the chosen data collection technique
Clarke (2007)	Semi-structured interviews	The purpose of this study was to explore the behaviour associated with the phenomenon of the giving and receiving of gifts as part of hospitality, leisure and tourism experiences.	The aim of this exploratory research was to shape initial understanding of the behaviour associated with the giving and receiving of experiences, as opposed to physical goods. Interviews would give the opportunity to explore the real experience of gift-giving behaviour, with informants recalling and describing actual events.
Anderson (2006)	Semi-structured interviews	This paper describes the preparedness of organizations to respond to crisis events; the personnel or human resource (HR) strategies implemented; and the postscript, the organizational learning that occurred.	The semi-structured interview technique was considered most appropriate to describe and explore the complex issues associated with organizational responses to the events of 2001, namely, the collapse of the HIH Insurance Company, the World Trade Center attacks and the demise of Ansett Airlines. The use of semi-structured interviews, with a number of pre-determined questions, allowed some comparison between the responses of the participating senior managers, and also afforded the opportunity to digress and probe further, when appropriate.
Huang and Hsu (2005)	Focus group interviews	The purpose of this study was to identify mainland Chinese residents' perceptions, motivations and perceived behavioral inhibitors when visiting Hong Kong.	It was thought that focus group interviews would encourage Chinese residents to discuss and explore questions amongst themselves, and produce a lot of information quickly, identifying and exploring beliefs, attitudes and behaviours, and providing ideas for further discussion.
Hardy and Beeton (2001)	Focus group interviews	The purpose of this study was to clarify stakeholder perceptions of tourism, in particular, perceptions of the tourism experience.	As the focus of the study was to understand stakeholder perceptions of sustainable tourism, focus group interviews with tourists would give the opportunity to gather insights into the issues they felt were

Authors	Data collection technique	Aim of the study	Justification for the chosen data collection technique
			relevant and, second, to explore these issues in detail by giving tourists the chance to comment on each other's views and stimulate discussion.
Choi *et al.* (2007)	Content analysis	This study attempted to identify the image representations of Macau on the Internet by analysing the content of a variety of web information sources – the Macau official tourism website, tour operators' and travel agents' websites, online travel magazine and guide websites, and online travel 'blogs'.	With the increasingly rich and readily available text data on the web, qualitative assessments such as content analysis of image formation and other tourism phenomena is gaining in popularity. The examination of the effects of projected images through various information channels could become an integral part of image formation research.
Altinay (2006)	Observation	This study aims to provide an insight into the process of selecting potential franchise partners in the European division of an international organization.	It was essential to check if data obtained from the interviews accurately reflected the real-time experience of participants involved in the process. Therefore, observation was utilized to support the interviews. Twelve meetings were attended in the capacity of participant/observer in the host countries (Belgium, Germany, Spain and Turkey) and at corporate levels (UK). Notes were taken to provide a condensed version of events. Shadowing of a number of key informants was adopted to get close to the phenomenal world of the key actors.
Alleyne *et al.* (2007)	Questionnaires	This study aims to measure the effect of human resource management (HRM) on performance in the hotel industry in Barbados.	The literature reveals that the dominant method of researching the links between HRM and performance has been surveys through questionnaires; questionnaires enable easy comparisons because a standard set of questions and appear to be authoritative – the researcher has more control over the research process.

Authors	Data collection technique	Aim of the study	Justification for the chosen data collection technique
Lam *et al.* (2007)	Question-naires	The purpose of this study was to explore the influence of perceived IT beliefs, the task–technology fit, attitude, self-efficacy, and subjective norms on behavioural intentions in adopting informa-tion technology in hotels in Hang Zhou, China.	Questionnaires were chosen to allow the collection of a large amount of data from a sizeable population in a highly economical way.

References

Alleyne, P., Doherty, L. and Greenidge, D. (2007). Human resource management and perform-ance in the Barbados hotel industry. *International Journal of Hospitality Management*, 25(4), 623–646.

Altinay, L. (2006). Selecting partners in an international franchise organization. *International Journal of Hospitality Management*, 25, 108–125.

Anderson, A. B. (2006). Crisis management in the Australian tourism industry: preparedness, personnel and postscript. *Tourism Management*, 27, 1290–1297.

Bowen, D. (2002). Research through participant observation in tourism: a creative solution to the measurement of consumer satisfaction/dissatisfaction among tourists. *Journal of Travel Research*, 41, 4–14.

Choi, S., Lehto, Y. X. and Morrison, M. A. (2007). Destination image representation on the web: content analysis of Macau travel related websites. *Tourism Management*, 28(1), 118–129.

Ciraulo, M. (2002). 'An Investigation into the New Product Development Practice in the Cruise Industry'. Unpublished MSc Dissertation, Oxford Brookes University.

Clarke, J. (2007). The Four 'S's of experience gift giving behaviour. *International Journal of Hospitality Management*, 26(1), 98–116.

Correia, L, Ascenção, M. J. P. and Mw, S. C. (2004). Wine routes in Portugal: a case study of the Bairrada wine route. *Journal of Wine Research*, 15(1), 15–25.

Deng, J. (2005). 'The Provision of Emotional Labour in China's Tourism and Hospitality Industry'. Unpublished MSc Dissertation, Oxford Brookes University.

Easterby-Smith, M., Thorpe, R. and Lowe, A. (1991). *Management Research: An Introduction*. London: Sage Publications.

Gilbert, D. and Horsnell, S. (1998). Customer satisfaction measurement practice in United Kingdom hotels. *Journal of Hospitality and Tourism Research*, 22(4), 450–464.

Guerrier, Y. and Adib, A. (2003). Work at leisure and leisure at work: a study of the emotional labour of tour reps. *Human Relations*, 56(11), 1399–1417.

Hardy, L. A. and Beeton, S. J. R. (2001). Sustainable tourism or maintainable tourism: man-aging resources for more than average outcomes. *Journal of Sustainable Tourism*, 9(3), 168–192.

Huang, S. and Hsu, C. H. C. (2005). Mainland Chinese residents' perceptions and motivations for visiting Hong Kong: evidence from focus group interviews. *Asia Pacific Journal of Tourism Research*, 10(2), 191–205.

Kayat, K. (2002). Power, social exchanges and tourism in Langkawi: rethinking resident perceptions. *International Journal of Tourism Research*, 4(3), 171–191.

Lam, T., Cho, V. and Qu, H. (2007). A study of hotel employee behavioral intentions towards adoption of information technology. *International Journal of Hospitality Management*, 26(1), 49–65.

May, T. (1997). *Social Research: Issues, Methods and Process*, 2nd edn. Buckingham: Open University Press.

Patton, M. Q. (2002). *Qualitative Research and Evaluation Methods*. Thousand Oaks, CA: Sage Publications.

Prideaux, B. and Crosswell, M. (2006). The value of visitor surveys: the case of Norfolk Island. *Journal of Vacation Marketing*, 12(4), 359–370.

Robson, C. (1993). *Real World Research*. Oxford: Blackwell.

Sackmann, A. S. (1991). Uncovering culture in organizations. *Journal of Applied Behavioural Science*, 27(3), 295–317.

Saunders, M., Lewis, P. and Thornhill, A. (2007). *Research Methods for Business Students*. London: Prentice Hall Financial Times.

Schein, H. E. (1992). *Organizational Culture and Leadership*. San Francisco, CA: Jossey-Bass.

Strauss, A. L. and Corbin, J. (1990). *The Basics of Qualitative Research: Grounded Theory Procedures and Techniques*. Newbury Park, CA: Sage Publications.

Su, Y. A. (2004). Customer satisfaction measurement practice in Taiwan hotels. *International Journal of Hospitality Management*, 23(4), 397–408.

Vernon, J., Essex, S., Pinder, D. and Curry, K. (2003). The 'greening' of tourism micro-business: outcomes of focus group investigations in southeast Cornwall. *Business Strategy and the Environment*, 12(1), 49–69.

Yin, K. R. (1994). *Case Study Research: Design and Methods*. London: Sage Publications.

Chapter 7
Writing your research proposal

The time to begin writing an article is when you have finished it to your satisfaction. By that time you begin to clearly and logically perceive what it is you really want to say.

(Mark Twain, cited in Ayres, 2005: 252)

The research proposal is a very important milestone in your research journey. Many consider to be as an implicit contract between you and your research committee (or supervisor) about your research. We would like you to think of it more as your 'selling pitch', your first formal attempt to convince the people who overview your research that you have what it takes to go on, that you are ready to leave the classroom and get out into the field. For many students, this is a quite scary stage. Bowen and Rudenstein (1992) see the period between the end of the planning stage and the actual engagement with the research as one of the most fraught and difficult for students. In their account of the genesis of a research proposal, they emphasize the words 'anxiety' and 'paralysis'. This is often the situation with students who have not taken a systematic approach to the development of their research – but it should not be the case for you!

Mark Twain's quotation above couldn't be more appropriate for this stage of your research. Having followed the steps described in the previous chapters, you should now be in the position to 'clearly and logically perceive what is you really want to say' about your research. You have already done most of the work needed; you are familiar with the relevant literature, you have identified the gap, clarified the aim of the study and thought about how to achieve it (your research design). Now all you have to do is to tie these together on paper and convince your research supervisor that you are ready to actually engage with your research. Moreover, this proposal will serve as a blueprint for your research. Although its length and format may vary from institution to institution, it usually consists of three sections.

Section One

As in every written piece of work, you will first need to introduce the reader to the proposal. In Section One, you will include a brief introduction, provide the background/rationale of the study, state your aim and objectives, and argue the originality of your research and its contribution to the body of knowledge.

Introduction

The introduction should be one or two brief paragraph(s) presenting the problem or question that you'll be exploring, and drawing the reader into your research. It is not advisable to start your proposal with perplexing concepts. The most straightforward approach is to state the aim of the proposed study. You have seen how you can broadly articulate the overall aim of your research in Chapter 3, but here you need to be quite specific. Depending on your research approach, your introduction might be as follows:

> This research proposal puts forward a _____ (exploratory, explanatory) study that will seek to _____ (understand? describe? analyse? test? determine?) the _____ (phenomenon to be studied, theory on the relationship between variables) for _____ (the sample, participants, organizations, groups) in _____ (research context, region, sector). This first section of the proposal introduces the proposed study.

Background and rationale of the study

This is the part that gives the reader the context of your study. It should be a narrative, structured in such a way that it answers the six questions regarding research topic selection (see Box 1.3), basically describing what is happening in the industry that has attracted your attention. When describing the general state of knowledge on the research area, it is appropriate to refer to key researchers and their work – but don't overdo it; the literature review has its place later in the proposal. Here, limit the references to the key ones and use them selectively in order to discuss the deficiencies of current studies. This discussion should lead to the formulation of the problem that your study is going to address.

The problem statement

All research projects are guided by a general research question, which can be either single or followed by two or more specific questions. As suggested in Chapter 3, it is preferable to avoid the 'kitchen sink' approach of broad questions. However, should you choose this method to frame your problem statement, make sure that you structure it as an open-ended question. Here is an example:

> In what ways can a tourism destination website create a social relationship with its on-line visitors?

In order to achieve better specificity, you may as well opt to frame the problem using an open-ended question supported by relevant and more specific questions:

> The overall aim of the study is an attempt to answer the question: 'What is the role of regional headquarters for international hotel chains in the Asia-Pacific region?', with more specific focus on the following questions:
>
> 1. What are the company's motives in setting up regional headquarters in this region?
> 2. How does the company's centric (EPRG) profile influence the function of regional headquarters in this region?

If the aim of your research is to test a specific theory, then you are likely to have to include some hypotheses in your problem statement. A hypothesis is a testable statement derived from the theory that proposes a possible explanation to some phenomenon or event. A hypothesis should not be confused with a theory. Theories are general explanations based on a large amount of data. Researchers may also propose a number of hypotheses to test. For example, when Reisinger and Mavondo (2004) were looking at how the psychographic make-up of tourists may influence tourist behaviour, they proposed and tested as many as nine hypotheses:

H1: There is a positive relationship between values and personality.

H2: There is a positive relationship between values and travel motivation.

H3: There is a positive relationship between values and activities.

H4: There is a positive relationship between personality and travel motivation.

H5: There is a positive relationship between personality and activities.

H6: There is a positive relationship between personality and lifestyle.

H7: There is a positive relationship between travel motivation and activities.

H8: There is a positive relationship between travel motivation and lifestyle.

H9: There is a positive relationship between activities and lifestyle.

The number of hypotheses depends on the number of variables that need to be tested. In the above example, there were five variables that were examined: cultural values, personality, travel motivation, preferences for activities, and lifestyle. You will notice that the relationship between values and lifestyle was not tested. This is because – according to the authors – this relationship has been proven by other studies.

Depending on its syntax, a hypothesis is termed a research hypothesis if it states that there is a relationship between the variables (positive or negative), or a null hypothesis if it states that there is no relationship between the variables. Many correlational (investigating whether a hypothetical relationship actually exists) and causal–comparative (attempting to identify the cause-effect relationships) studies frame the problem statement with a research question followed by a combination of research and null hypotheses. For example, in his investigation on budgetary design Yuen (2006) states his research problem as follows:

Research question: 'How can budgetary design be improved in order to enhance employees' job satisfaction in working environments of task difficulty and unclear goal setting, such as in a hotel?'

Research hypotheses:

H1 (null): There is no significant relationship between budgetary participation and job satisfaction.

H2: There is a positive relationship between budgetary participation and task difficulty.

H3 (null): There is no relationship between task difficulty and job satisfaction.

H4: There is a negative relationship between budgetary participation and task clarity.

H5 (null): There is no relationship between task clarity and job satisfaction.

H6: There is a negative relationship between improved design of a budgetary system and task difficulty.

H7: There is a positive relationship between improved design of a budgetary system and task clarity.

H8: There is a positive relationship between improved design of a budgetary system and job satisfaction.

Research objectives

There is always a degree of confusion among students regarding the distinction between the 'aim' of the research and the research 'objectives', because in many languages the two words have exactly the same meaning. To clarify this confusion we often use the analogy of trans-Siberian railway travel. The aim of the entire journey from Moscow is eventually to reach Vladivostok. However, in order to achieve this aim the train will need to stop at six stations between the two cities: Kazan, Yekaterinburg, Krasnoyarsk, Irkutsk, Ulan Ude, Birobidzhan and Khabarovsk. These are the objectives – in other words, the tasks that need to be achieved – during your journey in order to accomplish your aim.

For example, in a study where the research question is: 'how effective are the marketing communication tools used by the tourism authorities of Dalian in Northern China?', the objectives might be as follows:

- To undertake a literature review regarding marketing communication with emphasis on the available tools and the conditions that enhance or inhibit their effectiveness
- To develop a framework that evaluates the effectiveness of marketing communication tools in the context of a tourism destination
- To refine of this framework by a three-round Delphi of tourism marketing experts
- To apply the framework in the broader Dalian and Liaodong peninsula region in order to assess how effective the marketing communication tools used by the tourism authorities are
- Based on the findings, to propose changes to the local tourism authorities in their marketing communications strategy.

As you can see, the objectives provide a clear roadmap of how the research is going to be conducted. Try to make your objectives tightly focused and clear. Here, the literature review will start from the more generic business environment and then focus on tourism destinations. It is important for you to ensure that your objectives are realistically achievable within the available timeframe and word limitation. The three-round Delphi will be time-consuming and may present some challenges, as the application of the framework involves travel that may take some time. There is no right number of objectives, but, given the limits of the dissertation, it is safer not to try to have too many. As a rule of thumb, four to six objectives are usually enough.

Originality and contribution to knowledge

One of the fundamental elements of your research proposal is the defence of the originality and contribution to knowledge of your research. Note the emphasis on the word 'defence'. Your defence should include strong and convincing arguments regarding why your study is worthwhile, and what value you hope its results will offer to other researchers and practitioners.

All research projects are normally expected to show a certain degree of originality. This originality is usually attributed to the treatment of your subject (when you are using 'new eyes', a novel angle of investigation). The originality of your study itself makes a contribution to the body of knowledge.

However, apart from merely being original, your proposed study can make a contribution to knowledge in many different ways – by testing a theory that has not been tested in a hospitality and tourism context; by challenging conventional wisdom and establishing your beliefs; by offering a clearer understanding of a concept; providing additional theoretical or empirical insights on an issue; by proposing an alternative explanation to a particular phenomenon; by developing theory through your research for common practices in the field which do not yet have a rigid theoretical base; or by replicating a particular study in a different context. In simple terms, your research will make a contribution if, with your findings, something can be done differently – a practitioner can work differently, a researcher can research differently, and a teacher can teach a subject differently. This difference does not have to be huge; it can be very small.

This first section of your research proposal will most probably be the largest part of your dissertation's introductory chapter. So all the effort that you put in now will also bear fruit when you are writing up your dissertation.

Section Two

In a typical research proposal, this is where you will start to discuss your literature review in greater depth. The point here is to identify the literature that will establish the significance of your research. In other words, the discussion of the literature in this section should be sufficient for you to show how your project will extend current knowledge.

Literature review

In writing your literature review, use the literature map you developed at the earlier stages of your research and organize your discussion accordingly. It is not recommended that you start writing about how the research in the field was chronologically developed; rather, concentrate on the major streams of research within your field that are relevant to your research topic (i.e. the primary and perhaps the secondary focus areas in your map – not the peripheral ones). Present and briefly discuss the major theories that relate to your research problem, and then go into greater depth regarding the one or two theories you feel will be core in your research and will help you move your study to its next level.

Make sure that you do not simply list the literature, but also organize it in some coherent manner and 'engage in a dialogue' with it by exposing the variables that will be significant in your study, showing in every instance how these will influence your research, comparing and contrasting different views on the topic, explaining your rationale for accepting or rejecting them, etc. An effective dialogue with the literature should highlight all the concepts underlying your study, as well as the variables comprised in them.

Conceptual framework

A conceptual framework covers the main features (aspects, dimensions, factors, variables) of your research and their presumed relationships (Robson, 1993). There are five basic features that should be incorporated in any theoretical framework:

1. The variables considered relevant to the study, which should be clearly identified and labelled in the discussion (in the literature review chapter)
2. Discussion and statement regarding how two or more variables are related to one another; this should be done for the important relationships that are theorized to exist among the variables
3. If the nature and direction of the relationships can be theorized on the basis of the findings from previous research, an indication in the discussion as to whether the relationships would be positive or negative
4. A clear explanation of why these relationships are expected to exist (the arguments could be drawn from the previous research findings)
5. A schematic diagram of the theoretical framework, so that the reader can see and easily comprehend the theorized relationships (Sekaran, 2000: 103).

The conceptual framework should be the culmination of your literature review, at a more basic level in the proposal and a more advanced level in your final dissertation. Developing a conceptual framework forces you to be explicit about what you think you are doing. As Robson (1993: 150–151) states, it helps you to be selective, to decide which are the important features, and to determine which relationships are likely to be of importance or meaning – and hence what data you are going to collect and analyse.

An example of a conceptual framework of the factors that influence international hotel chains' decision-making regarding how they will enter new markets is presented in Figure 7.1. This framework clearly illustrates that there are a number of external and internal factors and generic strategies that influence an organization's choice of using different entry modes (franchising, management contracting, direct investment, joint venture partnerships).

Zhao's (1994) research stated how antecedent factors are related to entry modes based on the review of the literature:

1. Political instability is a major factor for wholly-owned subsidiaries and long-term leasing contracts, but it may not be a major factor for non-equity entry modes such as the management contract and franchise.
2. The strengths of intangible and tangible assets of multinational lodging companies help them win entries into the host countries' lodging industry with management contracts and franchise agreements, as well as wholly-owned or long-term leased lodging properties. However, multinational lodging companies rely mostly upon their intangible assets to win the entries rather than tangible assets (with one exception – reservation systems).
3. Multinational lodging chains have employed many generic international strategies, such as multidomestic, broad portfolio, combination of standardization and adaptation to local needs, and acquisition strategies. However, there is not enough evidence to illustrate the direct relationship between generic international strategies and the entry mode choices.

This helped him to remain focused and explicit during the data collection and analysis of his research findings.

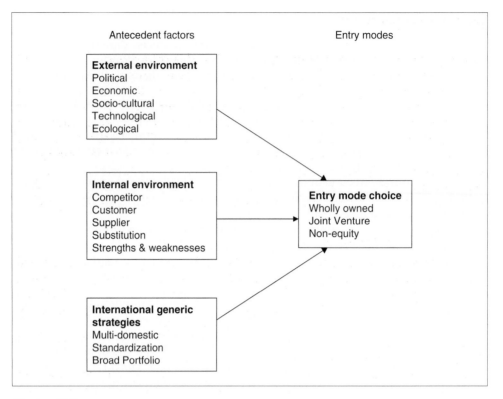

Figure 7.1
Conceptual framework of factors influencing entry mode choice
(Source: Zhao, 1994: 127).

Sometimes you may have a clear view about the possible relationships between variables, either through experience or because the theory or prior empirical work has already confirmed them within a certain context. In these cases, it is relatively easy to represent your conceptual framework visually. Your aim here will probably be to use this conceptual framework in a different context and see whether the variables are still adequate to describe the phenomenon you are investigating, and whether their interrelationships remain unaffected.

In other cases, the theory has not corroborated these relationships and you have to test them. If so, you have to provide conceptual definitions of key variables, state the hypotheses to be tested (something you may have already done with the problem statement), and offer an explanation/argument as to why the hypothesized relationships are plausible. Alternatively, you may be conducting an exploratory study in which you predict what the possible relationships might be between the variables, but wish to remain more tentative and open to the possibility that you may have misjudged these relationships, chosen variables that should not be included and/or missed variables that should. At the end of your study you will probably propose a new or revised model to be tested subsequently in a larger number of settings.

It is important to close this section by relating the literature review and the conceptual framework to your proposed study, making it clear to the reader how what is already known is connected with what your study aspires to reveal, or what the 'gap' is that your research is aiming to close.

Section Three

Normally this section is dedicated to the detailed description and justification of your research methodology. This is where you will demonstrate your understanding of what was described in Chapters 4–6 of this book – in other words, where you will show your supervisor and/or your research committee that you have a good grasp of research methodology and data collection techniques, and are capable of carrying out the proposed research. Again, this section will be largely the basis of your dissertation's methodology chapter; therefore the more effort you put into it now, the less you will need to add when writing up the actual dissertation. This section primarily involves four levels of concern: overall research design, data collection technique(s) and instrument(s), context and participants, and data analysis.

Overall research design

This section starts by restating the aim of the study, and explaining that you will describe the approaches, strategies and data collection techniques to be used in carrying it out. It is a good idea, at this point, also to state that although every effort has been made to present a detailed plan of the research process, this plan is continuously evolving and it will take its final shape during the fieldwork itself.

Next, you may explain your research approach – is it inductive or deductive? (see Chapter 4) – and why this is the appropriate approach for this study. In the same way, you have to justify your research strategy (ground theory, case study, survey, experiment, ethnography or action research). As mentioned above, this is the section where you demonstrate your learning and understanding of research methods. You should therefore be able to define the various terms you are using and also provide bibliographical references for these definitions. As in your literature review section, the more sources on research methods you use to support this methodology section the better, as this shows a wide range of reading and skills for independent literature search – generally, it is not advisable to use less than three sources.

Data collection technique(s) and research instrument(s)

Another key point in your proposal is justification of the techniques you will use for data collection, as well as a description of your research instruments' development. Here you need to explain why you have chosen the specific technique(s) and why these are appropriate to answer the particular research question or questions within your study. Obviously, to support your argument you will need to present, in some detail, the advantages of this technique for your particular research. However, you will need to show that you are also aware of the disadvantages inherent in this technique, that you have taken them into account, and that you considered special measures in order to eliminate them or minimize their negative effects on your study. The same advice as is given above regarding research methods literature also applies here.

The next step is to describe how you have developed the research instruments for these techniques. 'Research instruments' means the tools that you will use in each of your data collection techniques – so if, for example, you are planning to use participant or non-participant observation, your instrument will be the observation form, some guidelines and a schedule. Similarly, in a face-to-face interview you will need an interview plan with some general guidelines on how you will conduct the interview, the questions, and the recording devices; in a survey you will need a questionnaire, survey directions, etc.

In this part of your proposal you will need to show how you developed these tools – for example, how did you identify the behaviours, actions and points you will be observing during an observation? How did you develop the questions for your interview or questionnaire? It is evident here that you will have to relate the development of your research instruments to the conceptual framework of Section Two. Some supervisors explicitly require the linkage of each one of the research instrument's elements with the variables of the conceptual framework, and will question any omissions on either side. It is understood that the research instrument will require further refinement – and this is what you will work on with your supervisor during the process – but at this stage some initial work is required. Box 7.1 illustrates the first attempt of a student exploring the role of attitudinal loyalty in the implementation of CRM strategies within the hospitality industry.

Box 7.1	Developing the research instrument (initial thoughts)	
Concepts	**Literature source**	**Questions**
Company strategy: customer acquisition or customer retention?	O'Malley (1998)	1. As a service organization, what is your primary marketing objective – customer acquisition or customer retention? Can you explain why?
Company's understanding of customer loyalty: attitudinal or behavioural approach?	Fitzgibbon and White (2005)	2. In your own words, how would you define customer loyalty?
Frequency, recency, and monetary value (behavioural measures), or satisfaction (attitudinal measure)?	O'Malley (1998)	3. How does your company measure customer loyalty?
Full CRM integration with operations (customer centric processes; technology solutions; employee empowerment; customer databases)?	Jain and Jain (2005)	4. Where does CRM fit into the organization's plan?
Attitudinal vs behavioural loyalty	Fitzgibbon and White (2004)	5. What are the CRM strategies implemented by the hotel, and how is CRM used to achieve the overall goals of the business as well as loyalty-related objectives?
Customer database (financial activity, complaints/preferences, other information)	Jain and Jain (2005)	6. What CRM system does your hotel use? Can you explain briefly the main functions of such a system?

Concepts	Literature source	Questions
Uses: prospecting (leads to behavioural loyalty); personalized service (leads to attitudinal loyalty)	Bowen and Chen (2001)	7. What is the information gathered in your CRM system used for, and how accessible is the information by your staff?
Two-thirds of CRM projects fail to achieve their stated goals	Fitzgibbon and White (2004)	8. How would you evaluate the overall quality and usefulness of CRM systems?
CRM strategy focus: behavioural loyalty or attitudinal loyalty?	Jain and Jain (2005)	9. In your opinion, the organization's CRM strategies are designed to enhance repetitious purchases or strong emotional commitment to the brand? Why?
Loyalty programmes and database tracking technology prevail. Why not attitudinal loyalty? (starting point of my research)	Fitzgibbon and White (2004)	10. To retain valuable customers, does your hotel rely more on loyalty programmes and database-tracking technology or on the ability of the staff to create emotional bonds with the customers? Why?

One further issue you will need to address in this section is the reliability and validity of your research (see Chapter 4). One way of improving these two factors is by testing the instruments (i.e. piloting them). Describe how this pilot will be conducted, where, and who will participate. Robson (2002: 102) identifies four main causes of unreliability: participant error (where participants may give different answers at different times of the research); participant bias (where the participants say what they think you want to hear or follow the official company line rather than telling you what they really feel); observer error (where mistakes are made in recording the data); and observer bias (where the researcher interprets the data influenced by his or her own values and beliefs). Similarly, he identifies several threats to validity, such as history, testing, instrumentation, mortality, maturation, and ambiguity about causal direction, among others (Robson, 2002: 105–106). Your pilot will help you identify most (if not all) of these, and as a result you should either propose specific strategies that will minimize the impact of these causes of unreli-ability and threats to validity on your research or, as it is not always possible to eliminate them, acknowledge them as limitations of your research methodology.

Research context and participants

'Research context' means any information you can provide to help the reader to understand the 'where' and 'when' of your proposed research. The 'where' elements can range from the sector in which you will conduct your research (e.g. hotel, airline, cruise line, tour operating, catering, restaurant, etc.) to the geographic location (e.g. Southeast Asia, Europe, North America, or more specific regions, countries, cities and areas) and the size or other classification of the business under research (e.g. small and medium-sized restaurants, or four-star hotels). You generally need to include all the information the reader requires to understand the focus of your research. With regard to the 'when', the time horizon that your study will cover can either be longitudinal or cross-sectional. A longitudinal research study is one that studies the developmental trends of a phenomenon, organization or group of people across a period of time, whereas a cross-sectional study can be thought of as providing a 'snapshot' of the behaviour and characteristics of a phenomenon at a particular time (Saunders *et al.*, 2003: 96). You may also indicate the exact time period for the study – for example, 'the study will explore the new product/service development of TUI AG in the period 1997–2007' or 'the research will cover a two-month period, from 1 April 2008 to 31 May 2008'.

Before giving specific information about the participants, you need to explain your sampling technique – probability or non-probability (see Chapter 5) – as well as your sample type (e.g. quota, purposive, convenience, self-selection, etc.). Again, the same advice as given above regarding definitions and referencing applies here. You then need to provide specific information about the participants (characteristics that describe them to the satisfaction of the reader – i.e. financial controllers of five-star hotels, marketing managers of fast food restaurants), the number to be approached, and the process you will employ to locate them. An example of such a description is offered in Box 7.2.

Box 7.2	Sample description

The names and addresses of the subjects will be obtained from the 1996 membership directory of the Hellenic Management Association's Institute of Training and Development in Human Resources (ITDHR). The directory's overall population consists of 1255 members, most of whom are personnel managers. A random sample of 120 non-hospitality managers, covering a variety of sectors within the Greek industry and commerce, will be selected from this source, using Blalock's (1979: 598–562) exhibit of random numbers. A package containing a cover letter, three questionnaires and return stamped envelopes will be sent to each of the above subjects. The cover letter will explain the general purpose of the study, the sources of selection (the author is a member of ITDHR), will assure confidentiality and ask the recipients to fill out one questionnaire and forward the two other copies to a fellow member of ITDHR that they know is involved in hiring decisions for managerial positions. In this way, 360 questionnaires will be sent out to ITDHR members. Isaac and Michael (1981) suggest that in order to achieve a statistically representative sample from a population of 1255 members at least 350 subjects need to be approached. Some of the subjects will also be approached by telephone before the mailing of the package and all of them will be followed up again with a further call. { . . . } The same package (with only one questionnaire) will be sent to 25 first class and luxury hotel personnel managers.

(Source: Paraskevas, 2000: 248)

An issue that has been recently raised in many higher education institutions is that of ethics regarding research undertaken by staff and research students that involves human participants. Most universities have adopted a Code of Practice covering the ethical standards for research involving human participants, and have established research ethics committees to promote good practice and conduct formal ethics reviews of research (see Box 7.3). These standards mainly concern medical research, but they also have implications in the field of hospitality and tourism, since in most cases human participants are involved. Sometimes questionnaires, observation and interviews can be potentially intrusive and might provoke anxiety in participants. It is highly unlikely that your research processes will affect or violate human rights, cause any kind of harm or reveal the confidential nature of the participants' involvement. However, you need to take your supervisor's advice and follow the processes set by your institution with regard to ethical approval for your research.

Box 7.3	Example of Code of Practice for ethical standards in research

- No research should cause harm, and preferably it should benefit participants
- Potential participants normally have the right to receive clearly communicated information from the researcher in advance
- Participants should be free from coercion of any kind and should not be pressured to participate in a study
- Participants in a research study have the right to give their informed consent before participating
- Where third parties are affected by the research, informal consent should be obtained
- The consent of vulnerable participants' or their representatives' assent should be actively sought by researchers
- Honesty should be central to the relationship between researcher, participant and institutional representatives
- Participants' confidentiality and anonymity should be maintained
- The collection and storage of research data by researchers must comply with the Data Protection Act 1998
- Researchers have a duty to disseminate their research findings to all appropriate parties.

(Source: Oxford Brookes University, available at http://www.brookes.ac.uk/ rbdo/research/researchethics/ethics_codeofpractice.pdf)

Normally the research ethics committee will deal with staff and MPhil, MPhil/PhD, PhD or EdD student research, which involves people as research participants. In undergraduate and postgraduate research projects, the approval will usually be given (and documented, depending on the institution's regulations) by the research supervisor. However, one basic requirement in most institutions is that where research involves face-to-face interviews, focus groups, direct observation or similar methods of data collection, participants should be given an information sheet (or leaflet) and asked to sign a consent form. These are two elements that you will need to have designed – according to your methodology – by the stage of the proposal, and they should be discussed in this section.

The information sheet usually describes – in simple terms that can be easily understood by participants – what the study is about and what the role of the participant will be in it (see Box 7.4). It is important to try to avoid academic terms and jargon that may make the participant feel uneasy. The consent form should offer clear evidence that the participant has given informed consent to take part in the study – it can be a signed form, e-mail or letter, so long as it provides evidence that the participant has agreed to participate. Obviously, where participants are asked to complete and return a questionnaire no consent form is needed, as consent is implied by returning the questionnaire. However, an information sheet should be sent to the participants along with the questionnaire.

Box 7.4	Information sheet for participants

Study title: the title should be simple and self-explanatory to a lay person.

Invitation paragraph: explain that the individual is being asked to take part in a research study. The following is an example of how this may be phrased:

You are being invited to take part in a research study. Before you decide whether or not to take part, it is important for you to understand why the research is being done and what it will involve. Please take time to read the following information carefully.

What is the purpose of the study? Provide the background to and the aim of the study, along with details of how long it will run for and an outline of its overall design.

Why have I been invited to participate? Explain how the individual was chosen to take part in the study and how many other people will be asked to participate.

Do I have to take part? Explain that taking part in the research is entirely voluntary. For example, you could say:

It is up to you to decide whether or not to take part. If you do decide to take part, you will be given this information sheet to keep and asked to sign a consent form. If you decide to take part, you are still free to withdraw at any time and without giving a reason.

What will happen to me if I take part? Explain your methods of data collection, including what the individual will be asked to do and how much time will be involved.

What are the possible disadvantages and risks of taking part? (where appropriate)

Describe any disadvantages or 'costs' involved in taking part in the study, including the time involved.

What are the possible benefits of taking part? Outline any direct benefits for the individual and any other beneficial outcomes of the study, including furthering understanding of the topic.

> *Will what I say in this study be kept confidential?* Explain that all information collected about the individual will be kept strictly confidential, and describe how confidentiality, privacy and anonymity will be ensured in the collection, storage and publication of research material.
>
> *What will happen to the results of the research study?* Tell the individual what will happen to the results of the research. Will they be used in your dissertation or thesis? For what degree? Will they be published? How can they obtain a copy of the published research?
>
> *Who is organizing and funding the research?* Explain that you are conducting the research as a student or member of staff at (name of your institution). Give your department name as well, and state the organization that is funding the research, if appropriate.
>
> *Who has reviewed the study?* State that the research has been approved by your supervisor and give his or her details.
>
> *Contact for further information*: provide a contact point for further information – either your name or that of your supervisor.
>
> *'Thank you'*: remember to thank the individual for taking time to read the information sheet.
>
> *Date*: the information sheet should be dated.
>
> (Source: Adapted from Oxford Brookes University, available at http://www.brookes.ac.uk/rbdo/research/researchethics/researchstudentsandethics)

The above ethical issues should be taken into serious consideration when choosing the data collection techniques and developing your research instruments. Ensuring ethical clearance, consent and confidentiality are sensitive issues and crucial for your proposal as their consideration shows your own sense of involvement in and responsibility regarding your study.

Data analysis

Your study will eventually result in the collection of a quantity of raw data. These data will need to be analysed, and therefore when closing of Section Three of your proposal you will need to explain how this analysis will be handled (see Chapters 9 and 10).

The first step in this process is the documentation of the data in a form that allows further analysis. For example, interviews need to be transcribed, questionnaire answers need to be formatted in a way that can be counted or input to the analysis software, answers need to be recorded, etc. In a few lines, describe the process that you will follow, then explain briefly the process that you will follow for coding the data in order for it to be analysed. Finally, inform the readers about how you will conduct the analysis, and whether you are going to use specific software (such as ATLAS.ti, NUD*IST, NViVvo, SPSS, etc.).

Closing your proposal: the appendix

In this section you will detail any material that will be used to support your proposal. The requirements may vary from institution to institution, but it is suggested that the following be included.

Proposed structure of your dissertation

A proposed structure will give your supervisor and/or the research committee a sense of how you plan to organize your dissertation. You may simply provide a 'Table of Contents' or perhaps list your chapters, offering a brief summary of what you expect to include in each one.

Proposed time plan for activities

A tentative time plan will include all the activities you need to undertake, from the moment your proposal is approved till the completion of your research and the submission of your dissertation. It is a written evidence of the feasibility of your entire research, and you should therefore give it serious thought and be as realistic as possible with regard to the time allocated for each activity. It is always useful to start from the end (the date of your dissertation's submission) and plan backwards. The purpose of such a plan is to be a guide for both yourself and your supervisor with regard to your progress. It will be useful to both of you in arranging meetings, setting milestone dates and even recording days of absence (e.g. fieldwork period, supervisor's annual leave, etc.).

It is also useful to think about your resources (financial, time and access) and develop contingency plans in case things do not work according to the original proposal – for example, if you are planning to undertake your fieldwork in India and you realize that financial or other constraints may not allow this, you can consider using telephone interviews as a 'back-up' plan. Another example involves gaining access to the informants – if you realize that gaining and maintaining access to informants might not be possible or is too time-consuming, then you can consider the 'use of secondary data' as a contingency plan.

Information sheet and consent form

These items are described above, and relate to consideration of the ethical issues associated with your research.

References

Although the reference list appears in the last section of your dissertation proposal, this is one of the most crucial elements of your work and requires your special attention. You must make sure that you list all, and only, the sources you have cited in the main body of your proposal (in all three sections – do not forget the methodology). Cross-check your references by reading the proposal section by section, ticking off items on your reference list when they you come across citations in the text. This will allow you to identify any that are missing. Next, check the style and format of your referencing, within both the main body of your proposal and your list of references. Does it follow the referencing conventions of your institution? Are authors, publication dates, titles and other elements of the reference correct? In certain institutions you are encouraged to add sources that you have consulted but did not refer to while writing your proposal. In this case, list all these sources under the heading 'bibliography'.

Summary

- The research proposal is a very important milestone in your project. It will serve as a blueprint for your research, and ties together all the work that you have done so far on the literature review, the development of a rationale, the identification of a gap and the choices regarding your research design.

- Section One of the research proposal generally includes an introduction to the topic and the background/rationale of your research, as well as the research question (problem) statement. A clear rationale should also argue why your study is worthwhile, and what value you hope its results will offer to other researchers and practitioners. Proper articulation of your research aim and objectives will provide you with a clear roadmap regarding how your research is going to be conducted.

- Section Two normally includes a comprehensive summary of your preliminary literature review, organized in some coherent manner, exposing the variables that will be significant for your study, comparing and contrasting different views on the topic and showing how this literature is influencing your research. The literature review may also lead to a preliminary conceptual framework for your study, showing the relationships between the theories, concepts and variables surrounding your research topic.

- Section Three is largely the basis of your dissertation's research design chapter, and involves four areas: overall research design (including research approach and strategy), data collection techniques and research instruments, research context and participants, and data analysis. Depending on your institution's requirements, you may also need to discuss the ethical dimension of your project and how you will make sure that it will not affect or violate human rights, cause any kind of harm or reveal the confidential nature of the participants' involvement.

- The final section includes additional information in the form of appendices – generally a tentative structure of your dissertation, a time plan for your anticipated research activities, forms required by the ethics guidelines of your institution (such as a participant information sheet and a sample consent form), and, of course, a list of all the sources (references) used for your proposal.

Student experiences

An essential element of dissertation work is self-discipline and organization. Creating a time plan will help you to manage your time and monitor your progress towards the goals you have set for yourself. As your work evolves, you may need to re-consider these goals and perhaps renegotiate the timing of certain activities. Here, Yuan Wei, a student from Taiwan, describes how she attempted to plan her work from the outset of her dissertation.

Preparing a time plan for my dissertation

Although time management is not my strongest point, when I first realized how much work was still involved – at the time I was writing my proposal – I was really overwhelmed. My supervisor advised me to break down the work into manageable steps and to keep a weekly commitment with them. I knew that, if I wanted to keep myself in a 'sane' state throughout this dissertation, I should make sure that I use my work habits in the most productive possible manner and try to maintain a balance with the other aspects of my student life (both academic and social).

I had to make some decisions in order to plan the project. The first step I took was to double-check the deadline for the submission of my work and start planning backwards. Considering very honestly my strengths and weaknesses, I made the decision about how much time I need to devote to this project on a daily/weekly/monthly basis. If one day I could not make my 'time quota', I would have to work extra time another day, so that I made my 'weekly quota' (similarly 'monthly quota').

I then broke down and structured the project process into specific activities and deadlines (proposal approved, meeting with supervisor, further literature review, research instrument development, pilot, fieldwork, preliminary analysis, etc.). I used MS-project software to put all these into a Gantt chart with deadlines that I thought were realistic. Other students used simpler forms, but there are very effective Gantt chart tools in Excel (http://office.microsoft.com/en-gb/excel/HA010346051033.aspx). Obviously, when I later received the feedback for my proposal from my supervisor, I realized that I had underestimated some activities whereas I was more generous in time for activities that should be shorter.

Having visualized my research project in the Gantt chart, I then considered all my the other tasks and commitments (attending other courses, meeting coursework deadlines, tai-chi classes, etc.) to estimate the time available for my research project work and the used that time for a day-to-day version of my work plan. I had to evaluate the importance of my various activities and removed all those I felt were of low priority, making sure though that I had adequate time for rest and recreation, so that I could go on with the project. All these thoughts pushed me in developing a daily work schedule (four hours per day). Knowing myself (easily distracted), I decided that I would work in the University's library and that I would set daily achievement targets (such as articles read, pages written, etc.) rather than just sticking to the 'time' commitment alone in order to push myself to be more productive. My supervisor advised me that, as I progressed with my work, I might encounter 'writer's block', and I had to build in my plan some flexibility by saving the 'routine activities' such as formatting, interview transcribing, etc., for such periods.

I 'pilot tested' my original work plan by working on my research proposal for a little more than one week. Of course, things did not always work as planned, and I therefore had to re-evaluate and revise it, building 'buffers' into my plan for occasional setbacks and delays (such as illness, supervisor holiday, participants not able to be interviewed on planned dates) and also some incentives, such as a short holiday for myself if I met all my deadlines by then (I did!!!).

Review questions

1. What is the purpose of the background/rationale section in your research proposal?
2. If you were researching the topic for which the conceptual framework is presented in Figure 7.1, how would you state the research problem? How would you articulate the purpose (aim) of your research? How would you reveal your objectives?

3. Think about the originality of your own research topic and its contribution to the body of knowledge. Write a five-line paragraph 'defending' your topic with regard to these aspects. Give the paragraph to a colleague and ask if you have achieved your purpose.
4. Using your literature map, prepare a 750-word summary for your proposal. Do you 'engage in a dialogue' with the various authors you present by exposing the variables that will be significant for your study? Do you compare and contrast different views on the topic? Do you effectively justify your decisions for accepting or rejecting them?
5. How can the conceptual framework be used in the design of your research instruments?
6. Consider your own research project. What is the research approach that you will take? What research strategy will you select? What data collection tools are you going to use, and why are these more appropriate for your project? How are you going to address any drawbacks that these tools may have?
7. What would be an appropriate sample for the topic in Figure 7.1? How would you describe it in a research proposal?
8. Consider any possible ethical concerns in your study. Write an information sheet for your participants, using as example the template provided in Box 7.4.
9. What activities should be included in a Gantt chart for your project?

References

Ayres, A. (2005). *The Wit and Wisdom of Mark Twain*, 1st perennial edn. New York, NY: Harper & Row.

Blalock, H. M. (1979). *Social Statistics*, 2nd edn. New York, NY: McGraw-Hill.

Bowen, J. T. and Chen, S. L. (2001). The relationship between customer loyalty and customer satisfaction. *International Journal of Contemporary Hospitality Management*, 13(5), 213–217.

Bowen W. G. and Rudenstine N. L. (1992). *In Pursuit of the PhD*. Princeton, NJ: Princeton University Press.

Fitzgibbon, C. and White, L. (2005). The role of attitudinal loyalty in the development of customer relationship management strategy within service firms. *Journal of Financial Services Marketing*, 9(3), 214–230.

Isaac, S. and Michael, W. B. (1981). *Handbook in Research and Evaluation*, 2nd edn. San Diego, CA: EdITS.

Jain, R. and Jain, S. (2005). Towards relational exchange in services marketing: insights from the hospitality industry. *Journal of Services Research*, 5(2), 139–149.

Microsoft Office Online. *Create a Gantt chart in Excel* (online). Available at http://office.microsoft.com/en-gb/excel/HA010346051033.aspx (accessed 18 June 2007).

O'Malley, L. (1998). Can loyalty schemes really build loyalty? *Marketing Intelligence and Planning*, 16(1), 47–55.

Oxford Brookes University. *Research Students and Research Ethics Review* (online). Available at http://www.brookes.ac.uk/rbdo/research/researchethics/ethics_codeofpractice.pdf (accessed 18 June 2007).

Oxford Brookes University. *Research Students and Research Ethics Review* (online). Available at http://www.brookes.ac.uk/rbdo/research/researchethics/researchstudentsandethics (accessed 18 June 2007).

Paraskevas, A. (2000). Management selection practices in Greece: are hospitality recruiters any different? *International Journal of Hospitality Management*, 19(3), 241–259.

Paraskevas, A. (2006). Crisis management or crisis response system? A complexity science approach to organizational crisis. *Management Decisions*, 44(7), 892–907.

Reisinger, Y. and Mavondo, F. (2004). Modelling psychographic profiles: a study of the US and Australian student travel market. *Journal of Hospitality Tourism Research*, 28(1), 44–65.

Robson, C. (1993). *Real World Research*. Oxford: Blackwell.

Robson, C. (2002). *Real World Research*, 2nd edn. Oxford: Blackwell.

Saunders, M. N. K., Lewis, P. and Thornhill, A. (2003). *Research Methods for Business Students*, 3rd edn. Harlow: Prentice Hall Financial Times.

Sekaran, U. (2000). *Research Methods for Business: A Skill-Building Approach*. New York: John Wiley & Sons, Inc.

Yuen, D. (2006). The impact of a budgetary design system: direct and indirect models. *Managerial Auditing Journal*, 21(2), 148–165.

Zhao, J. L. (1994). 'The Antecedent Factors and Entry Mode Choice of Multinational Lodging Firms: The Case of Growth Strategies into New International Markets'. Unpublished PhD dissertation, Virginia Polytechnic Institute and State University, Blacksburg, Virginia.

Chapter 8
Conducting the fieldwork

The way to do fieldwork is never to come up for air until it is all over.
(Margaret Mead, American scientist, 1901–1978)

Although the quotation above is quite extreme, fieldwork (or data collection) is one of the most demanding stages of the research process. Depending on the nature of your research and your research approach, you may start your fieldwork either before or after completing your literature review, developing your conceptual framework and putting your hypothesis or hypotheses to test. Regardless of your approach, however, you will need to develop certain strategies in order to make the most of your fieldwork. If prepared for carefully, it can offer you a once-in-a-lifetime opportunity to explore new territories in hospitality and tourism and develop new insights, much as an explorer would.

The success of your fieldwork is directly proportional to your preparation for it. The preparation stage usually involves reviewing relevant literature in order to gain a wider view and fuller understanding of the relevant areas and concepts underpinning the research, developing the research instruments, and piloting them. The preparatory stage also involves discussions with other academics conducting research in related fields.

Negotiating access to organizations

One of the most significant problems that researchers face is gaining access to organizations, and it is often the case that a considerable amount of time and effort is spent on this task. Convincing busy executives and professionals to participate in or facilitate a study is a major undertaking for experienced researchers, let alone students. Okumus *et al.* (2007) have highlighted the difficulties of accessing hospitality and tourism organizations based on their experience as researchers, and their work may help you take a more structured approach towards this challenging undertaking.

Initial contact

The most important element in gaining and maintaining access to organizations is the establishment of a good and trusting relationship with the people who will act as gatekeepers during your fieldwork, facilitating your ability to conduct the investigation by arranging for you to enter and exit the field as needed, functioning like a 'hinge' between you and the organizations. Gatekeepers will introduce you to the relevant people and create an awareness of your project in the organization. But how do you get to these gatekeepers? Unless you already have contacts in the organizations you want to study, through your personal or even your supervisor's network, the only other way of gaining the attention of these people is by 'cold calling'. This is a term borrowed from the field of sales, and describes the process of approaching prospective informants, via mail, e-mail or telephone call, without their agreement for such an interaction. It involves simply sending a letter or an e-mail or making a telephone call to people that you deem appropriate as informants, inviting them to participate in your study. Another way to gain access to organizations is through their pubic relations office, which normally treats such requests quite favourably. This initial contact with the organization(s) you want study can be of great importance in building trust and confidence between you and key people in the research context, and you need to be fully prepared to impress people, as this may be your only chance. A well-structured and engaging letter or e-mail or a well-prepared and rehearsed telephone pitch may make all the difference between success and rejection. However, when using cold calling you will also have to be ready for the rejection that will occur regardless of the level of your preparation. There are variables associated with gaining entry that are out of your control, no matter how good your preparation. Okumus *et al.* (2007) cite Van Maanen and Kolb (1985: 11), who claim that access to organizations is a 'combination of planning and dumb luck'.

A successful cold call will turn the 'cold contact' into a 'warm contact' (i.e. a gatekeeper), and the next step for you is to show your level of professionalism and understanding of the context of your study. Even before your fieldwork, it is important that you collect and review relevant organization information, including annual reports and press releases. This is particularly valuable in terms of learning more about the context of your research and 'getting an initial taste' of how things are done in the organization, or what is going on there. This strategy will help you both to identify relevant questions and to appear well-informed in the eyes of both gatekeepers and other informants – something that will instil trust and confidence. The gatekeepers will appreciate that you have done your homework, which in turn means that you take the task seriously, and consequently the 'professional' attitude you display will make them feel it is worth spending time facilitating and participating in your research project.

Appreciating the role of gatekeepers

Impressing the gatekeepers is only the first step into the organization. These people will 'screen' you thoroughly before facilitating your access, so you must be ready to answer convincingly questions such as: What is the aim of your project? How can my organization help you? How is your project going to help my organization? What type of support and resources do you require from us? The information sheet will be helpful here, but the way in which you personally answer these questions can create a positive and professional impression which will give them the confidence to open the gates of their organization to your study. As part of the initial briefing process you might need to visit the organization, since gatekeepers will not always be satisfied with telephone conversations or email correspondence. They might still want to hear about your research and ask further questions in a face-to-face meeting. During such a meeting, gatekeepers will evaluate you and your study in order to ensure that the latter does not touch upon sensitive issues in their organizations. They may even guide you in identifying the most appropriate issues that can be investigated in the organization, and/or make suggestions regarding the most suitable time to approach informants. You may view this guidance as a threat to your autonomy that will probably influence not only the data collection process but also the whole direction of your study. However, Okumus *et al.* (2007) advise that there is a need to balance the maintenance of access against potential bias. You should not view gatekeepers as barriers, but rather as 'controllers' who are taking a risk in allowing access to a student who is going to ask perhaps sensitive or even irrelevant questions of informants at different levels and in various functional areas. You will therefore need to show some flexibility, since gatekeepers are risking their reputation and status in the organization by facilitating your access to these informants.

Building rapport and trust

The informants are a different 'kettle of fish' altogether. The fact that you have gained the trust and support of a gatekeeper does not guarantee that the same will automatically happen with all the informants. You will need to work hard in order for them to view you as someone worth spending time with. Building individual rapport with them goes beyond having a friendly face and dressing professionally; it is also important that you are on time for your meetings, stick to the agreed research plan and, as Okumus *et al.* (2007) suggest, convey the sense of 'I am here to learn from your experience and knowledge'. In every step of your research within an organization you have to follow a 'courtesy protocol' that will earn you the acceptance, if not respect, of the informants.

Understanding the internal dynamics of participant organizations

To achieve success in your study, it is beneficial to spend some time with people who are not directly involved in your research so that you can get a feel for the organizational culture. For example, in addition to the scheduled meetings with the key informants, you can plan to spend some time with other personnel – perhaps receptionists or personal assistants. This can be very helpful in your development of a wider understanding of the organization. Further useful techniques to gain a much clearer picture about the organization, its activities and style of operations include studying any relevant organizational documentation (such as pamphlets, brochures, etc.), reading notices on the noticeboards, observing everything around you and taking a tour (with permission) of the premises. This informal familiarization with the organization will also help you to identify key organizational dynamics, practices and politics. It will give you a feel for the bureaucratic obstacles and the potentially conservative or more liberal nature of the organization in terms of providing company-related information, and this will prove crucial to the success of your study.

Regardless of the data collection technique you have chosen, there are certain basic rules that you need to follow (courtesy protocol) which will help you not only to build your relationship with the informants but also to maintain access throughout and even after your research project. Details of how to conduct research using interviews, observation, questionnaires and document analysis were discussed at depth in Chapter 6. The following section describes the 'soft elements' that constitute the above mentioned courtesy protocol, as applied to interviews. Although the section focuses on interviews, it should give you a general feel for how to conduct research in organizations.

Professional conduct in the interview setting

The first objective for each interview is to establish a level of trust between you and the informants, to make them feel at ease with you so they will open up and provide the information that will help you to answer your research questions. These conditions will not be automatically created during your interview, and need to be worked upon way before that date. You should therefore start working towards this end even before you finalize your interview guide and start making your first contacts – perhaps two to three months before the fieldwork commences.

Initial contact

In the initial contact, your aim should be to explain why you want to talk to these informants. Although you may have already sent an information sheet to the informants, a face-to-face meeting or a conversation over the phone will give you the opportunity to clarify the aim of your study and the contribution they can make. It is also useful to discuss the possible outcomes of the project and how they can benefit from participating in your study. This should give you a more solid basis for your discussions, as well as motivating them. You need to carefully think through the 'selling points' and plan how you present them during this first encounter in order to stimulate potential informants' interest. One expectation common to most informants is that they will be provided with a copy of your findings or a summary of your entire project. This is a legitimate expectation, and it is advisable to honour it even if not explicitly requested. However, sharing the full set of findings is not good practice, for many reasons (it might be too long to read, and include complicated data analysis and discussions that may bore the non-academic reader, etc.); therefore, a summary of your study is more appropriate. It is a good idea to include in this summary a brief account of your rationale, your aim, your research method and sample (all in one page, if possible), along with a synopsis of your findings, conclusions and recommendation, free from academic jargon and written in a language that any practitioner can understand. Whatever you promise, make sure that you deliver!

You should then ask informants for their permission to tape-record interviews, explaining that this will enable you concentrate on the discussion rather than taking notes and will also help you transcribe their answers in their own words. This, in turn, will facilitate the analysis of their responses in order to elicit from them everything that can help you answer your research question(s). At this point you should also reassure them about the confidentiality of the overall process. Offer to send the transcript of the interview for their review and possible editing before any analysis on your part. It may also be worth informing informants that this transcript will not be shared with anyone besides your supervisor, and that in the final written report any potentially sensitive information about the informant and the organization will be disguised in such away that nobody will be able to recognize the source. This is the stage at which informants should be presented with a consent form and asked to sign it.

When scheduling the interview, make sure that you stick to the plan in terms of time, place and anticipated length of the interview. To the extent that this is within your control, choose a location which allows you to conduct the interview with minimum interruptions and noise from the external environment. Of particular importance, however, is your personal safety – a quiet and private location is desirable, but it is a good idea, especially for female interviewers, to travel in pairs (possibly with a male escort) when in areas known to be unsafe, or if interviews are being conducted in the evenings. You should also make sure that you conduct one interview per day, or at the most two, even if you are carrying out your research in a small city or location. The quality of your third interview in the same day will normally be of a low level, because when you are tired (and you will most certainly be after two interviews) you will not be able to follow the conversation effectively and ask the most appropriate questions.

Before the interview

Before you set off to meet an informant, check that your recording equipment is in a good working order (new batteries, enough cassettes for your tape recorder, extra supply of both – just in case!). A notebook and pens/pencils are always needed, even when the entire interview is to be taped or digitally recorded. Your interview guide should be clearly printed in a font that is readable from a distance (probably larger than the usual) so that you can ask questions with only at a quick glance at the guide.

You should arrive at the meeting venue about fifteen minutes earlier than scheduled. This will allow you some time to loosen up and concentrate on the upcoming interview by reflecting on why you want to interview this particular informant and what kind of information you hope to achieve. It also allows the opportunity to review your interview guide and ensure that you are confident you are well prepared.

The interview

It is always useful to break the ice by engaging in small talk with the informant. This will put both of you at ease, but remember that you also need to respect their time constraints. When you feel that you are both ready to start, thank the informant for allowing you an interview, and very briefly remind him or her of the purpose of your study and this interview in particular. If the consent form has not already been signed, make sure this is done now. Place your recording equipment in a strategic position that is effective in terms of both recording the conversation and being 'non-threatening' for the informant. Conduct the interview using all your communication skills (building rapport, being a good listener, etc.).

During the interview, remember that some people need more time than others to frame an answer, and do not be tempted to finish a sentence for an informant who answers slowly, as this may cause distraction. If you notice that the informant feels uneasy with a question, move on to the next; you can come back to this question later if you wish, but rephrase it rather than asking it in exactly the same way. Make sure that you maintain control of the interview – it is very easy for both parties (you and the informant) to become distracted and the interview to go off at a tangent. One common mistake made by interviewers is that rather than focusing on the informant's answer, they tend are thinking about their next question.

The interview ends only when the informant leaves, so make sure the recorder is not switched off until good-byes have been said. Experience has shown that a lot of interesting information comes up 'on the fly', when both interviewer and informant are standing up and preparing to leave. At this point, remember to thank your informant once again, restate your assurance of confidentiality, and explain the next steps in your research process.

If the informant does not grant you permission to tape-record the interview, you will have to take notes during the interview. To ensure that you maintain control of the process, avoid trying to note a full answer and opt for keywords. As long as the keywords reflect the essence of the conversation, you will be able to expand your notes after the interview while everything is still fresh in your mind.

After the interview

Experienced researchers allow themselves some time immediately after the interview to reflect on their experience. Think about how the whole process went, and write a brief evaluation in your notebook: Who was the informant? Where and when did the interview take place? What was the informant's disposition towards you? What was the level of communication between the two of you? Did the informant seem to understand the questions? Was the informant genuinely willing to answer and help your research? Was the environment conducive to a satisfactory interview?

Producing a complete, verbatim transcript of an interview is a laborious process – a one-hour interview may take as long as six hours to transcribe. However, you will benefit greatly from developing accurate transcripts of your interviews. These transcripts will provide you with full details of the informant's views and opinions, and will be a source of direct quotations when it comes to presenting your findings. Of course, you always need to consider that the informant may wish to alter some points in the transcript, and you should be ready to accept (and respect) that. Full transcripts can also be used to analyse the results of interviews in a more thorough and complete manner than is possible with notes.

It is good practice to keep in touch with your informants after the interview and update them on the progress of your project – something that displays both professionalism and commitment. A thank-you note by post or e-mail the next day is always welcome.

The international dimension

Undertaking research in an international context complicates the issues associated with gaining access even further. This is highlighted in many studies of research student experiences, and hospitality and tourism is not an exception (see for example, I'Anson and Smith, 2004). If you were a German student wishing to carry out an investigation in China, how would you start? What else would you need to consider above and beyond the potential value of your project for Chinese hotel practitioners or policy-makers? All researchers try to develop specific communication styles for gaining access to respondents which involve showing their trustworthiness, credibility, neutrality and rigour. However, a successful recipe for gaining access to organizations in one national and cultural context may not be as successful in another context. Gaining access to relevant people might therefore require that, in addition to having good interpersonal skills, you also possess a reasonable level of understanding of the culture and the role of networks in contacting people in the country concerned. For example, people in China, Italy, Greece and Turkey, particularly the older generation, often consider their business to be a private matter. They do not want to discuss their business with people outside the family, and in some circumstances they simply do not want to share information with others. It is quite hard for such people to break with tradition, even if you assure them of utmost confidentiality. In such cases you will have to negotiate access through their wider network, including community representatives, accountants, and even relatives and the friends of the business owner. Your first contact with the organization, whether personal, by letter or e-mail, or through referral, is likely to be the most decisive in terms of whether you will be granted access or not. If the gatekeepers are impressed and interested by your research topic at first contact, this will determine their decision about access. However, more often than not they will ask you, 'Who referred you to me?'

Personal contacts and networks are often the main way of gaining access to companies, especially in Eastern European and Middle Eastern countries. In these countries there are none of the reliable sources of information (such as databases, registers or archives) that researchers generally use to identify organization contacts (Michailova and Liuhto, 2000), and strong personal contacts and networks are the chief means of avoiding dependence on official (and consequently heavily bureaucratic and sometimes uncooperative) gatekeepers. Easterby-Smith and Malina (1999: 79), in an examination of the methodological and philosophical implications of cross-cultural management research, compared conducting a field study collaboratively in the United Kingdom and China, and noted:

> *Expecting at the outset that access to Chinese organizations would prove very difficult, the UK researchers were most surprised to discover that this was not the case. A key factor in gaining access was that the senior Chinese researchers worked in prestigious universities and had therefore developed excellent networks that included former students who were by now senior managers in the target companies. Because of these personal links, the project was not reliant on the official gatekeepers who normally allow access for foreign researchers only to showcase organizations {…} and this advantage enabled the team to reach areas that would not normally be accessible.*
>
> *Access to UK companies proved much more difficult, and three of the four companies named in the original research proposal were unable to confirm their provisional commitments.*

It is a considerable challenge for young researchers to form international networks and make personal contacts. How should you do it? Fellow students and researchers originating from the country under study provide a good starting point. The former are easy to access in the context of your institution, while the latter can be met during coffee breaks and lunches at international conferences – yet another incentive for you to attend such conferences!

In many countries you will have to meet the respondents personally more than once before the formal research study. Referrals can get you to the door of the organization, but you may also have to do some work yourself. Building relationships may take longer in countries where people are 'dialogue-oriented' (such as Latin American countries, Spain, Italy, etc.) rather than 'data-oriented' (Oliveira, 2001), or have a long tradition of collaboration with academic institutions, such as the Nordic countries (Björkman and Forsgren, 2000). In certain cases your referral may be considered 'suspicious', and potential respondents will want to weigh you up before opening up to your study. Welch *et al.* (2002) report that in certain cases the researcher may be seen as a 'headquarter's spy' if referred to an organization's unit by a top executive. In countries of a particular political orientation, potential respondents may be suspicious of your intentions. Lisa Wynn, a tourism PhD student from the University of Michigan, describes her experience of fieldwork in Egypt:

> *My {Egyptian} friends joked about {me being a spy} often, and once, finally, I asked a close friend if he really thought I was working for the CIA. 'Look', he said, 'I don't really think that you are, but I don't know for sure. Let's say I think there's a 90 percent chance that you're not working for the CIA. But there's still that 10 percent chance that you are, so I would be a fool not to keep it in mind. But even if you're not actually working for them, your research will still be used by the CIA and other US government organizations to compile information on Egypt.'*
>
> *(Wynn, 2003: 27, cited in Gillespie and Riddle, 2006)*

Therefore, gaining access goes way beyond explaining the overall aim and objectives of a project in a clear and straightforward way and assuring confidentiality. It may also involve socializing with the potential respondents even before the fieldwork, gaining their trust by, for example, having a number of meals together or attending social occasions. It may also involve identifying common interests, and organizing activities. For example, exploiting your golf skills in countries such as China or Taiwan can help to build trust. In countries such as Greece, having late dinners with respondents may be the answer. In the UK, adapting to the widespread pub culture can have some value. Such activities, of course, cost time and money, and an international researcher therefore has the problem of assessing the balance between the benefits of access and the costs of gaining it.

Contrary to common belief, being a foreigner may be an advantage rather than a disadvantage in access negotiations. Ghauri (2004) argues that having to rely on a second language simplifies the communication protocol between researcher and respondent, making it more straightforward and direct. Nevertheless, relying only on English in carrying out international business research may be a restrictive factor in terms of access, as it may exclude key respondents from your study. Some researchers maintain that this factor may have an impact on the validity of the study, as respondents who are fluent in English may have different attitudes and behaviours from those of their non-English speaking colleagues (Wright, 1996). You should therefore seriously consider language as an access factor, and if you are multilingual then make use of your linguistic skills in the most appropriate way.

Irrespective of cultural context, one thing you must always remember is that access to organizations is a special privilege granted to you, and as such it may be revoked at any time. Building and maintaining trust with the gatekeepers and the respondents is of paramount importance. As a general rule, you only achieve this when you respect all participants, comply with the restrictions regarding areas and topics that cannot be broached, follow the organization's protocols, maintain the privacy and confidentiality you promised, and provide some benefits to the organization. Following these simple rules will guarantee you a successful international research project.

Summary

- You need to allocate considerable time to gaining access and collecting data. Planning and preparation are essential.
- You need to have certain interpersonal communication and research skills, and a good understanding of the complexities and challenges of organizational and/or community settings, when trying to gain access.

- It is crucial to establish of a good and trusting relationship with the people who will act as gatekeepers during your fieldwork and facilitate your investigation by arranging for you to enter and exit the field.
- The determination of what can be researched and what is seen as worth researching is by no means straightforward, even if access is gained to the organizations. You need to understand the internal dynamics of the organizations – namely, the organizational culture and structure and the power relationship between different members of the organizations.
- Undertaking research in an international context complicates the issues associated with gaining access even further. You need to be aware of the social fabric, informal networks and culture of the host society, and also to make use of your linguistic skills in the most appropriate way.

Student experiences

Easterby-Smith *et al.* (1999: 45) state that 'the determination of what can be researched and what is seen as worth researching is by no means straightforward'. You can always develop research questions and explain convincingly why a particular topic is worth researching, but you cannot really be sure that you can carry out your research until you have secured access and ensured that you can overcome possible resource constraints (time and money). It is therefore important that you develop contingency plans for your fieldwork, in case things do not work out as originally planned. For example, the organization you were planning to study might go through turbulence because of restructuring, a merger or a crisis, and may not grant you access – or, even worse, your granted access may be revoked. The need for alternative contacts and subjects is evident. Another issue worth considering regards the practicalities of conducting research in multiple locations. If your research is to be conducted in different countries in Europe, you will need to consider different methods for pursuing your research (such as conducting telephone interviews or using postal questionnaires) in order to be able to manage your limited resources effectively and efficiently.

You should also be prepared to face various challenges that may be related to your chosen data collection technique or the context of your study. Here, Greg, a South African student, describes the challenges he faced when conducting group interviews in the UK.

Challenges in the preparation and conduct of group interviews

I used group interviews as an idea-generating technique in the preliminary phase of my research. The first challenge I faced was familiarizing myself with the focus group technique itself. I began reading research methodology textbooks with a particular emphasis on group interview preparation and procedure. However, it seems that while some methodology textbooks offer interesting tips on overcoming the difficulties of group interviews, some offer conflicting advice. I decided that the best way to learn about the practical issues involved with focus groups was to test the technique within my research area. Using fellow students for this test seemed ideal because they were in close proximity and relatively easy to contact. However, I felt that Master's level and PhD students were closer to the population sample that I would be using for my main focus groups than undergraduates would be. So, I began by speaking to a few of the postgraduate students in my university and asking them if they, or any of their classmates, would be interested in attending a pilot focus-group session. One postgraduate was particularly keen to assist me, and this student played an important role in recruiting other people for the group through word-of-mouth. After I had prepared a topic guide and booked a meeting room for the pilot group, my next consideration was food preparation. I felt that asking participants to spend an hour of their time in a group without compensation would be difficult. I therefore decided that it would be a polite gesture to offer the participants at least some light snacks and beverages. I did not want, however, to spend a lot of money, as my student budget was quite tight. The cost of food and beverages for the pilot group interview amounted to approximately £40 (€60). I found in subsequent focus groups that it was sufficient to budget on half that amount of money. Also, I found budgeting to be essential for items such as group worksheets, consent forms and other print material.

While conducting the pilot group interviews, I also became aware of several issues that I had not initially thought of. These included: participants' difficulties in understanding the research aim; some participants speaking more than others; difficulty in approaching certain discussion topics; the presence of leading questions in my interview guide; some participants contradicting what they had said previously; and some participants apparently following the opinions of other participants. These issues were resolved by providing some time after the group interview session for participants to discuss their general feelings about how the group was conducted. I also conducted follow-up interviews with certain participants to find out why they had contradicting viewpoints. Keeping a detailed notebook of issues helped me to reduce problems occurring in subsequent focus groups. Some of these notes included issues related to the way I moderated the group. For example, I found that I rushed to completed people's answers and that to resolve this issue I needed to allow people more time to speak. I also found that I had a tendency to change discussion topics just at the time when people were becoming familiar with the previous topic. This meant I needed to reduce the number of discussion topics and reallocate more time to some topics and less to others. Keeping notes of all these issues assisted me in amending my interview guide.

When I started my main fieldwork, I was presented with some new challenges regarding access. Instead of recruiting students, as I did in the pilot group, this time I had to recruit people from outside the university, people with whom I had no previous relationship. To achieve this I designed A4 posters which invited participants to my group interviews. After printing these posters, I had to tactfully negotiate with managers at various bookshops and coffee shops for their permission to display them in prominent areas of their shops. I found that the clarity of the topic was of fundamental importance at this stage. When communicating with people unfamiliar with my research area, it was crucial to use everyday language rather than topic-specific terminology. This also meant reducing long-winded academic phrases to short simple sentences. Perhaps the most valuable all-encompassing lesson that I have learned with regard to overcoming challenges in group interviews is to try things out in practice and to learn from previous mistakes.

Ina, a French student, describes the challenges she encountered while conducting her fieldwork in Lebanon:

Real-life complexities of doing fieldwork in Lebanon

Reflecting on my fieldwork in Lebanon, I feel I have experienced a fascinating educational journey that I could never have been fully prepared for. I had made quite detailed plans about the fieldwork, but the reality of coming face-to-face with industry professionals was far from preparing interview questions at home. After the first interviews, I realized I had to change some of the questions as they led to almost the same answer, whereas others were receiving too broad or too short answers. My pilot was conducted with British and French informants back in UK, and now my participants were pre-dominantly Lebanese who, although fluent in English and French, responded in a very different manner to my questions. I took a more 'open-minded', less structured view, and modified my questions according to the flow of the discussion. This approach gave me the freedom to derive experiences and feelings from my informants, to gather rich information about specific subjects, and gain flexibility in terms of the respondents' answers. Gaining access to possible candidates was problematic from the UK, but once I had arrived in Lebanon and interviewed one or two professionals, I found people were happy to help out and provide access to their networks. I discovered that being persistent by knocking on doors or calling people on the phone was far more effective than e-mailing (though this may vary from country to country). I achieved my best results by asking my first informants to help me find other people for my study. Once you know someone who knows someone else, the door is wide open, and most people will try their best to help. When I arrived in Lebanon I had only one planned interview, with a representative of the local tourism authorities, but in the course of three weeks I managed to interview thirteen informants from all possible local tourism stakeholders through the network I developed during my stay in Beirut.

Review questions

1. What are the possible constraints involved in doing fieldwork?
2. What are the possible difficulties of gaining access to smaller organizations, or to customers?
3. What might be possible strategies for coping with these difficulties?

4. What are the skills needed to facilitate and maintain access to organizations?
5. Would the difference between your cultural background (for example, Italian) and the culture of the research context (for example, undertaking research in China) influence your fieldwork? If so, how would you manage this?

References

Björkman, I. and Forsgren, M. (2000). Nordic international business research. *International Studies of Management and Organization*, 30(1), 6–24.

Easterby-Smith, M. and Malina, D. (1999). Cross-cultural collaborative research: toward reflexivity. *Academy of Management Journal*, 42(1), 76–86.

Easterby-Smith, M., Thorpe, R. and Lowe, A. (1999). *Management Research: An Introduction*. London: Sage Publications.

Ghauri, P. (2004). Designing and conducting case studies in international business research. In: R. Marschan-Piekkari and C. Welch (eds), *Handbook of Qualitative Business Research: Methods for International Business*. Camberley: Edward Elgar Publishing, pp. 109–125.

Gillespie, K. and Riddle, L. (2006). Case-based teaching in business education in the Arab Middle East and North Africa. In: I. Alon and J. R. McIntyre (eds), *Business Education and Emerging Market Economies Perspectives and Best Practices*. Norwell, MA: Kluwer Academic Publishers, pp. 141–155.

I'Anson, R. A. and Smith, K. A. (2004). Undergraduate research projects and dissertations: issues of topic selection, access and data collections amongst tourism management students. *Journal of Hospitality, Leisure, Sport and Tourism Education*, 3(1), 19–32.

Michailova, S. and Liuhto, K. (2000). Organization and management research in transition economies: towards improved research methodologies. *Journal of East–West Business*, 6(3), 7–46.

Okumus, F., Altinay, L. and Roper, A. (2007). Gaining access for case study research: reflections from experience. *Annals of Tourism Research*, 34(1), 7–26.

Oliveira, J. (2001). *Brazil: A Guide for Businesspeople*. Yarmouth, ME: Intercultural Press.

Van Maanen, J. and Kolb, D. (1985). The professional apprentice: observations on fieldwork role into organizational settings. *Research in the Sociology of Organizations*, 4, 1–33.

Welch, C., Marschan-Piekkari, R., Penttinen, H. and Tahvanainen, M. (2002). Corporate elites as informants in qualitative international business research. *International Business Review*, 11(5), 611–628.

Wright, L. L. (1996). Qualitative international management research. In: B. J. Punnett and O. Shenkar (eds), *Handbook for International Management Research*. Cambridge, MA: Blackwell, pp. 63–81.

Wynn, L. (2003). 'From the Pyramids to Pyramid Road: An Ethnography of the Idea of Egypt'. Unpublished Doctoral Dissertation, University of Michigan, Dissertation Abstracts International (UMI No. 3078644).

Chapter 9

Analysis of qualitative data

Get the habit of analysis – analysis will in time enable synthesis to become your habit of mind.
(Frank Lloyd Wright, American architect, 1867–1959)

Researchers usually feel exhausted by the time they have finished their fieldwork and reached the data analysis stage. Data collection is a time-consuming process, and researchers assume that once it is over, the research findings can be easily put together and presented. This is a wrong assumption, and problems may arise if you underestimate the importance of data analysis and the extent of time and effort it requires to clarify the meaning of the data collected.

Qualitative data

Qualitative data come in various forms. In many qualitative hospitality and tourism studies, the data come predominantly from interview transcripts; however, there is no limit to what could constitute a qualitative database, and increasingly researchers are using other techniques – such as recorded observation (both participant and non-participant), focus groups, document analysis, Internet websites (see, for example, Davidson and Yu, 2005), photographs (MacKay and Couldwell, 2004), videos (Brown, 2007) and multimedia (Viken, 2006). The term 'qualitative data' refers to data that is not quantitative (i.e. represented in a numerical form). Qualitative data are not produced only by qualitative research; numerous quantitative studies include open-ended questions and other forms of qualitative data.

Qualitative data analysis is the conceptual interpretation of the dataset as a whole, using specific analytic strategies to convert the raw data into a logical description and explanation of the phenomenon under study. In simple terms, data analysis is all about making sense of what the data say about your research topic. It requires making your own interpretations and highlighting patterns grounded in the data in a way that can be recognized and understood by the readers of your research. As in many instances in qualitative research, the processes of data collection and analysis tend to be simultaneous, with analysis continually informing the process of additional data collection and new data informing the process of analysis. It is important to recognize that the process of data analysis is not entirely discernible from the actual data. The analysis of your data will largely be influenced by your theoretical perspective of the phenomenon under study, your research strategy and your understanding about what data might be relevant and important in answering your research question.

Different approaches to qualitative data analysis

Qualitative studies aim to describe and explain a pattern of relationships and interactions (Miles and Huberman, 1994), and if you are using a qualitative methodology you may find yourself in the position of having a staggering volume of data in hand. The data analysis strategy that you will follow must therefore ensure that you neither die of data asphyxiation (Pettigrew, 1988) nor leap to quick conclusions (Nisbett and Ross, 1980; Miles and Huberman, 1994). Thus it would be sensible to start with a deductive (theory-driven) approach to data analysis and then mix it with the inductive (findings-driven) approach (see Chapter 4 for an explanation of terms 'inductive' and 'deductive').

Deductive (theory-driven) approach to qualitative data analysis

If you opt to follow the deductive approach, you must develop a coding schema or template which reflects the codes deriving from your research (conceptual) framework and emphasizes the key themes that emerge from the literature review. A code is a 'label attached to a section of text to index it as relating to a theme or issue in the data which the researcher has identified as important to the interpretation' (King, 1988: 119). These codes can be used as a set of 'lenses' to view the collected data, and in this case the data analysis consists of breaking down the interview transcripts, observation notes or collected documentation into manageable clusters with the purpose of classifying them under each code. As the simultaneous data collection and analysis proceed, you can adopt a 'cut-and-paste' approach (Ritchie and Spencer, 1994) whereby you continuously re-group 'chunks' of verbatim text or observation notes. Consequently, you will also revise, modify and augment the place and level of the codes in the template hierarchy. From the start of the analysis, you should also record your comments or thoughts on incidents and linkages between the variables, updating these notes as the analysis moves on. In this way new and deeper understanding of the phenomenon continually emerges, in an iterative process of knowledge creation.

Employing a theory-driven approach is particularly important in a research study for the following reasons:

- The theory-driven approach helps you to describe and explain the pattern of relationships and interactions better, because you group the data according to clearly defined codes which derive from your research (conceptual) framework
- The theory-driven approach helps to bring to the surface themes that might not emerge from the inductive mode of analysis.

Zhao and Olsen (1997) used a theory-driven approach in their study of the relationships among the antecedent factors and market-entry mode choices (direct investment, franchising, management contracting, joint venture partnership) of multinational hospitality companies planning their expansion into existing and/or new international markets. Their research effort was designed to answer the following questions:

1. What are the antecedent factors in the external environment that influence the entry mode choices of a hotel firm?
2. What are the antecedent factors in the task environment that affect the entry mode choices of a hotel firm?
3. How do these factors influence a hotel firm's choice of using particular entry mode methods?

A coding schema was derived from the literature, which reflected the research framework of the study and highlighted the key elements that emerged (see Box 9.1). This coding schema, which consisted of a number of codes, highlighted the broad areas (based on the literature review) according to which factors in the external and task environments could be grouped. In other words, in this schema each environmental element was treated as a code/pattern. This coding schema was then used to group the study findings gathered through interviews and documents. The data analysis consisted of breaking down the fieldwork findings into manageable blocks in order to classify them under each code/grouping. This stage of the analysis enabled the researchers to identify the issues in both the external and task environments of the hotel firm, and provide answers for the first two research questions.

Box 9.1	Coding schema
External environment	• Political • Economic • Socio-cultural • Technological
Task environment	• Customers • Competitors • Organization's resources and characteristics

A matrix was then developed with environmental elements versus entry mode choices (see Box 9.2). This matrix helped to cross-classify the variables logically, to generate themes, and to illustrate inter-relationships between different environmental factors and entry modes. More specifically, this matrix helped to answer the third research question by explaining how these factors influence a hotel company's

Box 9.2	Analysis matrix: company environment vs entry mode	
International expansion modes	Wholly-owned subsidiary (direct investment)	Non-equity or partial involvement (franchising, management contracting, joint venture partnerships)
Environmental elements		
External environment		
Internal environment		

choice of using particular market entry modes, based on the views of the informants and other evidence from other sources. The comments and the researchers' notes on their interpretation of the linkages and relationships between the environmental elements and the different market entry modes played an influential role in explaining how these elements affect a hotel organization's choice of market entry mode. For example, by using this approach the researchers were able to answer questions such as 'Why does a hotel company prefers to invest in a politically and economically stable country?', or 'Why does a hotel company prefers to use franchising or management contracting over direct investment in a politically or economically unstable country?'

Inductive approach to qualitative data analysis

As well as the deductive (theory-driven) approach to analysing qualitative data, you can also use an inductive approach. After spending some time viewing your data through the lens of a schema, you may put your theory-driven tool to one side and try to explore your study's findings in order to generate new knowledge about your research topic. When you are doing this, you should try to have a relatively open mind towards the topic, and prevent yourself from becoming over-structured by any preconceptions. This is particularly important in terms of avoiding bias and limiting the findings and themes that could emerge from your raw data.

There are different models (Miles and Huberman, 1994; Ritchie and Spencer, 1994) and different stages (Walker, 1985; Easterby-Smith *et al.*, 1991) that can be followed by researchers engaging in inductive qualitative data analysis. An amalgamated version of these frameworks and stages for qualitative data analysis will be presented here. By adhering to the following principles and practices you will not only improve the quality and depth of your qualitative data, but also increase the validity and reliability of your research. The data analysis should take place in the following stages.

1. Familiarization with the data
2. Coding, conceptualization and ordering:
   - open coding
   - axial coding
   - selective coding
   - enfolding literature.

Stage 1: Familiarization with the data

During this stage, you need to become familiar with the data. Doing this enables some first thoughts to emerge, and helps you to become aware of interesting points. You should try to review all the data at this point. The following activities can help you with the review process:

- Listen to each interview recording several times and note your impressions and intuitions with regard to both interviewee and the content of the interview. Notes of possible interpretations must be taken, and you need to identify the emerging themes.
- Alternatively, re-read the interview transcripts and/or observation documentation. Re-reading these materials can accelerate the process of locating concepts

and the links between them. If your research is carried out in an organizational setting, you can also review the organization's documents, and published reports regarding the participant organization. This can provide the background of the organization, and aspects of the business perceived as important. However, while reviewing secondary sources you should remember that they are not always reliable and accurate (Mason, 1998).

Stage 2: Coding, conceptualization and ordering

Analysis of each dataset involves the generation of concepts through the process of coding. According to Strauss and Corbin (1990: 57), this process:

> *represents the operations by which data are broken down, conceptualized, and put back together in new ways. It is the central process by which theories are built from data.*

The coded data should derive from all possible types of sources, such as field notes, interview transcripts, documents and diaries, in order to identify significant incidents, such as events, issues, processes or relationships. Three types of coding can be employed in qualitative data analysis: open coding, axial coding and selective coding.

Open coding

Strauss and Corbin (1990: 61) define 'open coding' as 'the process of breaking down, examining, comparing, conceptualizing and categorizing data', or simply selecting and naming categories for the data. Variables involved in the phenomenon are identified, labelled, categorized and related in an outline form. This is the initial stage of data analysis, and is about describing overall features of the phenomenon under study. The data are broken down by asking simple questions such as what, where, how, when and how much?

Case example

Plummer *et al.* (2006), in their study of the causes of the rise and fall of the Waterloo–Wellington Ale Trail (similar to a wine route but for ales) located in south central Ontario, Canada, employed open coding in the qualitative analysis of the interviews they conducted with key informants (brewery and non-brewery representatives). Regarding the decision to discontinue the Ale Trail, despite its success, the variables (reasons) that were identified labelled, categorized and related to one another in an outline form to explain the decision were as follows:

- for the brewers, economics (not making enough money), expansion (plans to expand their operations) and withdrawal of other breweries
- for the non-brewers, expansion and cost, change in leadership, dissatisfaction among breweries, incorrect structure of the Ale Trail, and lack of commitment from the brewers.

These reasons are presented diagrammatically in Figure 9.1.

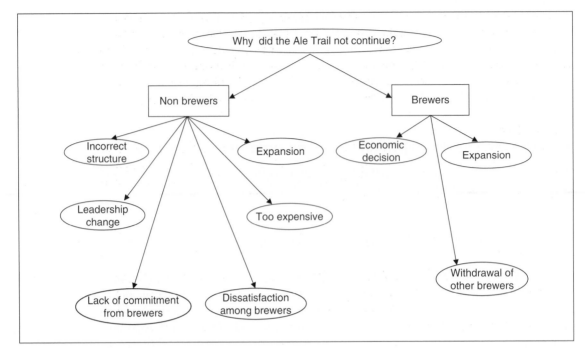

Figure 9.1
Why the Waterloo–Wellington Ale Trail was discontinued (source: Plummer *et al.*, 2006: 199).

Axial coding

Axial coding is the next stage after open coding. Whereas open coding divides the data into concepts and categories, axial coding puts them back together in new ways by making explicit connections between a category and its subcategories in order to understand the phenomenon to which they relate (Dey, 1998). This is achieved by utilizing a 'coding paradigm', i.e. a system of coding that seeks to identify causal relationships between the various categories and subcategories.

Case example

Mackay and Kerstetter (2005) used a multi-step coding process in their study of the role that tourism spaces (a cruise ship in particular) play in the development of social interaction among passengers. The researchers used both open coding and axial coding to identify phrases, words and ideas that were later funnelled into broad themes. They carried on this analytical process until saturation was reached and no new themes emerged. The researchers also used diagrams as a cross-check to work backwards from the themes. Starting with a theme, they made sure that the specific ideas, phrases and words belonged under a particular thematic umbrella. These diagrams helped them to make visual linkages by shifting words, phrases, and ideas within focused themes, and to clarify their thinking about patterns and relationships between the emerging concepts.

Memos, which are the written form of the researcher's ideas regarding the codes and their relationships (Strauss and Corbin, 1990), are also kept throughout the analysis process as they strike the researcher. Comments or thoughts on incidents and linkages are recorded initially as one sentence, and as the analysis moves on they are updated and expanded. This process of open coding, axial coding and writing and developing memos leads to a number of finalized and saturated categories.

Selective coding

Selective coding involves the integration of the abovementioned categories (axial) to form an initial theoretical framework (arrive at a grounded theory). The codes and categories are explored further by revisiting the coded statements, with attention being given to understanding inter-relationships.

Case example

Hansen *et al.* (2005), in their study of factors that form customers' meal experiences in *à la carte* restaurants, took a multi-step qualitative analysis approach. In the first step, the seven semi-structured interviews were coded and divided into 613 comment codes, with memos connected to each code. Each text sequence was given up to five comment codes, in order to extract more information and meaning from the text. The 'comment coding' helped with tracking the original quotation and in remembering thoughts and comments that were made by the researchers at the time the raw data were developed. Next came the open coding process of the comment codes, which yielded seventy-seven open codes. The open codes were then analysed and separated into seventeen categories for axial coding. Axial coding of the categories followed, and data were reassembled in new ways on a higher abstraction level. Finally, the selective coding that followed was based on the selection of the core category, systematically relating it to other categories and filling in categories that needed further refinement and development.

An 'open approach' to data analysis tackles the central cognitive problems of qualitative data analysis by bringing data out into the open. You are therefore advised to record different facets of the research data on cards or slips of paper and then convert them into a concrete, workable form which can be analysed by means of consciously adopted strategies rather than hidden, intuitive means.

Enfolding literature

As the data analysis process begins to yield a number of themes, concepts and relationships, these can be compared these with the extant literature (Creswell, 1998). Enfolding the literature involves asking what these themes are similar to, what they contradict, and why. During this stage you need to review a broad range of literature, and sometimes you will have to study areas that may be distant from your own direct research interest. As a result of this inductive logic, data analysis may lead you into less familiar or even entirely unfamiliar fields. This process will increase the level of uncertainty in your research process, and you will sometimes feel 'lost'.

However, it will facilitate an understanding of how to conceptualize and integrate the data. Enfolding literature, comparing and contrasting the research findings against the literature, and identifying the similarities and differences between the two all improve construct definitions, and therefore internal validity.

In summary, it is necessary to compare the emergent concepts, themes and relationships with extant literature for the following reasons:

- Identification of similarities will allow you to tie together underlying similarities in phenomena not normally associated with one another. This is particularly important in terms of achieving stronger internal validity, wider generalizability and a higher conceptual level (Eisenhardt, 1989).
- At the same time, juxtaposition of conflicting results will force you into a more creative, frame-breaking mode of thinking than you might otherwise be able to achieve. The results will deepen insight into both the emergent theory and the conflicting literature.
- Recognition of the conflicting findings will also build confidence in the results. If this is not reflected, readers might assume that, for example, the results are incorrect, which is a challenge to internal validity (Eisenhardt, 1989).

It is also appropriate to supplement these activities by placing your findings (in the case of both deductive and inductive data analysis approaches) in the public domain and sharing them with friends, supervisors, other academics and people from the industry. This is particularly important, because this will give you the opportunity to strengthen your analysis by having your research questions subjected to dialectical examination by others, thus helping to ensure validity.

Using Computer-Assisted Qualitative Data Analysis Software (CAQDAS)

Manual analysis of qualitative data can be quite challenging, especially when the data are recorded on several tapes or digital recorders and there are handwritten field notes. Of course, you will transcribe your tapes and probably devise your own way of organizing your data in one or more files together with other documents and perhaps photos you may have collected during your fieldwork in order to analyse them. You may even start your analysis on the very files, writing in the margins, crossing sections out, highlighting words, moving pages to match themes, drawing arrows to connect words, etc. The result of all these actions can be quite messy, and may cost you valuable time spent reorganizing your field notes or even deciphering your writing.

One answer to this problem is the use of information technology, which offer various types of software packages collectively called Qualitative Data Analysis Software (QDAS or QDA software) or even Computer-Assisted Qualitative Data Analysis Software (CAQDAS). The different types of software most frequently used in institutions are ATLAS.ti, MAXqda, N6, NVivo, QDA Miner and Qualrus. Although they have their differences, these software packages typically enable you to search, organize, label and annotate textual and visual data. Depending on how you use them, the packages will assist you in linking and comparing patterns within and across documents, giving you more freedom to play with ideas and even build your theories by visualizing the relationships between variables you have identified in your data.

CAQDAS functionalities

One of the main CAQDAS functionalities is that it helps you to structure your work. You will usually start by creating a 'project', which acts as the database for all the data collected during fieldwork. Through various tools offered in the package you can then structure and organize your data as you feel more appropriate, and access it instantaneously. Text search tools offer a number of ways to search for a single word or a phrase, or even a set of words relevant to a topic area. Such searches help you access the parts in your documents where these keywords appear, select them and retrieve them without any difficulty, one by one or as a set of paragraphs. The organization of your data within the project enables you to focus each time on a particular subset of data (or combinations of subsets), thereby facilitating comparison of the findings and leading you to the building of theory.

Next, you need to import your documents (e.g. interview transcripts) into the project. It is preferable to edit and spell-check your transcript doing this, because CAQDAS frequently does not offer a spell-checker or edit/find and replace tools. The latter are required when you have to 'anonymize' your data and replace company and respondent names with fictitious ones, and it is far easier to complete this activity using a word-processing program (e.g. MS Word, Kword, EZWord, etc.) than doing it manually. Using the edit/find and replace tools in Word, you can replace all basic respondent identities with codified information – for instance, 12-M-GM-INTHC (respondent 12, male, general manager, international hotel chain). Later, you may use text search or autocoding tools in order to identify and code all the GM respondents and their responses in a particular question. The uniformity of your transcripts in terms of spelling and spacing, as well as other features such as respondent identifiers and headers (question headers, section headers, topic headers, etc.) is very important.

The transcript should be in electronic, text-based format, and saved using either a text-only format extension (.txt) or rich text format (.rtf). If you are able to establish the format of the data file yourself – for example, in the case of interview transcripts – you should modify this format to one acceptable by the CAQDAS chosen. If you collect data from the Internet, or use data from other sources that are formatted in a different manner, you should keep an appropriate file format-converter program. Box 9.3 shows the text formats acceptable by various CAQDAS.

Box 9.3	Text format accepted by various CAQDAS packages

Atlas.ti V4.2	Text only with line breaks
Atlas.ti V5	.rtf or Word
HyperRESEARCH	Plain text
N5/N6	Text only
Nvivo Version 1-2	.rtf (text only, plain text, text only with line breaks)
MAXqda	Rich text format (.rtf)
MAXqda2	.rtf
QDA Miner	Word, .rtf, text only
QUALRUS	.rtf
The Ethnograph	Word (copied and pasted into an editor window)

Coding of the data can be performed relatively easily by applying keywords to embedded sections of the text, labelling certain aspects of your data, and sorting the information into clearly distinct categories that are defined based on the research topic. This will also enable you to keep track of your ideas and of sections in your data that address specific topics, and to explore them further if you think they will add value to your study.

Many researchers code their transcripts line-by-line. By taking this approach, you will focus on the content of the text in the line and what it is about. Line-by-line coding tends to yield descriptive codes; nevertheless, a good number of the codes that you produce using this approach will be more analytic, and with further effort you will be able to develop more of them, as well as recode some of the descriptive codes to make them more analytic. Other common coding techniques include:

- *Free coding*, which allows you to mark sections of data and attach a code to these sections.
- In vivo *coding*, which is a subtype of free coding where a portion of text to be coded becomes the label (code) of the text itself. This is a very efficient technique; however, it should be used with caution.
- *Free memos*, which are not really codes but rather little comments that can be attached to data or codes – similar to Post-It™ notes on hard copies.
- *Coding of variables*, which is where variables are defined and document-wide attributes (such as the gender or the position of the interviewee) can be stored.
- *Automatic coding* (available in most programs), which enables you perform text and/or code searches and assign a code to the search results. Some CAQDAS packages have more advanced features in this area. For example, Qualrus uses algorithms borrowed from artificial intelligence and generates coding suggestions on the basis of previously co-occurring codes (i.e. the software continuously 'learns' how to code), while ATLAS.ti allows you to store search queries in so-called 'supercodes' (i.e. your entire query itself becomes a code to search and retrieve in the future) with the added benefit that any new or changed data added to a project will be automatically coded through these codes.
- *Coding annotation*, which allows you to annotate your codes in many different ways (you find the one most appropriate for your analysis).
- *Coding of multimedia*, which is a feature currently available only in certain CAQDAS packages (HyperRESEARCH, Qualrus and Atlas.ti) and allows you to apply codes to sequences of certain video and audio files.

An important aspect of CAQDAS functionality is the way in which the output of your analysis is presented. You will normally be able to view the results of your searches both in output format and within the software, integrated into the working project. If the software supports the use of mapping for more graphic representations of coding schema, etc., you will usually be able to be export and paste them into Word files. A range of reports that allows you to view coded segments using either one code or a selection of codes in hard copy or to integrate them into other applications (such as Word, Excel or SPSS) is fairly standard to all packages. Normally these reports have the form of tables that may vary from simple word-frequency counts to more elaborate tables presenting each segment labelled with code, source document and paragraph numbers. You may also produce tables that display the frequency of codes by documents, which you can further filter to show comparisons between document subsets and coding subsets. Some packages (such as N6) also offer the ability to carry out qualitative cross-tabulations (matrix searches), which may be useful for theory building.

Benefits of using CAQDAS

The most obvious benefit of CAQDAS is that it can help you in organizing and maintaining a controllable dataset. This is especially useful when your research project becomes larger and the material collected increasingly bulky and unmanageable, with notes, comments, bookmarks and diagrams or even sometimes with multimedia (audio and video recordings). CAQDAS packages can store most of this material and, with their organizing functions (nodes, trees, sets, families and groups, etc.) and, most importantly, their coding functionality, they will help to keep everything neatly organized.

The CAQDAS search tools can locate and retrieve material (text or codes) quickly, so whatever you are looking for will always be only a couple of clicks away. Code searching in particular is a very useful tool for looking for the relationships between coded text sections – for example, you can look for text that is coded as 'destination image' and also as 'pollution' to find sections where respondents talk about pollution associated with their perception of a destination.

An equally important benefit of using CAQDAS is that, with its coding functionality, you can keep track of your analytic thoughts about your dataset, using the software as a platform (with its coding hierarchies, comments and memos, groupings, networks and linkages, etc.) to develop your analysis through better understanding and interpretation of the material collected throughout your project. You can take this a step forward by comparing responses or cases that are coded in the same or similar ways. If you have large datasets, CAQDAS makes such comparisons a lot easier than by working with numerous pieces of paper.

An added bonus of CAQDAS is that you can, if you wish, link your qualitative data to quantitative data. Most packages offer tools that facilitate the import of data from quantitative datasets and link it directly with relevant qualitative data in your project. You may, for example, be undertaking a project exploring the behaviour of long-haul premium-class air travellers. If you have quantitative data about these travellers (e.g. age, income, dietary habits, seating preferences, departure time preferences, etc.), CAQDAS will allow you to import this information in such as way that the narrative obtained from the traveller is linked with the quantitative data pertaining to that particular traveller.

A few words of caution

One of the most common drawbacks of using CAQDAS is the temptation to code everything, which in most cases leads to the substitution of analysis with coding.

It is very important not to be lured to the 'coding trap'; it is very tempting simply to attach codes to data, develop a well-structured coding tree and stop there, thinking that this analytical ordering of data. It often occurs when you use *in vivo* coding (i.e. the coding of text to itself), which may lead you to just a summary of descriptions rather than proper analysis of the responses. You must always remember that coding is only a precursor for your analysis.

Another risk of over-coding is that you end up with far too great a number of codes and, consequently, cluttered coding trees, which, rather than facilitating your analysis, make it even more difficult.

More significantly, you should ask yourself whether there is a point to using CAQDAS in the first place. Several approaches to analysis, such as conversation, discourse and narrative analyses, do not really take a thematic approach, and therefore the thematic coding offered by such software packages is not relevant. Equally, you may have just a small number of interviews and quite short responses, in which case the need for software is limited. Remember also that the use of CAQDAS requires (sometimes considerable) investment on your part, of both time (learning how to use it) and money (if your institution does not offer it and you have to buy it). Of course, there is an abundance of training manuals and courses in the use of CAQDAS, and higher education institutions are increasingly offering training in analytical software packages. Nevertheless, you should spend time considering whether or not to use CAQDAS, and your supervisor's advice will always be helpful in this decision and especially when purchasing software from your own personal budget. In this case, there are several aspects that you need to consider. These are summarized by Lewins and Silver (2006) and reproduced in Box 9.4.

Box 9.4	Questions to ask when choosing a CAQDAS package

- What kind(s) and amount of data do you have, and how do you want to handle them?
- What is your preferred style of working?
- What is your theoretical approach to analysis, and how well developed is it at the outset?
- Do you have a well-defined methodology?
- Do you want simple-to-use software that will mainly help you to manage your thinking and thematic coding?
- Are you more concerned with the language, the terminology used in the data, or the comparison and occurrence of words and phrases across cases or between different variables?
- Do you wish to consider tools which offer suggestions for coding, using Artificial Intelligence devices?
- Do you want both thematic and quantitative content information from the data?
- Do you want a multiplicity of tools (not quite so simple) enabling many ways of handling and interrogating data?
- How much time do you have to 'learn' the software?
- How much analysis time has been built into the project?
- Are you working individually on the project, or as part of a team?
- Is this just one phase of a larger project – do you already have quantitative data?
- Is there a package (and peer support) already available at your institution or place of work?

(Source: adapted from Lewins and Silver, 2006)

The international dimension: language and 'language equivalence'

There is an ongoing debate in the research community regarding the extent to which researchers should distance themselves from their findings in order to avoid bias. In the case of qualitative research, though, it is essential that researchers have direct association and interaction with the data in order to be able to clarify its meaning.

Researchers bring their own interpretations of the informants' views, behaviours and attitudes to the research topic, and also interpret the contents of the documents in such a way that the data helps them to build up a full picture of the topic area. One of the issues with regard to the interpretation of the data is the 'use of language' and 'language equivalence' in an international context.

When different languages are used by researchers, informants, clients or evaluators of research, translation is supposed to lead to equivalent meanings (Usunier, 1998). The most widely employed method for reaching translation equivalence in cross-cultural research is by the 'back-translation' technique (Campell and Werner, 1970). According to this method, one translator translates from the source language (S) into a target language (T), then another translator, ignorant of the source-language text, translates the first translator's target language text back to the source language (S). The two source-language versions are then compared. Whilst back-translating, discrepancies may arise from translation mistakes in either direction, or from actual translation equivalence problems. These are then discussed and addressed by the researcher (who speaks the source language) and two translators, and a final target language (T) version of the interview is prepared. The advantages and disadvantages of direct and back-translation are listed in Box 9.5.

Box 9.5	Advantages and disadvantages of direct and back-translation	
	Direct translation	**Back-translation**
Process	S → T	a) S → T; T → S b) Compare of S with S c) Modifications lead to the final version of T
Advantages	Easy to implement	Ensures the discovery of most inadequacies
Drawbacks/constraints	Leads to translation errors and discrepancies between S and T	Requires the availability of two translators, one native in S and one in T

Note: S = source language, T = target language (translated language)
(Source: adapted from Usunier, 1998)

To illustrate the above, consider a Thai student who studied for her PhD in the UK. For her research, she conducted interviews with the company executives of Thai hotel chains. The interviews were in the Thai language, because these executives were all Thai, and conducting the interviews in their own language would ease communication. She transcribed the tape-recorded interviews straight afterwards, whilst everything was fresh in her mind. She then sent the interview transcripts to the informants to ensure that the transcripts were an accurate representation of what they had said. Once this was completed, the transcripts were sent to the Department of Western Language and Linguistics for back-translation. Two translators were assigned to this; one translator was responsible for translating transcripts from Thai to English, and the other for translating them back from English to Thai. A comparison was made between these translations to identify and address the discrepancies and avoid the loss of meanings during the translation.

Another important issue is the comparison of culture-bound concepts and culturally embedded findings in the process of enfolding literature. For example, we all know that Total Quality Management (TQM) is a Japanese culture-bound concept, as it is underpinned by Japanese beliefs concerning lifelong employment, seeing the organization as a family, and widespread trust in the organization.

Since this concept was successfully implemented by the Japanese, many research studies have arisen in this area trying to investigate how TQM has been implemented in different country contexts. However, in many of these studies the researchers failed to explain the unsuccessful attempts of organizations to implement TQM practices because, during the enfolding of the literature, they missed the fact that TQM was perceived differently by the Japanese than by Americans, Spanish, Italians, Germans and Arabs. Another interesting example is the area of relationship marketing and differences in people's perceptions of 'relationship' in different cultures. Relationship marketing in Chinese organizations is underpinned by the concept of *Guanxi*, which describes the personal connections between people in Chinese society. As a result of the *Guanxi* concept, Chinese employees and organizations place stronger emphasis on emotional connectivity as well as mutual trust than in Western cultures. Obviously, these cross-cultural issues must be issued in order to be able to interpret the findings properly and reflect an accurate picture of what happens in different country contexts.

Overall, it is important for you to clarify the types of differences and similarities you are seeking between the literature and the research findings when you are doing research in different cultural contexts: are you seeking variations/similarities along conceptual/theoretical dimensions, or are you seeking variations/similarities on the basis of peoples' perceptions/interpretations of certain concepts? Or both?

Summary

- Preparation of data for qualitative data analysis is important, as lack of clarity in the findings can lead to the loss and/or misinterpretation of important messages.
- Both deductive and inductive approaches should be applied to qualitative data analysis in order to overcome the disadvantages of each.
- It is advisable that inexperienced researchers employ deductive data analysis before using inductive data analysis in order to ensure that they neither die of data asphyxiation nor leap to early conclusions.
- Data analysis can be facilitated by placing the findings in the public domain (such as friends, supervisors, other academics and people from the industry) and receiving feedback on interpretations of the research findings.
- The quality of qualitative analysis, whether computer-based, manual, mechanistic or observant of coding procedures, will always depend on the experience, creativity and theoretical awareness of the investigator.

Review questions

1. How should you prepare your findings for the data analysis?
2. What are the advantages and the disadvantages of deductive and inductive approaches to data analysis?

3. How does a coding schema help in the deductive data analysis process?
4. Why do you need to take notes and write memos during the data analysis process?
5. What is the purpose of enfolding literature in data analysis?

Annex: Extended example of inductive analysis

This section provides an extended example of the inductive analysis of a study carried out by two hospitality and tourism researchers (Mehmetoglu and Altinay, 2006).

The study

The study's research process was drawn from a wider doctoral research project by Altinay (2001), whose aim was to answer two broad research questions:

1. How does an international hotel group expand internationally?
2. Which factors influence the international expansion of the organization?

Such a definition of the research questions within a broad topic facilitated selection of the specification, the kind of decisions to be investigated and the types of data to be gathered, whilst leaving room for a theory-building study.

The investigation focused on the European division of an international hotel organization. The data collection methods chosen for the study were semi-structured in-depth interviews, observation, and complementary documentary analysis, all of which were considered to be appropriate strategies for obtaining in-depth context-specific information about particular subject areas (Yin, 1994). More than forty-five semi-structured in-depth interviews were conducted with relevant organizational members, both at host country and corporate levels (see Box 9.6 for a summary of the research sample).

Box 9.6	The research sample

- Development directors – Germany, France, Benelux, Turkey, UK and Ireland, Spain, Italy, Central Europe, Middle East and Africa
- Business support managers
- Legal counsels
- Franchise managers
- Operations managers
- Technical services managers
- VP sales and marketing
- VP development and investment
- VP mergers and acquisitions
- Other senior people who are involved in the international expansion process

Observation and participant observation were particularly important methods used to support the interview data (Schein, 1996). Twelve meetings were attended in the capacity of an ordinary participant and a participant observer both at host country and corporate levels in a number of countries, such as the UK, Belgium, Germany and Turkey. During the meetings, notes were taken to provide a condensed version of what actually occurred. Shadowing a number of key informants was an especially appropriate strategy to get close to the world of the key actors. Documentary analysis was also used as a complementary data collection method (see Box 9.7 for the various data sources and types analysed). These data were compared and analysed in conjunction with interviews and observations. This kind of approach was thought to be particularly useful in terms of increasing the richness of the case study data and constructing the 'full picture' of the organization's international expansion practice.

Box 9.7	Various data sources and types

Fieldwork data
Company documents collected:

- Job descriptions of the organizational members, international expansion proposals, annual reports, letters, memoranda, agendas, minutes of meetings and formal reports.

Publications about the participant organization:

- Reports and other press releases
- Brokers' reports about the participant organization from different investment and research organizations
- Publications of trade journals and newspaper articles
- A wide range of publications about the hotel industry in general, and the hotel organization in particular, through a number of databases such as Infotrac, Emerald, CD-ROM databases such as ABI/INFORM, Business Source Premier, and articles in Hospitality and Tourism database.

A case study database was created for the data collected via multiple data collection techniques. This was particularly important, because preparation of a case study database enhances reliability. Other researchers should be able to review the evidence directly and not be limited to the written reports. In this way, the database can increase the reliability of an entire case study.

Preparation of data for analysis

Every effort was made to transcribe interview and observation notes and tapes *verbatim* during the data collection period. The researcher was aware of the fact that it would have been difficult and time-consuming to capture and reflect all verbal and non-verbal aspects of the interviews and observations from abbreviated and poorly written notes. The researcher also kept the details of all documentation and supplementary information. It was important to clarify the notes about the relationships established between the researcher and the people interviewed, the general attitude of the interviewee, and the level of confidence felt about the data offered.

The data analysis process in practice

Although the analysis process is presented in a linear fashion here, it took place simultaneously in accordance with the main principles of grounded theory. The analysis process consisted of three concurrent stages or activities: familiarization; coding, conceptualizing and ordering; and enfolding the literature.

Stage 1: Familiarization

The data were all reviewed at this point. The researcher:

- listened to each audiocassette several times in order to note down the interpretations and identify emerging themes
- reviewed the organization's documents and brokers' reports regarding the organization which illuminated the context of the organization and those aspects of the business perceived as important; this helped to accelerate the process of locating concepts and links between them.

Stage 2: Coding, conceptualization and ordering

The researcher included field notes, interview transcripts, documents and diaries in the coded data in order to identify significant incidents, such as events, issues, processes or relationships. Three types of coding were employed: open, axial and selective. The following section will provide the information about what actually took place in this project in terms of the coding process.

Open coding

Open coding comprised approximately 250–300 pages. During the open coding process, data were initially broken down by asking simple questions such as what, where, how, when, how much, etc. Box 9.8 provides a brief example illustrating how the initial coding process was actually used, and how it worked in practice. Re-reading the transcripts several times contributed a great deal to making sense of the data and breaking them down into manageable forms.

As a reader outside the research, you are not expected to understand in any detail the notes contained in this table. The point to emphasize is that in your own research, you will need to use such methods to organize your data and ideas for your own future reference. In this case, the first column of the table included the raw data from the interviews, observations and documents. As the researcher broke down the data and moved from the first column to the others, he made an initial attempt to introduce his own interpretation and understand what was actually happening within the international expansion decision-making process. In the case of interviews and observations this was particularly important, because the process helped the researcher to discover the meanings informants attached to different events, objects and people. For example, in the last row of the table it is noted that the rationale behind the demand of the business support manager for information was to be able to justify a project at committee level. This close look at the data helped the researcher to identify the importance attached by the organizational members to information and information sharing, and to where and how that information was used.

During the categorizing, data that had been initially broken down were then compared, and similar incidents were grouped together and given the same conceptual label. For example, it was obvious that a fair amount of the data was about the

Box 9.8	Open coding process	
Included terms	**Semantic relationship**	**Cover term**
What is email doing in this company? It is destroying the relationships between people.	is a kind of	importance given to face-to-face communication
I did just after, I asked my VP to come and I made him sleep in this hotel after the refusal.	is a kind of	informal lobbying attempt
He said yes, so it means that a misunderstanding between the real value of the property and the decision was in the committee.	is a kind of	misperception, misjudgment, or the expectations of the people do not match
This project was good; it was right to enter at that time, in our brand, but was refused because people read the papers said oh, rooms are small. But the guy slept there he said, no this is right. The reality of the hotel, it was different.	is a way of	making a good decision through interacting with environment
I will have regular phone calls from the development directors, finding out what is happening, where they have new projects, price for the building and land, revenue numbers, occupancy, staffing costs.	are kinds of	information and knowledge needed to find out whether or not it will be a value-creative project
A desire that, once they have agreed a deal or price for a deal, that they've done the job and that Bass should just approve that deal and believe everything they say rather than actually go through an approval process for that deal.	is a kind of	frustration business support managers have with development directors
There will be a lot of dialogue about the proposal before we even get to the stage where an official proposal is put together. So many weeks beforehand, I would know that they would want to put forward a proposal. I know that will be happening.	is a way of	sharing information
I am asking for the information, I would say we need this information in order to convince the capital committee that this is a good project.	is a reason	Why business support manager uses information and knowledge
(Source: Mehmetoglu and Altinay, 2006: 20)		

organization's major characteristics in terms of doing business in different markets. 'Company-related factors' was therefore given as a conceptual label for this category. Moreover, there was a category of information related to the different sorts of decision-making criteria used by decision-makers. This category was therefore named 'Decision-making criteria'.

Many categories emerged during this process, although not all of these were within the major focus of the investigation. Those ones that did not recur in the data were considered unimportant and dropped from the list, while those that were closely associated with each other were combined. For example, categories such as 'Stages in the international expansion process', 'Decision-making criteria' and 'People getting involved in the process' were brought together in order to form a more substantial category leading to a better in-depth understanding of what was actually happening in the organization.

Axial coding

During axial coding, the main categories and their subcategories were combined into new variations according to the connections between them. For example, the components of the construct 'Education' were brought together through this process. As can be seen in Figure 9.2, the reasons why education took place both

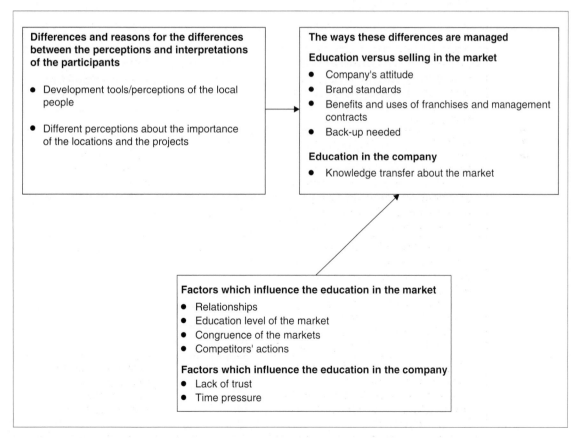

Figure 9.2
The components of the construct 'Education' (source: Mehmetoglu and Altinay, 2006).

in the organization and outside in the market, the forms and types of education, and the factors which influenced education both in the company and in the market, were all combined in order to develop a more substantial understanding of this category.

During axial coding, the emerging categories, themes or patterns were validated by selected informants, particularly influential organizational figures. This was important because what the researcher as a newcomer learnt at entry revealed only the surface layers of the organization's activities. Collaborating with the informants helped him to develop an understanding of what really went on in the organization, and how to think about it. Two additional procedures also ensured that the data analysis was not entirely subjective:

1. The researcher had hours of discussion of themes with the supervisors who met with him, usually on a two-weekly basis.
2. The researcher made different presentations both at the school and at conferences, and shared his views with a wide audience. This provided him with the opportunity to have the analysis subjected to dialectical questioning.

The analytic procedure was not a simple indexing process, since the researcher created memos (e.g. insights) throughout it as they occurred. Box 9.9 provides an example of a sample theoretical memo. This memo explains the importance of communication in the decision-making process, and the problems faced with regard to communication.

Box 9.9	Theoretical memo – the importance of communication in the process, and the problems faced with regard to communication

There is evidence that people tend to exchange information continuously throughout the international expansion process. Information travels between people. The authorizers – people on the committee – generally lack the in-depth knowledge that the development directors have. Information comes to the divisional level largely in the form of arguments supporting a course of action. It is likely to be presented by someone who is, for personal or subgroup reasons, trying to persuade the organization to do something. Decision-makers at the divisional level tend to give feedback to the development directors regarding their projects in order to bring the project to a stronger position or ask them to suggest a better alternative. There is evidence that investigation and the sharing of information in the international expansion process relies on both formal and informal channels of communication, but largely on the latter. Development directors channel information through business support coordinators; however, informal interactions take place as well. Development directors, the Senior Development Director and the VP are involved in discussions on the phone, over lunch or elsewhere. Communication can take place in different forms – lobbying, writing letters, and face-to-face communication – and facilitates the decision-making in the organization. In particular, it closes the knowledge gap between the host country and corporate decision-makers. The process is a cycle in which decision-makers try to find the optimal solution rather than the perfect one, because the information they receive is most likely incomplete, decisions are taken under time pressure, and different people have different expectations. In spite of the fact that parties communicate and interact through both formal and informal methods, people at divisional level seem to be cautious about the activities of the development directors. This is because most of the information presented by the development directors to those at divisional level is subject to misinterpretation. Although development directors are given incentives in order to motivate them, there is an impression in the company that they are salesmen and are thinking of their bonus. This impression within the company creates a bad working environment for them, and contributes to a deterioration of the situation. There is, however, evidence that these sorts of attitudes towards development directors influence their motivation adversely and isolate them from the rest of the company. Development directors take the role of gathering, interpreting and synthesizing information about the local cultures. However, the information does not seem to be considered by those people at company level. Communication between the development directors and the company seems to be limited – for instance, development directors are not granted the right to challenge the committee's views and decisions, therefore the committee dominates the decision-making process and fails properly to encompass the strategic views of development directors. Although people in the company do not know enough about the local market, because of their lack of trust in the development directors they cannot learn enough about it or make effective decisions, and sometimes miss opportunities. The organization seems not to benefit enough from the development directors in learning about the local market; rather, it uses development directors as salesmen or promoters to transfer their ideas and views to the local culture, to teach local people the company's way of doing business. Effective communication would lead to a better balancing of global efficiency and local responsiveness. The company cannot judge the strategic importance of cities or sites; it cannot assess whether it is using right tool for that site.

In the market, development directors and development partners have different expectations. Therefore, they attempt to bridge the gap between what development partners want and what development directors can give, or what development directors' want and what development partners can give. In order to bridge that gap, negotiations take place between the development directors and development partners regarding the financial viability of the project and the time issue. The way development directors negotiate or communicate is influenced by their own culture; however, the negotiation guidelines have been strictly determined by the company. To exploit the differences between local and divisional levels, the strategic mission assigned to the local representatives should be locally responsive. In addition to this, it is essential to show the local investors and cultures that the company is sincere, to make them feel that enough importance is assigned to local cultures. Giving an office to your development directors is important both for their motivation and for the image of the company in that culture. This suggests that decisions and strategies should be relatively in line with the expectations of local cultures.

(Source: Mehmetoglu and Altinay, 2006)

Taking this theoretical memo as an example, it can be seen that writing up and developing this particular memo was useful for the following reasons:

- It helped to identify where the communication dimension fitted within the overall international expansion picture of the organization, particularly its relationship to international expansion both internally and externally. For example, the following two pieces of text clearly illustrate that communication had two dimensions, internal and external:

and facilitates the decision-making in the organization. In particular, it closes the knowledge gap between the host country and corporate decision-makers

and

In the market, development directors and development partners have different expectations. Therefore, they attempt to bridge the gap between what development partners want and what development directors can give, or what development directors want and what development partners can give.

Moreover, the same sentences illustrate the importance and influence of communication in the international expansion process. It was an important aspect, and facilitated the decision-making process both internally and externally (Mehmetoglu and Altinay, 2006: 23).

- It helped to identify the relationship between the other categories and construct the overall international expansion picture of the organization. The following excerpt shows that communication in the market with development partners involved negotiation, and this helped to form a common ground for the partnership:

In order to bridge that gap, negotiations take place between the development directors and the development partners about the financial viability of the project and the time issue. The way development directors negotiate or communicate is influenced by their own culture; however, the negotiation guidelines have been strictly determined by the company.

Deal negotiation was an important stage of the international expansion process, and was investigated and evaluated as a separate category. However, as the theoretical memo indicates, categories were closely inter-related. Moreover, the memo also illustrated how members' orientations towards each other (this was another important category which had come out of the analysis process) influenced communication between them and ultimately the international expansion process (Mehmetoglu and Altinay, 2006: 25):

Although people in the company do not know enough about the local market, because of their lack of trust in the development directors they cannot learn enough about it or make effective decisions, and sometimes miss opportunities.

The processes of open coding, axial coding and writing and developing memos led to a number of finalized and saturated categories (Mehmetoglu and Altinay, 2006: 25; see also Figure 9.3):

- International expansion decision-making process (incorporated the stages of the process and the parties involved in the process)
- Communication (explored the importance of communication in the decision-making process)

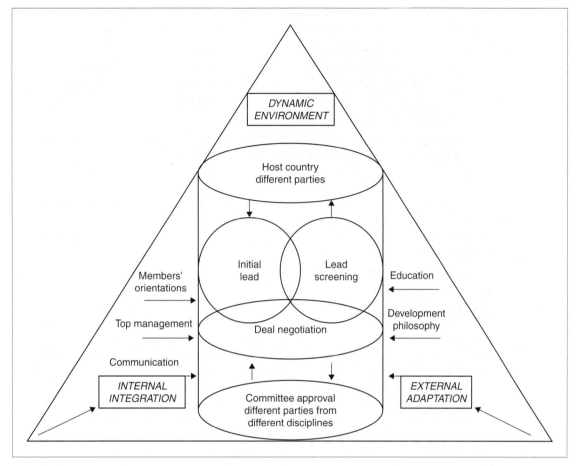

Figure 9.3
International expansion decision-making process (source: Mehmetoglu and Altinay, 2006).

- Top management (explored the consequences of recruiting one or two country nationals to key positions)
- Members' orientations (reflected on the organization's members' perceptions about the role and status of each other in the organization)
- International expansion philosophy (reflected in the dominant, widespread philosophy or organization's assumptions underpinning its international expansion activities)
- Education (explored the importance of the transfer of organization- and market-specific knowledge between parties involved in the decision-making process)'

Selective coding
This stage of coding involved using the abovementioned categories (axial) to form an initial theoretical framework. During this stage, the researcher placed emphasis on the diagrammatic illustration of constructs and categories in order to redefine the key concepts, map the range and nature of phenomena, and seek associations between and explanations for the constructs. Memos played an important role,

assisting in the processes of creating order from the data and making sense of it. Whilst integrating categories, creating order and making sense of the data, the 'International expansion decision-making process' emerged as a core category. This category had a pervasive presence in the data, and was the broadest category that could be related to as many lower-level categories as possible. For example, categories such as Decision-making criteria, Stages of the process, and Parties who were involved in the process, which were broad in themselves, could be brought together and accommodated within this broadest category. This was because they were closely and strongly inter-related. In addition, as a core category it could easily be related to subcategories. For example, categories such as Communication, Education, and Members' orientations towards each other influenced the core category, the International decision-making process. At the same time they were influenced by the process itself. Moreover, during the ordering stage it was realized that there was a clear distinction between two groups of categories. One group of categories related to the internal functioning of the organization, and the other to the external. The researcher therefore decided to structure the concepts under two broad headings: internal integration and external adaptation (see Figure 9.3).

Stage 3: Enfolding the literature

During this stage, the researcher started to compare different literature review areas with the themes, concepts and relationships that emerged from the analysis process undertaken above. Enfolding the literature involved asking what it was similar to, what it contradicted, and why. A broad range of literature was reviewed, and the data analysis led the researcher into less familiar and even completely unfamiliar fields. The comparison between the extant literature and the analysis of the findings helped to link the research with the existing body of knowledge in the subject area and supply an analytical framework. The emergent theory of the international expansion process (see Figure 9.4) included newly identified themes regarding, for example, decision-making processes and key players which had not been previously discussed in the international expansion literature. A comparison was conducted with extant theories in the broader field of strategic management on the subjects of entrepreneurship, strategy implementation and control, franchising and management contracting, and organizational environment. The similarities and contradictions identified were recorded as memos, and the researcher sorted the memos into batches and linked them up so as to create a theoretical outline of the connections across the categories.

Learning from the above study

As stated, the existing literature did not provide much detailed company information regarding the international expansion of hospitality organizations. Utilizing grounded theory methodology provided an opportunity to develop new insights into the internationalization of hospitality organizations, with particular focus on the role of entrepreneurship and the influence of different stakeholder groups in the internationalization process.

The research process of this study started with the identification of a research question within a broad topic. No attempt was made to specify potentially important variables through reference to extant literature, and thinking about specific relationships between variables and theories was avoided as much as possible, in order to maximize the likelihood of new discoveries.

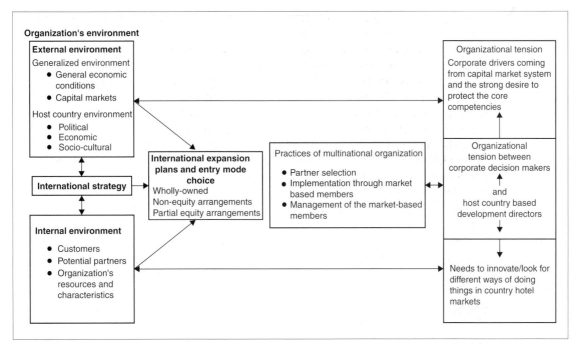

Figure 9.4
International expansion framework (source: Mehmetoglu and Altinay, 2006).

In this study there was a natural overlap of research idea formulation, crafting of instruments, entering the field, data analysis and literature review. Theoretical categories were not created on a single step basis, but rather through a process of creating categories and aligning them with new data. The researcher concurrently collected, coded and analysed the data, and decided what data to collect next and where to locate them. Categories were therefore redefined as relationships became clearer. As categories became saturated with evidence, they formed a foundation on which to ask further questions about the underlying process.

Despite the important advantages associated with the use of a very inductively-driven data analysis strategy such as grounded theory, this analytical approach should by no means be considered the sole solution to data analysis problems since, despite its strengths, it also has some methodological and practical limitations. For instance, in the later stages of the abovementioned study it was realized that employment of the inductive data analysis approach involves a great deal of complexity and ambiguity, which is difficult for an inexperienced researcher to handle. It is very likely that an inexperienced researcher will introduce bias to the research if he or she is expected to analyse an enormous amount of primary and secondary data within a limited period of time. More importantly, utilizing such an unstructured approach to research might limit an inexperienced researcher's ability to identify some of the important themes and aspects in the research findings, which might emerge if the researcher undertakes a 'tight', more theoretically-driven approach. A solely inductively-driven approach to data analysis, such as the grounded theory approach, can be better employed by a team of researchers or a more experienced researcher who could deal with the complexities and contradictions of this approach within a limited period of time.

References

Altinay, L. (2001). 'International Expansion of a Hotel Company'. Unpublished PhD Thesis, Oxford Brookes University.

Brown, B. (2007). Working the problems of tourism. *Annals of Tourism Research*, 34(2), 364–383.

Campbell, D. T. and Werner, O. (1970). Translating working through interpreters and the problem of decentering. In: R. Naroll and R. Cohen (eds), *A Handbook of Method in Cultural Anthropology*. New York, NY: Natural History Press, pp. 398–420.

Creswell, J. W. (1998). *Qualitative Inquiry and Research Design Choosing Among Five Traditions*. London: Sage Publications.

Davidson, A. P. and Yu, Y. (2005). The Internet and the occidental tourist: an analysis of Taiwan's tourism websites from the perspective of Western tourists. *Information Technology and Tourism*, 7(2), 91–102.

Dey, I. (1998*). Qualitative Data Analysis: A User Friendly Guide for Social Scientists*. London: Routledge.

Easterby-Smith, M., Thorpe, R. and Lowe, A. (1991). *Management Research: An Introduction*. London: Sage Publications.

Eisenhardt, K. M. (1989). Building theories from case study research. *Academy of Management Review*, 14(4), 532–550.

Hansen, K. V., Jensen, Ø. and Gustafsson, I. B (2005). The meal experiences of à la carte restaurant customers. *Scandinavian Journal of Hospitality and Tourism*, 5(2), 135–151.

King, N. (1998). Template analysis. In: G. Symon and C. Cassell (eds), *Qualitative Methods and Analysis in Organizational Research*. Thousand Oaks, CA: Sage Publications, pp. 118–134.

Lewins, A. and Silver, C. (2006). *Choosing a CAQDAS Package. A Working Paper*, 5th edn. Guildford: CAQDAS Networking Project, University of Surrey. Available at http://caqdas.soc.surrey.ac.uk/index.htm.

MacKay, K. J. and Couldwell, C. M. (2004). Using visitor-employed photography to investigate destination image. *Journal of Travel Research*, 42(4), 390–396.

Mackay, C. Y. and Kerstetter, D. (2005). Casting off: an exploration of cruise ship space, group tour behavior, and social interaction. *Journal of Travel Research*, 43(4), 368–379.

Mason, J. (1998). *Qualitative Researching*. London: Sage Publications.

Mehmetoglu, M. and Altinay, L. (2006). Examination of grounded theory analysis with an application to hospitality research. *International Journal of Hospitality Management*, 25, 12–33.

Miles, M. B. and Huberman, A. M. (1994). *Qualitative Data Analysis*. London: Sage Publications.

Nisbett, R. and Ross, L. (1980). *Human Inference: Strategies and Shortcomings of Social Judgement*. Englewood Cliffs, NJ: Prentice-Hall.

Pettigrew, A. (1988). 'Longitudinal Field Research on Change: Theory and Practice'. Paper presented at the National Science Foundation Conference on Longitudinal Research Methods in Organizations, Austin, Texas.

Plummer, R., Telfer, D. and Hashimoto, A. (2006). The rise and fall of the Waterloo–Wellington Ale Trail: a study of collaboration within the tourism industry. *Current Issues in Tourism*, 9(3), 191–205.

Ritchie, J. and Spencer, L. (1994). Qualitative data analysis for applied policy research. In: A. Bryman and R. G. Burgess (eds), *Analysing Qualitative Data*. London: Routledge, pp. 173–194.

Schein, E. H. (1996). Culture: the missing concept in organisation studies. *Administrative Science Quarterly*, 41, 229–240.

Strauss, A. L. and Corbin, J. (1990). *The Basics of Qualitative Research: Grounded Theory Procedures and Techniques*. Newbury Park, CA: Sage Publications.

Usunier, J. C. (1998). *International & Cross-Cultural Management Research*. London: Sage Publications.

Viken, A. (2006). Tourism and Sámi identity – an analysis of the tourism–identity nexus in a Sámi community. *Scandinavian Journal of Hospitality and Tourism*, 6(1), 7–24.

Walker, R. (1985). *Applied Qualitative Research*, Aldershot: Gower.

Yin, K. R. (1994). *Case Study Research: Design and Methods*. London: Sage Publications.

Zhao, J. L. and Olsen, M. D. (1997). The antecedent factors influencing entry mode choices of multinational lodging firms. *International Journal of Hospitality Management*, 16(1), 79–98.

Chapter 10

Analysis of quantitative data

The analysis of concepts is for the understanding nothing more than what the magnifying glass is for sight.
(Moses Mendelssohn, German philosopher, 1729–1786)

Quantitative data analysis helps researchers to answer their research questions and achieve their research objectives by expressing the opinions, attitudes and behaviours of people or characteristics of organizations in quantitative terms. Quantitative data can be a product of different research strategies, but mainly come from surveys and experiments.

For example, you may undertake a study investigating the extent to which tourists' personal motivates as well as socio-demographic characteristics such as gender, age, level of education, income and social class affect their perception of a particular destination. You survey 150 tourists at random by means of a structured questionnaire in the destination's main airport, having established a system of quotas relative to the dimensions (gender, age and nationality), with proportional allocation of tourists in each of those dimensions. To measure the various components of destination image formation, a thirty-item, five-point Likert scale from the typology of attributes proposed by the literature is used. How are you going to make sense of different types of data and present them to your audience (such as destination marketing managers and planners) so that they can modify their marketing and planning strategies accordingly?

There are a number of issues to consider in this scenario:

1. It is important to take into account the type of data collected by using various scales, because different scales play an influential role in deciding the type of analysis that can be carried out.
2. The preparation of data for analysis is imperative. As in qualitative analysis, data must be prepared for analysis by being organized, coded and entered into software packages.
3. It is important to consider the vehicles that can be used for quantitative data analysis. In the past, data were analysed manually, using paper and pencil, or perhaps with the help of a calculator and statistical tables. However, this approach was extremely time-consuming and errors were almost inevitable. It is no longer necessary to calculate statistics by hand, as this can be done quickly and efficiently by using computers and software packages such as Excel and SPSS (Statistical Package for the Social Sciences).

Scales in quantitative analysis

Variables can be measured using a number of different scales. These scales help to generate quantitative data for our analysis. Box 10.1 outlines the different types of scales and illustrates their use. The scales generate quantitative data, and these data can be coded and analysed through various statistical methods.

Box 10.1	Different types of scales	
Type of scales	**Key characteristics**	**Examples**
Nominal	Illustrates the key characteristics of objects or individuals; allows the researcher to assign subjects to certain categories or groups	Sex Colour of eyes or hair Occupation of the individual Department of employee in an organization
Ordinal	Illustrates the importance attached or preference for certain variables; categorizes the variables in such a way as to denote differences among the various categories; rank-orders the categories in a meaningful way	An individual's preference regarding hotel brands A hospitality student's preference regarding hospitality courses The importance attached to different job characteristics.
Interval	Illustrates the ranking of objects or individuals with numbers indicating same intervals; allows measurement of the distance between any two points on the scale.	Measurement of temperature Any attitude survey that measures a variable based on a point (five-point, seven-point, etc.) scale (e.g. Likert scale)
Ratio	Illustrates the absolute value and size of the objects or individuals	Sales turnover Number of customers Weight Time

Nominal scale

A nominal scale only indicates the key characteristics of objects or individuals. It is not possible to carry out any ranking with the data emerging from nominal scale, because this type of data does not give any indication about importance and/or amount. For example, a questionnaire may contain a question with a nominal scale regarding the respondent's nationality, and could be posed as:

Your nationality: ❐ British   ❐ Chinese   ❐ Other (please state): _____

Another example of a variable that lends itself to nominal scaling is the occupation of an individual. This would normally be scaled as follows:

Teacher	❐
Doctor	❐
Marketing manager	❐
Lawyer	❐
Construction worker	❐
Financial controller	❐
Other	❐

Note that every respondent has to fit into one of these categories, and the scale will allow calculation of the numbers and percentages of respondents that fit into each.

Ordinal (ranked) scale

An ordinal scale is used to order the categories of a variable according to some preference. The preference is ranked (for example, from best to worst; highest to lowest) and numbered as 1, 2 and so on. Ordinal scales are seen in questions that call for ratings of quality (very good, good, fair, poor, very poor) and agreement (strongly agree, agree, disagree, strongly disagree). For example, customers may be asked to rate the quality of pizza offered according to a scale of 1 to 5, where 5 = very good, 4 = good, 3 = average, 2 = poor and 1 = very poor.

Another example of a variable that lends itself to ordinal scaling is the ranking of the importance students attach to five distinct benefits that a hospitality course offers:

Rank the following characteristics of a hospitality course in terms of how important they are to you. You should rank the most important item as 1, the next in importance as 2, and so on, until you have ranked each of them 1, 2, 3, 4, 5.

Course benefit	Ranking
Offers work experience opportunity	
Develops customer service skills	
Develops numerical skills	
Develops IT skills	
Improves cultural awareness	

Here, the ordinal scale helps the researcher to determine the percentages of students that consider work experience to be most important, cultural awareness to be most important, and so on. Such knowledge may help in designing courses that would attract future students.

Compared with a nominal scale, an ordinal scale provides more information. An ordinal scale goes beyond categorizing information to providing information on how respondents differentiate aspects by rank-ordering them.

Note that an ordinal scale does not tell you anything about the magnitude of the difference among the ranks. In the hospitality course characteristics example above, the first-ranked characteristic might be only marginally preferred over the second-ranked course characteristic, while the characteristic that is ranked third might be considered far more important than that ranked fourth. Therefore, although ordinal scaling will indicate differences in ranking of objects, persons and events, it will not indicate the magnitude of these differences.

Interval scale

An interval scale has all the characteristics of an ordinal (ranked) scale except that the distances between the points on the scale (i.e. intervals) represent equal quantities of the measured variable (e.g. degrees Fahrenheit on a thermometer) (Gill and Johnson, 1997: 90). An interval scale allows measurement of the distance between any two points on the scale, and facilitates the calculations of certain arithmetical operations on the data. For example, it helps with calculating the means and standard deviations of the responses regarding the variables in order to measure the magnitude of the differences in preference among individuals (Sekaran, 2000). More specifically, taking the example above, if students think that (1) it is more important for them to gain work experience than develop numerical skills, and (2) it is more important for them to develop IT skills than improve cultural awareness, then an interval scale will indicate whether the first preference is of the same extent, a lesser extent, or a greater extent than the second (Sekaran, 2000). For example, the ordinal scale used above might be changed to an interval scale as follows:

Indicate the extent to which you agree with the following statements as they relate to a hospitality course by circling the appropriate number against each, using the scale given below:

Strongly disagree	Disagree	Neither agree nor disagree	Agree	Strongly agree
1	2	3	4	5

The following opportunities offered by a hospitality course are very important to me:

a. Work experience opportunity	1	2	3	4	5
b. Developing customer service skills	1	2	3	4	5
c. Developing numerical skills	1	2	3	4	5
d. Developing IT skills	1	2	3	4	5
e. Improving cultural awareness	1	2	3	4	5

The interval scale can help researchers to establish the equality of the magnitude of differences in the scale points. Suppose that students circle the numbers 3, 1, 2, 4 and 5 for the five characteristics of a hospitality course. This indicates that the extent of their preference for developing customer service skills over developing numerical skills is the same as the extent of their preference for developing IT skills over improving cultural awareness. In other words, the magnitude of difference represented by the space between points 1 and 2 on the scale is the same as the magnitude of difference represented by the space between points 4 and 5.

An obvious example of an interval scale is a thermometer used to measure body temperature. The starting point is an arbitrary number, and the magnitude of difference between 37°C degrees (supposed to be the normal body temperature) and 38°C is the same as the magnitude of difference between 42°C and 43°C.

An interval scale incorporates the differences, order and equality of the magnitude of differences in the variable. Therefore, it is considered to be more powerful than nominal and ordinal scales in calculating statistics.

Ratio scale

In addition to the above, some research methodology textbooks (e.g. Gill and Johnson, 1997; Robson, 1999) identify another type of scale – the ratio scale. This is the most powerful of the four scales, as it possesses all the properties of other three. Its distinctive characteristic is its unique zero origin, which allows the multiplication and division of points on a ratio scale possible and meaningful. For example, with ratio scales it makes sense to form ratios of observations, and it is thus meaningful to say that a 60-year-old person is twice as old as a 30-year-old. A ratio scale can also allow us to compare the weight of two individuals – a person weighing 100 kg is twice as heavy as one who weighs 50 kg.

Ratio scales are usually used in organizational research in hospitality and tourism industry when exact numbers can be obtained regarding objective factors, as in the following questions:

Please provide information about your sales turnover and employee number:

1a. What was the sales turnover for the start-up year? £_____

1b. What is the sales turnover for 2006? £_____

2a. How many people did you employ in the start-up year? _____

2c. How many people do/did you employ in 2006? _____

Please indicate the number of employees you have in each of the following categories:

Employee type	Full-time	Part-time	Casual	Total
Family-member	——	——	——	——
Non-family member Turkish	——	——	——	——
Other origins	——	——	——	——
Total	——	——	——	——

Please provide an approximate breakdown of sources of your start-up capital:

Personal savings	___%
Capital from family	___%
Loans from British banks	___%
Government grants	___%
Commercial credit	___%
Loan from a friend	___%
Other (please state)	___%

Organization, coding and entering data for analysis

Once you have become familiar with the above scales and the type of data generated by them, you can move to an important stage of quantitative data analysis – the organization, coding and entering data for analysis.

As it is the case with qualitative data, different research strategies may yield large amounts of quantitative data. An *ad hoc* approach to preparing data for analysis can result in a number of errors that will eventually affect the quality of your analysis. Therefore, you need to have a systematic approach to organizing the information, coding it and entering the data for analysis in statistical software packages. The range of programs available for data analysis varies from simple spreadsheet packages such as MS-Excel to more advanced statistical packages such as SPSS. Regardless of the software package chosen, you must follow a simple logic for formatting and organizing the information. The first step for this process is to sort the data into variables. A variable is an indicator of interest in a research project, and may take the form of any of a specified set of values, perceptions, attitudes and attributes. A variable can be anything, as long as it has differing or varying values. Examples of variables include job satisfaction, employee motivation, absenteeism, number of passengers, and length of stay in a hotel. Variables can be discrete (e.g. gender: male/female, nationality: British, German, Turkish) or continuous (e.g. age of employees, income of customers).

The following example includes both discrete (nationality and sectors of operations) and continuous (sales turnover and employee numbers) variables as presented in a questionnaire.

What is your nationality? Please tick.

Your nationality: ❐ British   ❐ Chinese   ❐ Other (please state): _____

Please tick the sector you are in:

Manufacturing of food products and beverages, textiles	❐
Professional services (doctor, accountant, insurance, IT, etc.)	❐
Wholesale trade and commission trade	❐
Retail trade	❐
Hotels, restaurants, takeaways and cafés	❐
Other (please state)	❐

Please provide the following information on sales turnover and employee number since start-up:

Period	Sales turnover	Employee number
At start-up In 2001 In 2005 In 2007		

Variables can also be grouped in an abstract or a numerical manner. For example, consider a study on the job satisfaction of employees at a hotel. You may be interested in the age of employees, their salary, and the extent to which they are satisfied with their job. Numerical values can be easily assigned to variables such as age and salary (numerical variables), but the concept of job satisfaction (abstract variable) has to be converted from an abstract format into a variable to which a value can be assigned so that you can measure it. The level of an employee's job satisfaction can be measured, for example, on a ten-point Likert scale, with the level of satisfaction varying from (1) 'very low' to (10) if 'very high'.

Furthermore, variables can be grouped as independent and dependent variables. An independent variable is one that causes changes to a dependent variable or variables (Saunders *et al.*, 2007) – for example, staff training or lack of staff training (independent variable) might influence service quality (dependent variable). The dependent variable changes in response to any alteration in the independent variable – for example, in an organization offering poor service quality as a result of lack of training, more emphasis on training may result in the improvement of service quality. The relationship between the two variables can be measured by the number of training hours per employee on the one hand, and the number of customer complaints on the other. An increase in hours of training may result in service quality and thus a decrease in customer complaints.

The next stage is to code your data. By coding, we mean assigning a numerical value (code) to the different possible answers (observations) that a variable or question can take within a questionnaire. Each observation is represented in such a simple and consistent way that it can be entered easily into the software package for analysis. When you start to code your data, it is better to use numbers for coding than letters or a combination of letters and numbers, as this may lead to confusion later (Saunders *et al.*, 2007). By assigning a number to each observation, you are developing a coding scheme. The following coding scheme illustrates how possible answers (observations) regarding the first two variables of the example above can be coded.

Chinese	Turkish	British	Other
1	2	3	4

Manufacturing	Professional Services	Wholesaling	Retailing	Catering	Other
1	2	3	4	5	6

If you have a question with a scale, you can code it in a similar manner by assigning a number or using the scale numbers of the question. Suppose, for example, that you have the following question in your questionnaire:

How important have the following been in the growth of your business?					
	Very important				Unim-portant
Factors	5	4	3	2	1
Development of new products Business diversification Low costs Low prices Producing high-quality products Intensive marketing of products Other (please state)					

You can code the possible answers using numbers that indicate the importance attached to different factors affecting the growth of business, as follows:

Very important				Unimportant
5	4	3	2	1

You can always shorten the names of the variables and give them a label that can be easily remembered and understood – for example, the variable 'development of new products' may be labelled 'DevNewPro', and 'producing high-quality products' may be labelled 'ProHigQuaPro'.

The data gathered from the respondents are then entered on a spreadsheet, as illustrated below. Each row holds the data for an individual, while each column represents the data for a variable. In this example, row 1 represents a person who is Chinese (coded 1), whose business is in the catering sector (code 5), who thinks that 'development of new products' is very important for business growth and has thus coded it 5, that 'business diversification' is less important (coded 1), and that 'low prices', 'producing high-quality products' and 'intensive marketing' are of high importance (coded 4).

Respondent	Nationality	Sector	DevNewPro	BusDiv	LowPri	HiQua	IntMark	Other
1	1	5	5	1	4	4	4	1
2	2	3	5	2	3	3	1	1
3	1	2	1	1	4	2	1	1
4	4	1	2	3	4	3	2	1
5	3	6	3	.	3	4	1	.

You will have noticed the small dot, which appears twice in the last row of the table. This indicates missing data. There are a number of reasons for missing data.

One common cause is that a respondent might refuse to answer the question because of confidentiality. Another is that the respondent does not know the answer or does not have an opinion. The respondent might simply have missed the question by mistake, or his or her answer may be unclear. Statistical analysis software often reserves a special code for missing data (Saunders *et al.*, 2007: 416). Cases with missing data can be excluded from your analysis if necessary.

Regardless of how careful you are, you may make errors when you are inputting and coding your data. While some types of errors hardly matter, others can seriously affect your results. For example, consider a study of the effects that part-time employment has on the performance of hospitality and tourism students. You might decide to enter the marks of the students as a decimal (e.g. 0.70 to represent 70 per cent) – but if you enter 70 instead of 0.70 for just one student, your results will change dramatically. You can minimize the risk of errors such as this by checking the data and looking for illegitimate codes (Saunders *et al.*, 2007). For example, for every coding scheme you should only assign certain numbers to the possible answers; numbers other than these will not indicate anything. More specifically, in the above nationality question, if you detect in the input an answer coded as 5 this is clearly an error, since this question is only coded 1–4.

Analysing quantitative data

Once you have completed the basic 'housekeeping' work of inputting, coding the data, cleaning and correcting the inconsistencies, you can move on to analysis of the data. There is no need to perform any statistical tests manually; statistical software packages are widely available in all higher institutions. The layout of the various software packages available in the market might differ, but they all perform the same basic functions. It is important to familiarize yourselves with these variable layouts and understand clearly the types of statistical tests that you should use to answer your research question.

Remember that different types of scales generate different types of data, and these will determine which statistical tests to use (see Box 10.2). The lowest level of measurement is the nominal scale and the highest is the ratio scale, while the power of statistics increases as you move from the nominal to the ratio scale – that is, information on the variables can be obtained with a greater degree of precision in relation to your research questions when you use interval or ratio scales.

Exploring data

The first stage in any data analysis is to explore the data collected in order to get some idea of any patterns within it. Usually, you should look at descriptive statistics such as minimum, maximum, mean, mode and median, and standard deviation and variance. Minimum, maximum, mean and mode are the measures of central tendencies in your data. Standard deviation and variance represent the extent of dispersion in your data.

Mode and median are obtained from nominal- and ordinal-scaled variables, whereas maximum, minimum, means, standard deviations and variance are obtained from interval-scaled variables.

The *minimum* and *maximum* may alert you to data that are impossible or are outliers – for example, a customer with an age below 0 or above 150, a price of below 0, etc.

Box 10.2	Different scales of measurement and their use

Scale of measurement	Measures of central tendency	Measures of dispersion	Some tests of significance between the variables
Nominal	Mode	Variance	Chi square (χ^2)
Ordinal	Mode, median	Variance	Chi square (χ^2)
Interval	Mode, median, mean	Standard Deviation	Pearson Correlation test, analysis of variance (ANOVA), *t*-test
Ratio	Mode, median, mean	Standard deviation	analysis of variance (ANOVA), *t*-test, multiple regression analysis (coefficient of multiple determination)

(Source: Adapted from Sekaran, 2000)

The *mode* can be found for all types of scales and data. It represents the value that occurs most frequently in your dataset – so in a dataset where the answers for a question are:

$$4, 6, 1, 2, 6, 3, 4, 5, 2, 6, 6, 3, 3, 3, 6, 4, 6, 4, 2, 6$$

the mode is 6.

The *median* is simply the middle piece of data, after you have sorted the data from the smallest to the largest. The median only requires the data to be ordered, and can therefore be used with ordinal as well as ratio- and interval-scaled data. Suppose, for example, that in your dataset you have the following answers to a question:

$$1, 2, 2, 2, 3, 3, 3, 3, 4, 4, 4, 4, 5, 6, 6, 6, 6, 6, 6, 6.$$

There is an even number of values, and the middle (or median) is therefore between the second and third 4s. Because they are the same, you can easily claim that the median is four; however, if they were different – say if the median was between 3 and a 4 – you would have to calculate $(3 + 4)/2$ to find a median of 3.5.

The *mean* (often called the arithmetic mean) of a set of values is the sum of all the values, divided by their number. The mean requires numeric representation, and can therefore only be calculated for interval- and ratio-scaled data. In the example above, the mean would be:

$$(4 + 6 + 1 + 2 + 6 + 3 + 4 + 5 + 2 + 6 + 6 + 3 + 3 + 3 + 6 + 4 + 6 + 4 + 2 + 6)/20 = 4.1$$

Standard deviation is a measure of the deviation from the mean. A small standard deviation means that the data are tightly grouped around the mean, whereas a large standard deviation implies that the data are widely scattered around the mean. In the example, which consists of a small number of observations, the standard deviation is 1.68. By running descriptive statistics, you can locate these errors and correct them. The standard deviation is a measure of dispersion for interval- and ratio-scale data.

Variance indicates the extent to which a variable is dispersed in the dataset. It can be calculated by subtracting the mean from each of the observations, squaring the results, summing them, and dividing the total by the number of observations. Variance is unique to nominal- and interval-scale data.

For example, suppose that you are undertaking a study on entrepreneurial growth in your city. One of the questions in your survey asks the participating entrepreneurs to rank the importance of different factors (such as price reduction, new product development, etc.) in business growth, using a five-point scale. After collecting the questionnaires you code the answers and enter them in SPSS. One of the steps you could take next is to produce descriptive statistics for this answer, choosing (from the software's dialog box):

Analyze
    Descriptive statistics
       Descriptives…
          (Select the variables)
             Options…
               (Choose the relevant statistics
               needed – i.e. mode, median,
               standard deviation and variance)

The results of a descriptive statistical analysis would look similar to Box 10.3.

Box 10.3	Descriptive statistics					
	N	Minimum	Maximum	Mean	Std deviation	Variance
Price reduction	173	1.00	5.00	2.379	0.756	0.570
New product development	173	1.00	4.33	2.671	0.521	0.271
Advertising	173	1.61	4.28	3.117	0.507	0.257
Relationship marketing	167	2.31	4.69	3.474	0.518	0.268
Analysing and predicting industry trends	174	1.00	4.00	2.511	0.673	0.453

From these results it is clear that the mean for price reduction is rather low (2.38 on a five-point scale), as is the mean for new product development (2.67). Advertising is about average (3.12), and relationship marketing is perceived as somewhat crucial (3.47). The mean of 2.511 on a five-point scale for analysing and predicting industry trends indicates that most of the respondents are neither bent on analysing and predicting trends nor surviving without this activity. The minimum 1.00 indicates that there are some who do not think that reducing price, developing new products, advertising and analysing and predicting industry trends are highly important to business growth. The maximum of 4.00 may be the smallest number in that column, but it is still very close to the upper end of the ranking scale – thus indicating that some people in your sample think that these marketing activities are highly important to growing their business. The variance for new product development, advertising and relationship marketing is not high. The variance for price reduction and for analysing and predicting industry trends is only slightly higher, indicating that most informants are very close to the mean on all the variables. In other words, if you take price reduction as a factor for business growth, you will notice that its variance from the mean (2.511) is 0.570. This suggests that most of the entrepreneurs in your sample rated this factor at anything from 1.941 (i.e. 2.511 − 0.570) to 3.081 (i.e. 2.511 + 0.570) or, more simply, they gave this factor an importance rating of either 2 (rounding up 1.941) or 3 (rounding down 3.081). The same happens with all the variables in your question; hence the conclusion that most of the people in the sample were very close to the mean.

In sum, the importance of price reduction is – in the opinion of your sample – relatively low (mean of 2.379), and the same stands for new product development as well as for analysis and prediction of industry trends (means of 2.671 and 2.51 respectively). On the other hand, advertising is perceived to be fairly important (mean of 3.117) and the relationship marketing appears to be the most important of all (mean of 3.474 – quite close to 4). You can also say that not one of these factors is viewed by your sample *as a whole* as being highly important, even if *some* (as indicated in the 'maximum' column) have chosen to rate the factors as being highly important.

Frequency distributions can also be obtained for all the personal data or classification variables. By running frequency distributions you can build a profile of respondents, which will be useful when you come to describe your sample in your research design section or chapter of your written report. You can produce a frequency table by using SPSS and choosing (from the dialog box):

Analyze
　　Descriptive statistics
　　　　Frequencies
　　　　　　(Select the relevant variables)
　　　　　　　　Choose needed:
　　　　　　　　　　Statistics . . . or Charts . . . (Bar and
　　　　　　　　　　pie charts, histograms, etc.)

Suppose that, as a financial controller, you are interested in exploring the number of employees for each department of a hotel, so that you can make your budgeting decisions accordingly. The frequencies of the number of individuals in the various departments for a sample hotel are shown in the Box 10.4 (based on your calculations of frequencies, using SPSS). It is clear that the greatest number of individuals in the sample came from Housekeeping (28.1 per cent), followed by Food & Beverage (25.3 per cent). Only three individuals (1.7 per cent) came from Reservations, and five from the Finance, Maintenance, and Guest Relations departments (2.9 per cent).

Box 10.4	**Frequencies output – respondent's department**			
	Frequency	**Percentage**	**Valid percentage**	**Cumulative percentage**
Sales & Marketing	13	7.5	7.5	7.5
Housekeeping	49	28.1	28.1	35.6
Food & Beverage	44	25.3	25.3	60.9
Finance	5	2.9	2.9	63.8
Front Office	34	19.5	19.5	83.3
Maintenance	5	2.9	2.9	86.2
Personnel	16	9.2	9.2	95.4
Reservations	3	1.7	1.7	97.1
Guest Relations	5	2.9	2.9	100.0
Total	174	100.0	100.0	100.0

The frequencies can also be visually displayed as bar charts or pie charts by clicking on CHARTS in the SPSS menu. Bar charts are suitable for data generated from descriptive (nominal) or ranked (ordinal) scales, and are often used to present data in reports. In a bar chart, the height of the bar represents the frequency of occurrence (Saunders *et al.*, 2007). For example, Figures 10.1 and 10.2 demonstrates the number of people who visited different regions and/or countries in 1998.

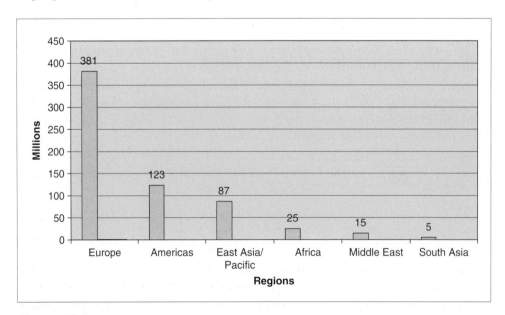

Figure 10.1
International tourist arrivals, 1998 (source: WTO, in Finnie *et al.*, 2000: 7).

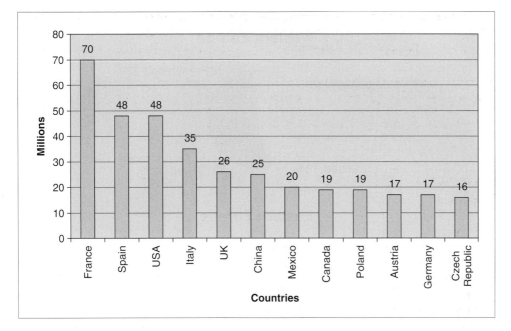

Figure 10.2
The world's top twelve tourism destinations (source: WTO, in Finnie *et al.*, 2000: 8). Figures exclude same-day visitors.

Pie charts can be used to demonstrate the proportion or share of occurrences in the data. A pie chart is divided into proportional segments according to the share each has in the total value (Saunders *et al.*, 2007: 427). For example, the pie charts in Figure 10.3 demonstrate the patterns of hotel affiliation modes in different regions of the world. They show the management structure (franchising, management contracting, owned, leased) of hotels in each region, and allow you to compare and contrast the nature of hotel industries in different parts of the world.

Explaining relationships between variables

It is often interesting to know whether there is a relationship between two and more variables and, if so, what relationship exists. For example, you might be interested in whether there is a relationship between the amount of time spent reading this book, and hospitality and tourism students' understanding of research methods. There are a number of ways in which these two variables might be related:

1. They may be positively related, which means that the more time students spent reading this book, the better their understanding of research methods becomes
2. They may not be related at all, which means that students' understanding of research methods remained the same regardless of how much time they spend reading this book
3. They may be negatively related, which means that the more time students spend reading this book, the worse their understanding of research methods becomes.

How can you tell whether two variables – such as (a) the amount of time spent reading and (b) understanding of research methods – are related? The following quantitative data analysis techniques will help you to decide.

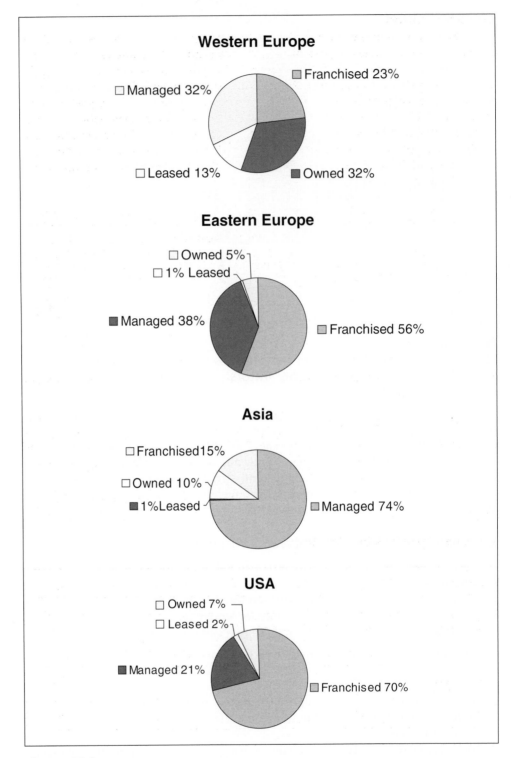

Figure 10.3
Patterns of hotel affiliation modes in different regions of the world (source: Slattery, 1996: 34).

Cross-tabulation

Cross-tabulation is the representation of two variables in a matrix where all the answers in one variable are presented in the rows, and all the answers in the other are presented in the columns. For example, consider a questionnaire seeking the opinions of customers in a pub on the smoking ban in England. You may want to see whether gender affects this opinion. This question can be explored by cross-tabulating the two variables, gender and opinion of customer. Data for these variables will normally be obtained by one question related to the respondents' demographics and another question where respondents may record their opinion in a scale from 1 to 3 (1 = agree and 3 = disagree). Prior to the entry of data, the table would look something like this:

Gender	Customer opinion			
	Agree (1)	Neutral (2)	Disagree (3)	Total
Male (1) Female (2) Total				

Suppose that, for this example, you have constructed the following cross-tabulation by choosing (from the dialog box):

Analyze
    Descriptive statistics
        Crosstabs...
            (Enter variables in the rows and columns boxes)

The result will look like Box 10.5.

Box 10.5	Cross-tabulation

Gender	Opinion of customer			Total
	Agree (1)	Neutral (2)	Disagree (3)	
Male (1)	8	8	5	21
Female (2)	5	6	12	23
Total	13	14	17	44

You can analyse the results of the cross-tabulation by identifying patterns of cells with small or large frequencies. If you can distinguish specific patterns in these cells, they will reflect a possible relationship between the variables. If there is no obvious pattern, and the frequencies are fairly even spread across the cells, then there is probably no relationship between two variables. If you consider Box 10.5, it is clear that most males (16 out of 21) have a positive opinion regarding the smoking ban, whilst most females (12 out of 23) appear to have a negative opinion. This indicates that the opinion of the customer regarding a smoking ban is dependent on the gender of the respondent – in other words, there is a relationship between the two variables, gender and opinion of customer regarding a smoking ban.

It is possible to cross-tabulate all questions in your questionnaire. However, this produces large amount of data and results in data overload.

Chi-square test

The chi-square test detects whether there is an association between two nominal variables. The first step is to develop two hypotheses to test; one is the null hypothesis H_0 and the other is the alternate hypothesis H_1. Rejecting a null hypothesis means rejecting a testable statement such as 'The growth of a business is independent of the owner's educational attainment', and accepting a testable statement like 'The owner's educational attainment is related to the growth of a business'.

When you are undertaking the chi-square test, you should pay particular attention to the P value (the significance value). If the significance value is below the conventional probability value (P), which is 0.05, then you reject the null hypothesis H_0 and accept the alternative hypothesis. If the P value is above 0.05, you accept the null hypothesis H_0 and conclude that there is no relationship between the variables.

Suppose that you are examining the possible relationship between different market scale brands (upscale luxury brand, mid-scale market brand and budget brand) and the employment status of employees (part-time versus full-time). Your hypotheses can be stated as null and alternate in the following way:

H_0: Employment status (part-time vs full-time) is not related to hotel brand scale
H_1: Employment status (part-time vs full-time) is related to hotel brand scale.

Since both variables are nominal, a chi-square test can be performed. Suppose that you run the statistical test by choosing (from the dialog box):

> Analyze
> > *Descriptive statistics*
> > > *Crosstabs...*
> > > > (Enter variables in the rows and column boxes)
> > > > Statistics...
> > > > > Select *Chi-square*

The output of your statistical analysis will then look like Box 10.6:

The cross-tabulation count indicates that, of the full-time employees, 103 work for the upscale luxury brand, 25 for the mid-scale market brand and 18 for the budget brand. Of the part-time employees, 16 work for the upscale luxury brand, 8 for the mid-scale market brand and 4 for the budget brand.

The P value, i.e. the value of significance, is presented in the Pearson chi-square row under the *Asymp. Significance (two-sided)* column. You can see that P here is 0.314, which is above the conventional probability value of 0.05. You can also see that the chi-square value in the first row and column is not high (2.312). This

---

Box 10.6 | Cross-tabulation

Employment status vs hotel brand scales

Employment status	Different types of brands			Total
	Upscale luxury brand	**Mid-scale market brand**	**Budget brand**	
Full Time	103	25	18	146
Part Time	16	8	4	28
Total	119	33	22	174

Chi-square test

	Value	df	Asymp. significance (two-sided)
Pearson chi-square	2.312	2	0.314
Likelihood ratio	2.163	2	0.339
Linear-by-linear association	1.103	1	0.294
No. of valid cases	174		

---

suggests that you have to accept the null hypothesis H_0 and conclude that there is no relationship between the employment status and hotel brand scales – in other words, the findings did not support hypothesis H_1.

Suppose now that you are undertaking another study examining the relationship between the educational attainment of business owners (such as, for example, a university degree) and their business growth. The following hypotheses were formulated for the study:

H_0: The educational attainment of a business owner is not related to his or her business growth

H_1: There is a relationship between the educational attainment of a business owner and his or her business growth.

The chi-square test generated the results presented in Box 10.7.

Box 10.7 | Chi-square tests

	Value	df	Asymp. Significance (two-sided)
Pearson chi-square	4.4010	1	0.0359
Continuity correction(a)	3.0818	1	0.0791
Likelihood ratio	4.3112	1	0.0378
Linear-by-linear association	4.3542	1	0.03691
No. of valid cases	94		

Here, you can clearly see that P value (0.0359) is below the conventional probability value (0.05), suggesting that you should reject the null hypothesis H_0 and accept the alternative hypothesis that there is a relationship between educational attainment and business growth. As the significance level increases (it is closer to zero), the chi-square value increases too (4.4010).

Pearson correlation test

Chi-square analysis shows whether there is a relationship between two categorical variables. However, it does not say anything about the strength of a relationship (whether it is strong or weak), or the nature or the direction of the relationship (positive or negative). A Pearson correlation test can allow you to measure the degree to which a change in a dependent variable is related to a change in one or more independent variables.

Suppose that you are interested in examining the relationship between the amount of time spent training employees on the job and the service quality offered by these employees in a restaurant. There are a number of ways in which these two variables (employee training and service quality) might be related. A positive relationship means that the more time spent on employee training, the better the service quality will be. Alternatively, there might be no relationship at all – which means that service quality will not change regardless of how much time restaurants spend on training (in other words, there is no relationship). The third scenario is a negative or inverse relationship, which means that the more time spent on training employees, the worse the service quality will become.

In order to examine the direction of a relationship, you need to use the data generated from the interval scale and calculate Pearson's correlation coefficient by using SPSS. You can do this by choosing (from the dialog box):

> Analyze
>> Correlate
>>> Bivariate...
>>>> (Select relevant variables)
>>>>> Option...
>>>>>> Select:
>>>>>> (a) Pearson correlation coefficient
>>>>>> (b) Test of significance – two-tailed, one-tailed

One-tailed tests should be used when there is a specific direction (positive or negative) to the hypothesis being tested (for example, if the amount of time spent on training increases, the productivity of the employees will increase/decrease). Two-tailed tests should be used when a relationship is expected, but the direction of the relationship is not predicted (Field, 2000).

These calculations enable quantification of the strength of a relationship between variables, and this value lies between −1 and +1. A coefficient of +1 indicates that the two variables are perfectly positively correlated – as one variable increases, the value of the other variable will increase. Conversely, a coefficient of −1 indicates a precise negative relationship – when the value of one variable increases, that of the other will decrease. Correlation coefficients between −1 and +1 represent positive and negative correlations, whereas a coefficient of zero indicates no linear relationship.

Suppose that your research investigates the customer and service provider interaction at front office. You are particularly interested in finding out whether the anxiety level of the service provider will influence service performance. Your research predicted that at higher levels of anxiety, service performance would be poor. Since you predicted a specific kind of relationship before the data were collected, the test for these variables should be one-tailed. Similarly, you predicted that the time spent on training would increase the service performance. Therefore, the test for these variables should be one-tailed too.

You run your statistical analysis according to the steps mentioned earlier, and the SPSS output provides a matrix of the correlation coefficients for the three variables (see Box 10.8).

Box 10.8	Correlations			
		Service performance	Service anxiety	Time spent training
Service performance	Pearson correlation	1.000	−0.424**	0.379**
	Sig. (one-tailed)	.	0.000	0.000
	N	106	106	106
Service anxiety	Pearson correlation	−0.424**	1.000	−0.706**
	Sig. (one-tailed)	0.000	.	0.000
	N	106	106	106
Time spent training	Pearson correlation	0.379**	−0.706**	1.000
	Sig. (one-tailed)	0.000	0.000	.
	N	106	106	106

**Correlation is significant at the 0.01 level (one-tailed).

The above results indicate that service performance is negatively related to service anxiety, with a Pearson correlation coefficient of $r = -0.424$. What is also important is that there is a less than 0.001 probability that a correlation coefficient this big would have occurred by chance in a sample of 106 people (as indicated by the ** after the coefficient). The figure is very close to zero (expressed as zero in the table), and with a probability value below 0.05 you should have confidence in your findings. Your results also show that service performance is positively related to the amount of time spent on training, with a coefficient of 0.379, which is also significant. Finally, service anxiety appears to be negatively related to the time spent on training ($r = -0.706$).

When it comes to communicating your results to your examiner and practitioners, your synthesis of the above results can be introduced as follows:

As anxiety about offering good quality service increases, the service performance decreases (e.g. the duration of service offer increases). Investment in training appears to be crucial because as the amount of employee training increases, the service performance increases. More importantly, as the amount of training increases the service provider's anxiety decreases.

t-test

There are many instances when you might be interested to know whether two groups are different from each other in relation to a variable which is measured on an interval or ratio scale. Research questions such as 'Do male and female consumers have different attitudes towards the "Starbucks" brand?', 'Do international students (who have had work experience overseas) perform better in organizational settings than students who have had only home country work experience?' or 'Do returning migrant entrepreneurs have a different investment pattern for their savings from that of those entrepreneurs who have lived and worked only in their own countries?' can be answered by using a *t*-test to see whether there are any significant differences in the means for the two groups in the variable of interest. In a *t*-test, a nominal variable that is split into two groups (male versus female consumers; students who have had work experience overseas versus students who have not; returning migrant entrepreneurs versus home entrepreneurs) is tested to examine whether there is a significant mean difference between the two groups on a dependent variable which is measured on an interval or ratio scale (attitudes towards the brand, work performance, investment pattern of savings).

When you use a *t*-test, you take into consideration the means and standard deviations of two groups on the variable and test whether the numerical difference in the means is significantly different (Sekaran, 2000). When you run the *t*-test (independent samples test), you choose (from the dialog box):

> Analyze
> > *Compare means*
> > > *Independent-samples* t-test...
> > > > Select a single grouping variable and click Define groups to specify groups to be compared
> > > > > *Options...*
> > > > > > (specify confidence level required – 0.05, 0.01, etc.)

Suppose that your study compares male and female (nominal variable) front-office employees in terms of their speed of check-in service (ratio variable). Your research question has been formulated as, 'Do female employees have different check-in service speed compared to male employees?' You have also developed your hypotheses – null and alternate:

H_0: There is no significant difference between the service speed of male and female employees

H_1: There is a significant difference between the service speed of male and female employees.

You have run your statistical analysis by following the steps described above, and have specified the confidence level as 0.05 (which will indicate the confidence level of your analysis). The output from the independent *t*-test consists of two tables. In Box 10.9 ('Group statistics'), you can find summary statistics for the two experimental conditions. From these, you can see that both groups had 30 subjects (column labelled *N*). Female employees who provide service to customers had a mean of

Box 10.9	Group statistics (example)				
	Sex	**N**	**Mean**	**Std deviation**	**Std error Mean**
Speed of service	Female	30	139.89	31.074	5.872
	Male	30	123.00	14.726	3.140

139.9, with a standard deviation of 31. Moreover, the standard error of that group (the standard deviation of the sampling distribution) is 5.87 ($SE = 31/\sqrt{30} = 5.87$). In addition, the table shows you that the average speed of service for male employees was 123, with a standard deviation of 14.726 and a standard error of 3.14.

By using the values in Box 10.9, you can easily tell whether variances are similar (for example, you know that standard deviations of the two groups are 31.074 and 14.726, and if you square these values then you get the variances). However, this measure would be very subjective and open to academic debate. Fortunately, the second table of output (Box 10.10) contains the main independent samples test statistics, including Levene's test, and can help to ease concerns.

Levene's test is similar to a *t*-test in that it tests the hypothesis that the variances in the two groups are equal (i.e. the difference between the variances is zero) (Field, 2005: 238). Therefore, if Levene's test is below the conventional *P* value, which is 0.05 (in other words, it is statistically significant), you can conclude that the null hypothesis is not correct and the variances are significantly different. This means that the assumption of equal variances has been violated. However, if Levene's test is above the conventional (0.05) *P* value (in other words it is not statistically significant), you must accept the null hypothesis, which suggests that there is no difference between the variances.

Suppose that the independent sample testing in the service speed/gender example produced the results shown in Box 10.10.

Box 10.10	Independent samples test								
		Levene's test for equality of variances		**t-test for equality of means**			**Mean differ- ence**	**Std error differ- ence**	**95 per cent confidence interval Difference**	
		F	**Sig.**	**t**	**df**	**Sig. (two- tailed)**			**Lower**	**Upper**
Speed of service	Equal variances assumed	15.769	0.000	2.347	48	0.023	16.89	7.196	2.424	31.362
	Equal variances not assumed			2.537	40.398	0.015	16.89	6.659	3.439	30.347

For the data in Box 10.10, Levene's test is significant (because $P = 0.000$, which is below 0.05). Therefore, you can conclude that the null hypothesis is not correct and the variances are significantly different. Given this result, you should read the test statistics in the row labelled 'Equal variances not assumed' (as indicated by the arrow in the table). Had Levene's test been insignificant, then you would have read the test statistics from the 'Equal variances assumed' row.

Having decided which variance row to read, you can move on to look at the *t*-test itself. When you are reading the *t*-test, you should be interested in whether the Sig. (two-tailed) value, known as the *t* value, is less than or greater than 0.05. In this case the two-tailed value of P is 0.015, which is less than 0.05. Therefore, you will have to conclude that there is a significant difference between the means of females and males. You can infer that there are differences between the female and male employees in terms of their speed of service at the front desk.

ANOVA (analysis of variance)

The *t*-test is an appropriate analysis technique for measuring the differences between two groups. However, there are circumstances when your research covers more than two groups and you need to compare them to examine the mean differences. ANOVA (analysis of variance) is a popular statistical technique among hospitality and tourism researchers, and allows you to test for significant mean differences in variables between more than two groups on an interval- or ratio-scaled dependent variable (Sekaran, 2000). For example, would there be a significant difference in the performance by the following groups of students?

- Those who attend the class every week and follow the course online
- Those who follow the course on-line only
- Those who have done none of the above.

Another example would be grouping a hotel's customers according to the frequency of their stay in a hotel (low, medium or high) and then examining the differences between these groups in terms of their attitudes towards the product; grouping them according to their educational attainment (i.e., primary school, secondary school, college and university graduates) and examine the differences between these groups in terms of their attitudes towards different marketing campaigns, and so on.

In order to be able to perform an ANOVA test, you have to ensure that each data value is independent and does not relate to any of the other values – for example, that the same person is not being tested repeatedly (Saunders *et al.*, 2007: 449). In addition, the number of cases in each group should be large (thirty or more). When you run your ANOVA test, you choose (from the dialog box):

Analyze

    Compare means

        One-way ANOVA...

            (Select the dependent variable(s) and select the grouping variable by clicking on factor)

In an ANOVA test, the F ratio or F statistic represents the differences between groups. If the likelihood of any difference between groups occurring by chance alone is low, this will be represented by a large F ratio with a probability of less than 0.05 (Saunders *et al.*, 2007: 448). Therefore, when you are reading the SPSS output of an ANOVA test you should pay attention to both the F value and significance. The F value shows the extent of differences between groups; which is the basic purpose of carrying out an ANOVA test; the *P* value shows the significance of the differences between groups and, as stated earlier, this should be less than 0.05 in order to be able to claim a statistically meaningful outcome.

Suppose that you are carrying out a study that investigates the differences between the marketing strategies of small businesses. Your research predicted that marketing strategies of small businesses differ according to the sector of operations, and the following hypotheses were developed accordingly:

H_1: The importance of business location will change according to small firms that operate in different sectors

H_2: The importance of production differentiation will change according to small firms that operate in different sectors.

Your grouping variable in this example is 'sectors' (catering, retailing, professional services, wholesaling and manufacturing), and dependent variables are 'business location' (measured as business owners' perception of importance) and 'product differentiation' (measured as business owners' perception of importance). Your sample was proportionally divided across different sectors, and each group consisted of more than thirty cases. You run your statistical analysis according to the steps mentioned earlier, and the SPSS output provides the ANOVA table shown in Box 10.11.

Box 10.11	ANOVA						
			Sum of squares	df	Mean square	F	Sig.
Business location * Café/restaurant/ takeaway = 1, Retail = 2, Service = 3, Wholesale = 4, Manufacture = 5	Between groups	(Combined)	107.345	4	26.836	9.729	0.000
	Within groups		612.329	222	2.758		
	Total		719.674	226			
Product differentiation * Café/restaurant/ takeaway = 1, Retail = 2, Service = 3, Wholesale = 4, Manufacture = 5	Between groups	(Combined)	9.343	4	2.336	.832	0.506
	Within groups		595.496	212	2.809		
	Total		604.839	216			

When you look at the F ratio for business location, you can clearly see that it is high ($F = 9.729$) and this value is significant at the 0.000 level. This implies that the first hypothesis is substantiated. Conversely, there are not significant differences in the mean importance of product differentiation with the F ratio, 0.832, which is not significant (P value is 0.506, i.e. above the conventional probability value of 0.05).

Multiple regression analysis

Pearson's correlation gives you the opportunity to assess the strength of relationship between two variables. However, it does not tell you how much of the variance in the dependent variable will be explained when several independent variables are proposed theoretically to influence it simultaneously (Sekaran, 2000). Multiple regression analysis gives you the opportunity to examine the simultaneous effects of several independent variables on a dependent variable – for example, when the variance in a dependent variable (e.g. sales growth of a small family-owned restaurant) is explained by five independent variables, A, B, C, D and E (e.g. educational background of the owner, employee training, marketing activities, incentives offered to the employees, use of informal networks such as friends and relatives to raise capital).

You should note that not only are the five independent variables correlated to the dependent variable (in other words have the potential to affect the sales growth of the small family-owned restaurant); they might also be inter-correlated. For example, the educational background of a small business owner might influence his or her attitude towards employee training or marketing – whether there is a need for a more professional approach to management and marketing. When these variables are jointly regressed against the dependent variable in an effort to explain the variance in it, the individual correlations are collapsed into what is called a multiple correlation (Sekaran, 2000: 406). The square of multiple r or R^2 can take on any value between 0 and +1, and it measures the proportion of the variation in a dependent variable (sales growth) that can be explained statistically by the independent variable(s) (attitude towards training, marketing).

Besides the R^2 value, you need to know the F statistic and its significance level in order to be able to interpret the results of multiple regression analysis. For example, if the R^2 is 0.70 with an F value of 31.20 and a significance level of $P < 0.001$, then you can say that 70 percent of the variance has been significantly explained by the set of independent variables. You can also claim that the confidence level of your results is high, because there is less than 0.01 per cent chance of this not happening.

When you are performing multiple regression analysis by using SPSS you choose (from the dialog box):

> Analyze
> > Regression
> > > Linear...
> > > > (Enter dependent and independent variables)

Suppose that your study examines the relationship between employment growth (increase in the number of employees) (dependent variable) of a small family firm and four independent variables:

1. Its approach to recruitment (whether through formal or informal channels)
2. Employee training

3. Employee incentives offered to the employees
4. Number of family member employees.

You have expressed your research ideas in the null and alternate hypotheses as follows:

H_0: The four independent variables will not significantly explain the variance in employment growth of the family firm

H_1: The four independent variables will significantly explain the variance in employment growth of the family firm.

Box 10.12 outlines the independent variables used to explain the variance in the dependent variable (employment growth).

Box 10.12	Independent variables
Variables	**Name of variable and transformation into codes**
Extent of family employees	Percentage of family employment
Employee training	If invested in employee business training = 1, otherwise = 0
Employee incentives	If invested in employee incentives = 1, otherwise = 0
Recruitment	Most favoured recruitment method is formal = 1; otherwise = 0

Your statistical analysis would then yield the results shown in Box 10.13.

Box 10.13 | Coefficients

Model		Unstandardized coefficients		Standardized coefficients	t	Sig.
		B	Std error	Beta		
1	(Constant)	−0.077	0.044		−1.725	0.09
	Familyemploy	−0.06	0.028	−0.183	−2.109	0.07
	Recruitment	0.042	0.031	0.121	1.364	0.18
	Incentemploy	−0.044	0.048	−0.085	−0.914	0.36
	Employeetrain	0.171	0.032	0.522	5.366	0
a	Dependent variable: Compound employment growth					

When you are interpreting the results of the analysis, you need to pay attention to the coefficients table – in particular the beta, significance results and t value. The significance value indicates how strong an independent variable (in terms of relationship) is in explaining a dependent variable. In the example given here, you can see that the highest number in the beta column is 0.5, for employee training, which is significant at the 0.001 level (presented as 0 in the table). You can also see that this is the only independent variable that is significant ($P < 0.001$). The t value indicates the direction of the relationship – whether it is positive or negative – and by looking at this you can infer that there is a positive relationship between firm training and firm growth. In other words, if you increase employee training, this will have a positive impact on the firm's growth.

Summary

- Quantitative data analysis allows you to represent the opinions, attitudes and behaviours of people or organizations in quantitative terms and draw interferences from numerical analysis.
- Different types of scales generating quantitative data determine the type of statistical test for quantitative data analysis.
- A variable is an indicator of interest in a research project, and may take any of a specified set of values.
- Coding your data involves representing each observation in a simple and consistent way so that it can be entered easily into the software for analysis.
- Examine the structure of your data before testing your hypotheses. Knowing which particular test to use is much more important than knowing how to calculate them by SPSS.
- You can explore your data by undertaking descriptive statistics.
- Bar charts are suitable for data that are generated from descriptive (or nominal) or ranked (ordinal) scales, and are often used to present data in the reports. Pie charts demonstrate the proportion or share of occurrences in the data.
- A cross-tabulation is the representation of two variables in a matrix where all answers in one variable are presented in rows, and all answers in the other are presented in columns.
- The chi-square test detects whether there is a relationship between two variables.
- A Pearson correlation test can allow you to measure the degree to which change in a dependent variable is related to a change in one or more independent variables.
- Independent samples t-tests and ANOVA are used to assess whether there is a difference between two or more groups.
- Multiple regression analysis enables you to assess the impact of two or more independent variables on one dependent variable.

Exercises: quantitative statistical analysis

The following exercises are based on a study of 112 British and Cypriot entrepreneurs who run small and medium-sized firms in different sectors of the catering industry, namely restaurants, cafés and takeaways. The spreadsheet at the end of this section is extracted from the 'Data view' of SPSS, and will represent your data for the exercises. Each column represents a variable for which data are available, and each row represents the data for an individual or case. In the spreadsheet, BR refers to 'British' and CY refers to 'Cypriot'. In the same spreadsheet, you will see that different groups of data are given different numerical numbers – in other words, they are coded (as is the case with variables such as country of origin, educational attainment, martial status and the others) in order to facilitate the analysis process. In the case of sales, the growth of sales over a period of time (if the sales of the firm have grown) is coded as 1, and the decline of sales is coded as 0 (amount of sales have declined). You have to make sure that you select the numerical statement of the variables (coded according to the numbers) whenever you are asked to select your variables for the analysis.

Before you use SPSS to carry out a number of tests and analysis, input the following data into SPSS. The details of the variables are not provided here, so your SPSS screen will only show the 'Data view' and not the details of the variables. However, this should not prevent you carrying out the following tasks. Make sure that you select coded data when you are undertaking the exercises.

1. Undertake a frequency distribution by clicking on Analyze/Descriptive statistics/Frequencies, selecting the 'Country of origin' variable and moving it into the Variable(s) box.
2. Calculate the mean, mode and other measures of central tendency by clicking on Analyze/Descriptive statistics/Descriptives and then selecting the 'Marital status' variable and moving it into the Variable(s) box. You can repeat this exercise by selecting 'Educational attainment', 'Country of origin' and 'Sectors' variables.
3. Produce a bar chart by clicking on Analyze/Descriptive statistics/Frequencies, selecting the variable 'Sector' and clicking on Charts and then Bar charts. You can practise this exercise by creating another bar chart for the same variable but with the vertical axis displaying percentages rather than frequencies. All you need to do is to change chart values from frequencies to percentages.
4. Calculate the standard deviation by clicking on Analyze/Descriptive statistics/Descriptives and then selecting the ratio-scaled data from the table.
5. Create a cross-tabulation of one variable against another by clicking on Analyze/Descriptive statistics/Crosstabs and then selecting Row(s) variable Educational attainment and Column(s) variable Sector (restaurant, takeaway, café) (coded sectors), using the same principles as when selecting frequencies.
6. Carry out a chi-square test to investigate whether there is a relationship between the sales growth of the firms and the sectors of operation.

You can use Field (2005) to run the statistical tests when working with SPSS.

Spreadsheet

Country of origin	Country of origin (coded)	Education level	Education (coded)	Marital status	Marital status (coded)	Sectors	Sectors (coded)	Sales growth (coded)
CY	1.00	PRIMARY	1.00	MARRIED	1.00	CAFE	1.00	1.00
CY	1.00	A LEVEL	3.00	MARRIED	1.00	TAKEAWAY	3.00	1.00
CY	1.00	PRIMARY	1.00	MARRIED	1.00	TAKEAWAY	3.00	1.00
BR	0.00	PRIMARY	1.00	MARRIED	1.00	TAKEAWAY	3.00	1.00
BR	0.00	PRIMARY	1.00	SINGLE	0.00	TAKEAWAY	3.00	1.00
BR	0.00	PRIMARY	1.00	MARRIED	1.00	TAKEAWAY	3.00	1.00
CY	1.00	A LEVEL	3.00	MARRIED	1.00	CAFE	1.00	0.00
CY	1.00	SECONDARY	2.00	MARRIED	1.00	RESTAURANT	2.00	0.00
CY	1.00	A LEVEL	3.00	MARRIED	1.00	RESTAURANT	2.00	1.00
CY	1.00	BACHELOR	4.00	MARRIED	1.00	RESTAURANT	2.00	0.00
BR	0.00	A LEVEL	3.00	MARRIED	1.00	CAFE	1.00	0.00
CY	1.00	PRIMARY	1.00	MARRIED	1.00	CAFE	1.00	1.00
BR	0.00	SECONDARY	2.00	SINGLE	0.00	CAFE	1.00	1.00
CY	1.00	BACHELOR	4.00	MARRIED	1.00	TAKEAWAY	3.00	1.00
CY	1.00	PRIMARY	1.00	MARRIED	1.00	CAFE	1.00	1.00
BR	0.00	SECONDARY	2.00	MARRIED	1.00	TAKEAWAY	3.00	1.00
CY	1.00	SECONDARY	2.00	MARRIED	1.00	CAFE	1.00	1.00
CY	1.00	A LEVEL	3.00	MARRIED	1.00	CAFE	1.00	1.00
CY	1.00	SECONDARY	2.00	MARRIED	1.00	RESTAURANT	2.00	0.00
BR	0.00	PRIMARY	1.00	MARRIED	1.00	TAKEAWAY	3.00	1.00
BR	0.00	PRIMARY	1.00	MARRIED	1.00	TAKEAWAY	3.00	1.00
CY	1.00	SECONDARY	2.00	MARRIED	1.00	TAKEAWAY	3.00	1.00
CY	1.00	SECONDARY	2.00	MARRIED	1.00	CAFE	1.00	0.00
CY	1.00	PRIMARY	1.00	MARRIED	1.00	TAKEAWAY	3.00	0.00
CY	1.00	SECONDARY	2.00	MARRIED	1.00	TAKEAWAY	3.00	1.00
CY	1.00	PRIMARY	1.00	MARRIED	1.00	TAKEAWAY	3.00	1.00
CY	1.00	SECONDARY	2.00	MARRIED	1.00	RESTAURANT	2.00	0.00
CY	1.00	SECONDARY	2.00	MARRIED	1.00	CAFE	1.00	0.00
CY	1.00	SECONDARY	2.00	MARRIED	1.00	TAKEAWAY	3.00	1.00
CY	1.00	SECONDARY	2.00	MARRIED	1.00	TAKEAWAY	3.00	1.00
BR	0.00	SECONDARY	2.00	MARRIED	1.00	TAKEAWAY	3.00	1.00
BR	0.00	PRIMARY	1.00	SINGLE	0.00	RESTAURANT	2.00	0.00

BR	0.00	PRIMARY	1.00	SINGLE	0.00	TAKEAWAY	3.00	1.00
BR	0.00	PRIMARY	1.00	MARRIED	1.00	TAKEAWAY	3.00	1.00
BR	0.00	PRIMARY	1.00	MARRIED	1.00	RESTAURANT	2.00	0.00
BR	0.00	BACHELOR	4.00	MARRIED	1.00	RESTAURANT	2.00	0.00
BR	0.00	SECONDARY	2.00	SINGLE	0.00	TAKEAWAY	3.00	1.00
CY	1.00	SECONDARY	2.00	MARRIED	1.00	RESTAURANT	2.00	0.00
CY	1.00	A LEVELS	3.00	MARRIED	1.00	RESTAURANT	2.00	0.00
CY	1.00	SECONDARY	2.00	MARRIED	1.00	RESTAURANT	2.00	0.00
CY	1.00	A LEVELS	3.00	MARRIED	1.00	RESTAURANT	2.00	0.00
CY	1.00	SECONDARY	2.00	MARRIED	1.00	RESTAURANT	2.00	0.00
CY	1.00	BACHELOR	4.00	MARRIED	1.00	TAKEAWAY	3.00	1.00
BR	0.00	A LEVELS	3.00	SINGLE	0.00	RESTAURANT	2.00	0.00
CY	1.00	SECONDARY	2.00	MARRIED	1.00	TAKEAWAY	3.00	0.00
BR	0.00	A LEVELS	3.00	MARRIED	1.00	CAFE	1.00	0.00
CY	1.00	SECONDARY	2.00	SINGLE	0.00	CAFE	1.00	1.00
BR	0.00	PRIMARY	1.00	MARRIED	1.00	TAKEAWAY	3.00	1.00
BR	0.00	A LEVELS	3.00	MARRIED	1.00	RESTAURANT	2.00	0.00
BR	0.00	NONE	1.00	MARRIED	1.00	RESTAURANT	2.00	0.00
BR	0.00	SECONDARY	2.00	MARRIED	1.00	TAKEAWAY	3.00	1.00
BR	0.00	PRIMARY	1.00	MARRIED	1.00	TAKEAWAY	3.00	1.00
CY	1.00	SECONDARY	2.00	MARRIED	1.00	CAFE	1.00	0.00
CY	1.00	SECONDARY	2.00	SINGLE	0.00	TAKEAWAY	3.00	1.00
BR	0.00	SECONDARY	2.00	MARRIED	1.00	CAFE	1.00	1.00
BR	0.00	PRIMARY	1.00	MARRIED	1.00	TAKEAWAY	3.00	1.00
BR	0.00	PRIMARY	1.00	MARRIED	1.00	CAFE	1.00	0.00
CY	1.00	SECONDARY	2.00	MARRIED	1.00	TAKEAWAY	3.00	1.00
CY	1.00	PRIMARY	1.00	MARRIED	1.00	TAKEAWAY	3.00	1.00
BR	0.00	SECONDARY	2.00	MARRIED	1.00	TAKEAWAY	3.00	1.00
BR	0.00	SECONDARY	2.00	SINGLE	0.00	TAKEAWAY	3.00	1.00
CY	1.00	SECONDARY	2.00	MARRIED	1.00	TAKEAWAY	3.00	1.00
BR	0.00	PRIMARY	1.00	MARRIED	1.00	CAFE	1.00	1.00
BR	0.00	PRIMARY	1.00	MARRIED	1.00	TAKEAWAY	3.00	1.00
CY	1.00	SECONDARY	2.00	MARRIED	1.00	CAFE	1.00	1.00
BR	0.00	SECONDARY	2.00	MARRIED	1.00	TAKEAWAY	3.00	1.00
BR	0.00	SECONDARY	2.00	MARRIED	1.00	TAKEAWAY	3.00	1.00
CY	1.00	SECONDARY	2.00	SINGLE	0.00	TAKEAWAY	3.00	0.00
BR	0.00	PRIMARY	1.00	MARRIED	1.00	TAKEAWAY	3.00	1.00
CY	1.00	PRIMARY	1.00	MARRIED	1.00	TAKEAWAY	3.00	1.00
BR	0.00	PRIMARY	1.00	MARRIED	1.00	CAFE	1.00	0.00
CY	1.00	SECONDARY	2.00	MARRIED	1.00	TAKEAWAY	3.00	1.00
CY	1.00	PRIMARY	1.00	MARRIED	1.00	TAKEAWAY	3.00	0.00
CY	1.00	PRIMARY	1.00	MARRIED	1.00	CAFE	1.00	1.00

(Continued)

Spreadsheet (Continued)

Country of origin	Country of origin (coded)	Education level	Education (coded)	Marital status	Marital status (coded)	Sectors	Sectors (coded)	Sales growth (coded)
CY	1.00	SECONDARY	2.00	MARRIED	1.00	TAKEAWAY	3.00	1.00
CY	1.00	PRIMARY	1.00	MARRIED	1.00	CAFE	1.00	1.00
BR	0.00	SECONDARY	2.00	MARRIED	1.00	TAKEAWAY	3.00	1.00
BR	0.00	PRIMARY	1.00	MARRIED	1.00	TAKEAWAY	3.00	1.00
CY	1.00	SECONDARY	2.00	MARRIED	1.00	TAKEAWAY	3.00	1.00
CY	1.00	SECONDARY	2.00	SINGLE	0.00	CAFE	1.00	1.00
BR	0.00	SECONDARY	2.00	MARRIED	1.00	RESTAURANT	2.00	0.00
BR	0.00	SECONDARY	2.00	MARRIED	1.00	CAFE	1.00	1.00
CY	1.00	SECONDARY	2.00	MARRIED	1.00	RESTAURANT	2.00	0.00
CY	1.00	SECONDARY	2.00	MARRIED	1.00	CAFE	1.00	1.00
CY	1.00	BACHELOR	4.00	MARRIED	1.00	CAFE	1.00	1.00
CY	1.00	A LEVELS	3.00	SINGLE	0.00	RESTAURANT	2.00	0.00
BR	0.00	A LEVELS	3.00	MARRIED	1.00	CAFE	1.00	1.00
BR	0.00	A LEVELS	3.00	SINGLE	0.00	CAFE	1.00	1.00
CY	1.00	SECONDARY	2.00	MARRIED	1.00	CAFE	1.00	1.00
BR	0.00	PRIMARY	1.00	MARRIED	1.00	TAKEAWAY	3.00	1.00
CY	1.00	A LEVELS	3.00	MARRIED	1.00	RESTAURANT	2.00	0.00
CY	0.00	A LEVELS	3.00	SINGLE	0.00	RESTAURANT BAR	2.00	0.00
BR	0.00	SECONDARY	2.00	MARRIED	1.00	RESTAURANT	2.00	0.00
CY	1.00	LYCE	3.00	MARRIED	1.00	TAKEAWAY	3.00	1.00
CY	1.00	A LEVELS	3.00	MARRIED	1.00	TAKEAWAY	3.00	1.00
BR	0.00	A LEVELS	3.00	MARRIED	1.00	RESTAURANT	2.00	0.00
BR	0.00	BACHELOR	4.00	SINGLE	0.00	RESTAURANT	2.00	0.00
CY	0.00	BACHELOR	4.00	SINGLE	0.00	RESTAURANT	2.00	1.00
BR	0.00	SECONDARY	2.00	MARRIED	1.00	RESTAURANT	2.00	0.00
BR	0.00	BACHELOR	4.00	MARRIED	1.00	RESTAURANT	2.00	1.00
CY	0.00	SECONDARY	2.00	MARRIED	1.00	CAFE	1.00	1.00
CY	1.00	BACHELOR	4.00	MARRIED	1.00	RESTAURANT	2.00	1.00
CY	1.00	A LEVELS	3.00	MARRIED	1.00	RESTAURANT	2.00	1.00
BR	0.00	A LEVELS	3.00	MARRIED	1.00	TAKEAWAY	3.00	1.00

CY	1.00	A LEVELS	3.00	MARRIED	1.00	RESTAURANT	2.00	0.00
BR	0.00	SECONDARY	2.00	MARRIED	1.00	RESTAURANT	2.00	0.00
CY	1.00	A LEVELS	3.00	MARRIED	1.00	CAFE	1.00	0.00
CY	1.00	A LEVELS	3.00	MARRIED	1.00	TAKEAWAY	3.00	1.00
BR	0.00	BACHELOR	4.00	SINGLE	0.00	TAKEAWAY	3.00	1.00
BR	0.00	A LEVELS	3.00	MARRIED	1.00	CAFE	1.00	1.00
CY	1.00	SECONDARY	2.00	MARRIED	1.00	CAFE	1.00	1.00
CY	1.00	SECONDARY	2.00	MARRIED	1.00	CAFE	1.00	1.00
CY	1.00	BACHELOR	4.00	MARRIED	1.00	TAKEAWAY	3.00	1.00
BR	0.00	BACHELOR	4.00	SINGLE	0.00	RESTAURANT	2.00	0.00
CY	1.00	BACHELOR	4.00	MARRIED	1.00	RESTAURANT	2.00	0.00
CY	0.00	PRIMARY	1.00	MARRIED	1.00	CAFE	1.00	0.00
CY	1.00	SECONDARY	2.00	MARRIED	1.00	CAFE	1.00	1.00

Review questions

1. What are the different types of scales?
2. Suggest two variables that would be natural candidates for nominal scales, and set up categories for each.
3. Develop an ordinal scale for consumer preferences for different budget brands of hotels.
4. The following list of statements reflects the attitudes/feelings/opinion of managers regarding their performance in terms of competition. Take the statements and devise an interval scale to measure them. Reword the questions if you wish, without changing their meaning.
   - Our business often leads the competition (our competitors have to follow us)
   - Because of the competition, our business must be very proactive in the marketplace in order to achieve our business objectives
   - When our competitors develop a new product or a new business method, our business quickly responds to it and adopts it
   - We are willing to try new ways of doing things and seek unusual, novel solutions
   - Our business constantly introduces new products/services in order to serve new customers/markets.
5. What type of analysis does each scale lead to?
6. What are the key steps a researcher needs to go through in order to organize, code and enter the data to SPSS?
7. What do you use bar charts and pie charts for?
8. How can cross-tabulation help your analysis?
9. When would you use a chi-square test?
10. What is the difference between a chi-square test and a Pearson correlation test?
11. When do you use a t-test?
12. When do you use an ANOVA test?
13. When do you use multiple regression analysis?

References

Field, A. (2005). *Discovering Statistics Using SPSS*, 2nd edn. London: Sage Publications.

Finnie, M., Champion, S., Holden, J., Collyer, G. and Noble, S. (2000). *Pan-European Hotels*. Deutsche Bank, 12 January.

Gill, J. and Johnson, P. (1997). *Research Methods for Managers*, 2nd edn. London: Sage Publications.

Robson, C. (1999). *Real World Research*. Oxford: Blackwell.

Saunders, M., Lewis, P. and Thornhill, A. (2007). *Research Methods for Business Students*. London: Prentice Hall Financial Times.

Sekaran, U. (2000). *Research Methods for Business: A Skill-Building Approach*. New York, NY: John Wiley & Sons, Inc.

Slattery, P. (1996). International development of hotel chains. In: R. Kotas, R. Teare, J. Logie, C. Jayawardena and J. Bowen (eds), *The International Hospitality Business*. London: Cassell, pp. 30–37.

Further reading

Bryman, A. and Cramer, C. (2001). *Quantitative Data Analysis with SPSS Release 10 for Windows: A Guide for Social Scientists*. London: Routledge.

Chung, K. H. and Shin, J. I. (2004). The relationship between destination cues of Asian countries and Korean tourist images. *Asia Pacific Journal of Marketing and Logistics*, 16(2), 82–100.

Israeli, A. A. (2002). A preliminary investigation of the importance of site accessibility factors for disabled tourists. *Journal of Travel Research*, 41(1), 101–104.

Chapter 11
Writing up the dissertation

He who has put a good finish to his undertaking is said to have placed a golden crown to the whole.
(Eustathius, Archbishop of Thessalonica, 1134–1194; commentary on the Iliad *cited in*
Eustathius, 1970: 75)

The dissertation (or research report) is the document that will evidence your research journey. Just like the photo album of your summer holidays, it should be structured with extra care in order for you to put 'a golden crown to the whole'. Indeed, the structure of your dissertation is very important, and all institutions emphasize this by providing all research students with very detailed guidelines regarding the document's style and appearance. A good starting point would be for you to review one or two well-written and -presented dissertations (your supervisor should be able to guide you in this). Pay particular attention to the overall style as well as the way the authors have used headings, subheadings, tables, graphs, etc. This way you will form a pretty clear idea of what your finished work should look like. Although presentation requirements may vary from institution to institution, the generally accepted structure of a dissertation is as follows:

- Cover page
- Abstract
- Acknowledgements
- Table of contents
- List of tables and figures
- Introduction
- Chapter(s) of literature review
- Chapter of methodology
- Chapter of findings and discussion
- Conclusion
- References
- Appendices

Writing up may appear a very daunting task, but if you have invested your time in writing a good proposal then a large part of your work is already in place (introduction, methodology, part of your literature review). You will only need to edit what you have already written (change the tense from future to past), taking into account the feedback that you received for the proposal and any other changes you made during your research.

The fact that the dissertation is a rigorously structured piece of work does not necessarily mean that the writing up has to be done in the same order – for example, you do not have to start writing your dissertation with the abstract. In fact, it is often advised that the preliminary sections should be the very last parts that are written. The most productive approach in writing the dissertation is to begin with those sections that you are most comfortable with and then build your dissertation around them. That said, the advice offered in this chapter follows the conventional order.

Cover page, abstract, acknowledgements and contents

These pages of your dissertation are often the last ones you worry about, after you have written up the rest of the work. Nevertheless, they are very important, as they will be the first ones your examiners read.

The format of the cover page is usually dictated by the institution, so there is not much you can do to change it. The only part where you have a role to play is in the title. As with every written work, the title needs to convey accurately the content of the work in a manner that will capture the attention of the audience. In Chapter 1, we discussed the 'working title' as a point of continuous reference and focus during your research. You will have to build on that and come up with a title that will better 'sell' your dissertation to your examiners. There are no specific rules for this, but you should keep in mind that the title must accurately depict your study (research question) and its context. Try to confine the title to ten to twelve words, eliminating articles and prepositions where they are not absolutely necessary. Avoid using general terms such as 'A Study of …'; 'A Survey of …'; 'An Investigation of …', etc.

The abstract is the summary of your dissertation. Its length may vary from 250 to 350 words, and within this limitation you must answer convincingly the following four questions:

1. WHAT? (What is the question I am trying to answer with this study?)
2. WHY? (Why is it an important question? What gap is it going to fill?)
3. HOW? (How did I conduct my research? What sample did I use? Where?)
4. SO WHAT? (What were my main findings and what are their implications?)

A popular approach to writing abstracts is to use a 'structured abstract', which consists of a number of set elements, thus helping researchers to provide the information that is most useful regarding their work (Box 11.1).

In the acknowledgements page, you just thank and recognize people who have supported you during your research. Usually these are your supervisor, your family, the participants, and other persons that possibly assisted you with your dissertation. This is also where you acknowledge any special permission granted to use published or unpublished material. Although this page is usually written with a smile on your face, it is important to remember that its tone must be academic and appropriate to scholarly work.

The table of contents and the list of tables and figures are the signposts of your dissertation for the reader. They can also be used as a checklist to help you ensure that you have not missed anything, and that your work follows a logical thread that can be easily understood by the reader. Examiners place high importance on the logical structure of a dissertation, and the first place they will look when evaluating this is

Box 11.1	The structured abstract

1. Choose a category for the paper (conceptual or empirical)
2. Purpose of this paper (reasons for writing the paper or the aims of the study)
3. Design/methodology/approach (main methods used for the research; approach to the topic; theoretical or subject scope of the paper)
4. Findings (what was found during this study)
5. Research limitations/implications for further research (if applicable)
6. Implications for practitioners (if applicable)
7. Originality/value of paper (what is new in the paper; who will benefit from it).

(Adapted from http://juno.emeraldinsight.com/vl=5309899/cl= 145/nw=1/rpsv/literaticlub/editors/editorialadmin/abstracts.htm)

your table of contents. The list of tables and figures can help you to check quickly that the tables and figures are all in their right place in the main body of your dissertation, and that each is followed by appropriate discussion. It can also help you to check that you have been consistent in their format, wording and description.

Introduction

This is the first section where you will be rewarded for all the hard work you did on the dissertation proposal. Unless any significant changes have taken place during the period between the submission of your proposal and the writing up of your dissertation, there should not be much for you to do here. The structure of the introductory chapter is exactly the same as was presented in Chapter 7. You should describe the background and rationale of your study, state the purpose of the research, articulate your research objectives, and defend the originality of your study and its contribution to knowledge. At the end of the introductory chapter you can include an overview of your dissertation with a brief chapter-by-chapter description.

Literature review chapters

Here, too, the work you undertook for your proposal will be of great help. However, you will have done a lot more 'in-depth' reading for your study since then. You may have to use more than one chapter for your literature review, depending on the number of concepts you are investigating. Tools you have used previously – such as the A, B, C lists, the annotated bibliography and the literature map – will help you to structure and develop your literature review chapters further. It is advisable to write these chapters using a 'general-to-specific' pattern – in other words, to start with the more generic management literature on the topic and then move to the more specific hospitality and tourism-related literature. We cannot over-emphasize the fact that the literature review is not just a simple structured listing of the relevant literature, but instead a record of your 'dialogue with the literature', organized in a logical discussion of *what* has been found out in previous research rather than by whom (unless this is necessary and appropriately justified). As general advice, avoid organizing your literature in chronological order, because this will automatically lead you to giving literature 'report' rather than 'review'. Box 11.2 lists the three principles of engaging in a dialogue with the literature.

Box 11.2	The three 'dialogue with the literature' principles

1. Follow through the set of concepts you are exploring, comparing the ways other studies deal with them
2. Include all views, even those that might be contrary to your perspective, and evaluate them critically, discussing their strengths and weaknesses (theoretical weaknesses, empirical problems, things that have been ignored, ways in which the argument could be improved)
3. Indicate how previous research relates to your own research in terms of methodology or some other factor.

Remember that you need to start each chapter with a three- to five-line introduction that connects the current chapter with the previous and briefly explains its purpose. You should also finish it with a summary of the main points the reader needs to take from the overall discussion in order to follow the 'thread' of your study.

The research design chapter

This is another part of your dissertation that will benefit greatly from your research proposal. The only changes that you will probably have to make (apart from the tense of the verbs) are those recommended during your supervisor's feedback on the proposal. There are four more things that you will need to add to your design: the results of the pilot, the actual data collection process, an explanation of how data analysis worked in practice, and your retrospective reflection on your research experience.

The pilot you ran must be accurately described – how many runs, who were the subjects, what were the findings? If the pilot indicated that modifications were required regarding your instrument, then these should also be reported in detail, with appropriate justification of the new course of action.

The explanation of the actual data collection process involves telling the reader your story of the real-life complexities of doing research. For example, readers will be curious to know how you prepared yourself for the fieldwork, how you gained access to customers or organizations, where and how you conducted your interviews, how long each interview lasted, and how you managed the problem of interruptions whilst you were conducting the interviews. Remember that you have a lot to offer to your examiner and the other students who will read your dissertation and benefit from your experience.

It is also important to explain the reader how the data analysis worked in practice. This involves explaining how the data were organized, coded, categorized and put together again in a meaningful format, how templates (coding schema) were used for the analysis, how you benefited from 'your notes of reflections and interpretations', and how your analysis was questioned dialectically by your supervisor or your colleagues. Your purpose should be twofold here: to show the extent of the transparency in your analysis, and to give other people the opportunity to learn from your experience.

The last part of your research design should be devoted to reflection on the research experience and the limitations of your methodology as revealed in the fieldwork. This reflection might, for example, cover procedural problems inherent in the data collection techniques, access challenges, unanticipated issues of validity and reliability, difficulties in the definition of codes for analysis, etc. The main point here is not simply to acknowledge these problems and their effect on the generalizability of your study, but also to answer the question: 'What would you do differently, were you to start all over again?'

Presenting and discussing your findings

There are two different ways to approach this part of your dissertation. Some researchers present and simultaneously interpret their findings, whereas others prefer first to present and explain their data, then to offer their interpretations in a separate chapter (the discussion chapter). The latter approach is often recommended, because the findings chapter will allow you to describe clearly what you have found while the discussion chapter will enable you present what these findings mean, in your view, and how they compare with the extant literature. This is where you demonstrate your 'higher-order thinking' skills (see Chapter 1). You do not want to dilute them with data tables and graphs!

Your research may have yielded a large amount of raw data that have you analysed for weeks or perhaps even months before reaching your conclusions. You will have to decide how many data you will present in this section, and how – too few may convey the image of sloppy research, whereas too many may result in boredom for the reader. A good balance between what is important and meaningful for the reader, and presentation in tables, figures or plain narrative, always provides a successful solution to these questions. Therefore, you will have to screen your data, summarize them in tables or figures (graphs, models, etc.) where possible, and decide which of these best support your argument in the discussion section.

The most common approach to structuring the findings chapter is by order of research question (if you have more than one) or by order of hypotheses. Your dissertation needs to be consistent all the way through. If your problem statement involves two research questions, then your research design should address these two questions, and subsequently your findings section should be guided by these two questions. In a longitudinal study, a chronological order of your findings may perhaps be more appropriate. If your study involves the interaction of many variables, ordering your results by variable may make better sense. Finally, many qualitative studies order their findings by the pattern of behaviour or emerging themes. Whatever your approach, your introduction to the chapter should explain to the reader how you structured this part of your dissertation.

When writing the main body of this section, it is always helpful to start with an overview that objectively sums up your findings in the area you are presenting. You should refer the reader to any table or graph you have provided as evidence, then move to the more specific findings in the particular areas of your study (as with the literature review, follow a 'general-to-specific' pattern). Remember that the narrative here should complement your tables and figures, and not duplicate them. In your narrative you should draw the readers' attention to any major findings rather than describing the tables and figures displayed in the chapter. As you move on from findings to discussion, always keep in mind that you are just presenting your findings; not what they mean to you.

The discussion chapter is perhaps the most significant part of any research, if you consider the amount of space that top-quality journals allow for it. Therefore, this is your opportunity to shine! You are now an expert in your area of research, and people will respect the work you have just completed. With the support of the general-to-specific pattern in the presentation of your results, your discussion should be relatively straightforward. Present your thoughts about the meaning, value and importance of your findings. Again, start with a general statement regarding what you think your findings mean, and then move on to the relevant specifics, providing evidence from the findings. As the interpretation of the findings is your own, the language you use should always be tentative and not assertive – i.e. it is more appropriate to say 'these findings appear to support the belief that …' rather than 'these findings confirm the belief that…'.

'Connect' is the operative verb in planning the writing of this chapter. In your discussion, everything should be connected with something. In providing evidence for your argument, you will have to move from one specific finding to another. Make sure that all relevant interpretations are well connected with each other. Towards that end, make sure you use transition words in the argument, such as first, second …, next, also, furthermore and finally, because they convey a sense of structure. Furthermore, you must always connect your interpretation of these findings with the extant theory (stemming from your conceptual framework) and evaluate whether they corroborate or refute it. Some students make the mistake of introducing new literature in this section to support their findings and overall argument, but this should be avoided. Apart from relating your findings to the theory, you have the opportunity to relate the findings to one another by looking at how they hang together and in which ways they seem consistent or inconsistent. Most importantly of all, your discussion needs to be connected with your problem statement and to show how you have succeeded in answering the research questions and testing your hypotheses.

In concluding this chapter, you may summarize your main findings from your perspective and state that the implications of your research will be discussed in detail in the subsequent chapter.

Conclusions and implications

This chapter is the 'cherry on the cake' of your dissertation. It is the last chapter, although perhaps not the last chapter you will write. This is the chapter where you give a full summary of your work and your findings; most importantly, this is where you present the implications of your study to both researchers and practitioners. This is where the 'expert researcher' offers recommendations and suggestions.

Conclusions

Overview of the study

The conclusions chapter usually starts, for the benefit of the reader (and in many cases the author too), with a restatement of the research problem and a brief review of the methodology employed in the study. Following this review, evaluate the extent to which you feel your overall aim and objectives were achieved. These may have been partially or fully achieved, or even exceeded. However, if you have failed to reach some of them, this is where you should report it. The reporting of failures to achieve some parts of your work and reflection on the reasons why things went wrong is generally considered to be a positive feature of a dissertation.

Insights from the study

This is where you share with reader the insights you have gained from the study – what you have really learned. You are expected to show where extant research has been endorsed, where gaps have appeared, and, as is to be expected, how your research responded to the emergence of those gaps. What is necessary here is an explicit and precise articulation of new, surprising and/or remarkable results and insights compared with existing theory.

You can also explain how or why these insights can help you to become a better researcher and/or a more effective manager. Keep the discussion general, and focus on your learning before moving to more specific findings. Additionally, you can flag any unexpected findings that emerged during your study. A quick reflection on why these emerged will add value to this part.

Implications of findings

Some students make the mistake of restating all their findings. What you really need to do here is highlight of the effect of these findings. You should aim at helping the readers to understand what these findings mean for their lives as academics, their understanding of a theory, their research, their teaching, or, as practitioners, their working practices and business environment. When discussing the implications, do not use assertive verbs. Instead, use verbs such as 'suggest' or 'imply', which have an element of uncertainty. This is the part of your dissertation where you have the opportunity (and obligation) to make specific recommendations to both communities (answer the SO WHAT? question) on how they can use your work as a basis to conduct further research (new areas of investigation prompted by your study findings; areas which were not researched during this study due to methodological or other constraints) or to modify/improve their business practices. Avoid the temptation to provide a series of recommendations, and focus instead on one or two major ones. Make sure, however, that you do make suggestions that could have been easily explored within your study, as this will show that you have not done all the work that you would like to in your own field of research.

Limitations of the study

This is where you discuss any weakness in study design – for example, issues that only became apparent during the conduct of the study. You will have to comment on how important these limitations are in the interpretation of your findings, and how they may affect their validity or generalizability. By tradition, the hallmarks of scholarship and scientific research are replicability (i.e. someone who conducts exactly the same research as you will find exactly the same results) and generalizability (i.e. the method and the findings can be generalized to all similar settings). Therefore, by tradition, you have to include a few lines stating the limitations of your study, but avoid using an apologetic tone and accept the study for what it is. Acknowledging your limitations in no way takes anything from the value of your research. As McNiff *et al.* (2003: 133) argue: 'It is neither possible nor desirable to aim for replication or generalization, since the aim {of research} is to understand rather than predict, to liberate rather than control'. If you have achieved something close to these ideas, then you have achieved a lot.

The last chapter: introduction revisited

After completing the writing up of your dissertation and before moving on to the 'final touches', you are advised you to re-read your introduction very carefully and check that what you actually delivered in the end is what you promised in the introductory chapter. Go through your introduction, bearing in mind that it should help the reader to move effortlessly in the direction of the conclusion. Make sure that all the important concepts necessary for understanding your conclusion are presented in the introductory chapter.

The final touches

Now that everything has been checked, you can move on to the final touches. You will obviously need to comply with the presentation requirements set by your institution in terms of format, length and style of your dissertation, and your supervisor is the best person to help you with these.

Appendices

One of the most common questions in this stage is, 'what do we include in the appendices, and what do we leave in the main body of the dissertation?' The answer is: any tables, graphs or other piece of information that are not critical to your argument, but that are relevant and useful in helping the reader to understand the concepts, methods and approaches used in your study, should be placed in the appendices. They can include letters sent to the informants, a sample of the contents of the documents analysed, and diagrams used for the data analysis. Normally it is an institution requirement to include at least one sample of an information sheet, a consent form and a questionnaire, and an interview transcript.

References

The crucial importance of references in your proposal has already been emphasized, and the same applies here. Make sure that all the sources for everything you have used in your dissertation are properly referenced. Check your references carefully in both the text and your reference list.

Editing your dissertation

Even if you are a regular user of your word processor's 'spell-check' functionality, you will have to proofread your dissertation several times. Spell-checkers are useful for initial checking, but do not catch words that sound the same but are spelt differently (e.g. sum, some) or other words with similar spelling. The following advice on editing you text will help, but the suggestions are certainly not exhaustive.

- While proofreading, make sure that you are consistent in the terminology you are using throughout your dissertation – so if you start your dissertation with 'travel comparison engines', make sure you do not use the term 'travel shopping websites' or 'travel shopping bots' in the sections that follow.
- Check your grammar – punctuation, sentence structure, subject–verb agreement (plural or singular), tense consistency, etc.
- Do not accept long-winded sentences that may confuse the reader, unless absolutely necessary; if you can, break them into parts using semicolons.
- Identify any repetitions in your text and eliminate them.
- Make sure that all your acronyms are explained the first time you use them.

Once you have proofread your work, it is always useful to ask another person to read it. A fresh pair of eyes will always catch points that you have missed. The reader can also evaluate the 'flow' of your thought and the logic of your structure. However, make sure that your institution allows such a practice. Some institutions consider proofreading by a third party to be collusion, which is an academic offence. Your institution may also offer alternative sources for proofreading and language editing.

Consider international readers

It is quite probable that your dissertation will have an international audience – an examiner (internal or external) from abroad, international students in your institution, or even international students abroad who have borrowed your dissertation through an inter-library loan. Therefore, if English language is one of your strengths, avoid writing complicated sentences to impress your examiners; this may have completely the completely opposite effect on them. Also, do not assume that all readers are familiar with the geography of the location(s) where you conducted your research. In the appendix, provide useful information about the area and a map clearly showing the region(s), city or cities of your study. In the main body of your dissertation, refer the reader – where necessary – to these appendices.

Other presentation conventions

There are some presentation conventions for dissertations that are pretty much common in all institutions. However, as these conventions can also vary, it is always wise to check your institution's presentation guidelines.

- *Fonts*. In most institutions, the standard size for fonts is 12-point for text and 10-point for footnotes and subscripts. You should avoid using fonts less than

10-point, even for superscripts and subscripts. If footnotes are permitted by your institution's guidelines, most software programs default to a font size smaller than 10-point. Remember, however, that the footnote number should not be less than 8-point.

- *Preliminary pages.* These are all the pages that precede the text of your dissertation. They usually include the title page (the format for which will be provided by your institution), the abstract, the copyright notice/declaration, the dedication page, the acknowledgments page, the table of contents, the list of figures and tables, and the key to symbols or abbreviations. Each heading of the main divisions of the dissertation should begin on a new page, with the heading typed in capital letters throughout and centred below the upper marginal line. The preliminary pages are usually written with single line spacing. The text should be 1.5 or double-spaced.

- *Page numbering.* Preliminary pages are normally numbered using lower-case roman numerals (i, ii, iii, iv, v, etc.). The title page is counted but not numbered (i.e. the number does not appear). Page numbers usually start appearing from the second page onwards, and are placed in the centre of the page. For text, appendices and the bibliography, all pages are counted and numbered with Arabic numerals (1, 2, 3, etc.). Page 1 should be the first page of your introductory chapter, Chapter 1.

- *Abbreviations.* All abbreviations must be defined the first time they are used, and after this the abbreviation is used (e.g., Customer Relationship Marketing, CRM). As a general rule, do not use an abbreviation unless a term appears at least three times in the dissertation.

- *Figures and tables.* The figures and tables in your work should be numbered using Arabic numerals and have a brief title, and they should be cited consecutively in your text. Normally, the title of a figure or table (as given in the list of figures and/or tables), should be placed ABOVE each table or figure, whereas the source of the information (if from secondary sources) should be placed BELOW each table or figure at the right-hand side.

- *Headings and subheadings.* On the first page of each chapter, the word CHAPTER (upper case and bold) and the appropriate number should be centred at the top of the page. Normally three levels of sub-headings should be used. First-order headings should be in bold underlined letters with two line spaces above and one line space below, and numbered 1.1, 1.2, 1.3, etc. Second-order headings should be in bold with one line space both above and below them, and numbered 1.1.1, 1.1.2, 1.1.3, etc. Third-order headings should be in italic type with one line space both above and below them, and numbered with roman numerals – (i), (ii), (iii), etc. You should avoid having headings and subheadings alone at the bottom of a page.

- *Past, present and future tenses.* Findings described in your dissertation should be described in the past tense (you have done the research), but your results are not yet accepted 'facts', so they can be written in the present tense. Findings from published papers should be described in the present tense (based on the assumption that published findings are 'facts').

- *Third vs first person.* Your dissertation should be written in the third person. However, avoid using the impersonal pronoun 'one' (e.g. 'One could …'). In this example, it is more appropriate to write: 'It is possible to …'. In addition, inanimate objects (like hotels, restaurants, destinations, etc.) should be described in the third person, and not with possessive terms (e.g. instead of writing 'its customers', write 'the restaurant's customers').

Summary

- Your dissertation is comprised of several chapters, of which the Introduction is the first. In this chapter, you should offer the background and rationale of your study, state the purpose of the research, articulate your research objectives, and defend the originality and contribution to knowledge of your study.
- The literature review chapter is where you offer a critical evaluation of the extant knowledge about your research topic.
- The research design chapter should cover your chosen research strategy, data collection techniques and sample, your pilot study, the actual data collection process, an explanation of how data analysis worked in practice, and your retrospective reflection on your research experience.
- The findings chapter allows you to describe what you have found from your fieldwork.
- The discussion chapter will enable you to present what, in your view, your findings mean, and how they compare with the extant literature.
- In the conclusions and implications chapter, you are expected to demonstrate how your research responded to the research gaps by articulating new, surprising and/or remarkable results and insights. You should also discuss the implications of your findings for the practitioners and policy-makers.

Turning a dissertation into an academic paper

Successful completion of your project does not necessarily mean that your research journey has ended. You may feel that through your research you have made a significant contribution to the body of knowledge, and want to challenge yourself further by sharing your findings with the rest of the research community through a conference paper or a journal article. Your supervisor can give you valuable advice on whether you should attempt such a challenge or not, and if so, how. You may opt to write the paper alone or co-author it with your supervisor, who is probably more experienced in publishing academic work. Either way, there are a few guidelines you can follow to help you overcome this challenge.

With your project already written up, you have already done most of the work for your paper. However, there are a few differences between a project and a scholarly paper. The main difference is that while in your research project you are trying to show your examiner that you have 'mastered' the topic you are researching and you know how to design and conduct research, in an academic paper you must 'capture' the interest of your audience. Therefore, the first important decision for you is the audience that you will target:

- Whose conference you are looking for? (Academics, practitioners, both?)
- What are its themes, and how does your topic fit with these themes?
- If you are writing a journal paper, what are the journal's mission and focus?

These questions will largely define the way you are going to write your article, from writing style to formatting. Presentation criteria differ from conference to conference, as they do from journal to journal. You will need to modify your writing each time and adhere to these criteria, because if you do not then the editor and reviewers will think that you were not ready to put the necessary effort into fulfilling the journal's requirements – and therefore wonder why they should put in the necessary effort to review your paper. Your writing style should also be adapted to the audience – for example, if you are writing for a conference (or journal) aimed at both researchers and practitioners, your style should be adapted to suit both audiences. However, even if your audience is purely academic you should avoid a complicated writing style, as an article that is difficult to follow is simply not achieving its aim: to inform the readers. Day and Gastel (2006) suggest that when writing for academic journals there is little need for ornamentation, as it is likely to cause confusion. The reviewers may also interpret a convoluting writing style as an effort to cover possible weaknesses in the research paper.

The next step is to convert your work from a 'competent research project' to an 'interesting research paper'. Barley (2006: 16) states that 'academic papers are a bit like rock and roll bands: whether an audience finds them interesting is a matter of perspective, if not taste'. However, he then offers the secret to success: difference is the root of all interest. Reviewers often complain that the introductions to certain papers read like an introductory chapter for a dissertation rather than a concept piece that suggests new thoughts or offers something different, unique, puzzling or contradictory about the paper to make it worthwhile (Yuksel, 2003). It does not have to be a groundbreaking difference, but it has to be pointed out early in your paper. Remember that your paper is not a novel, where the reader will wait till the end to read the 'happily ever after'; you will therefore have to revise your introduction by emphasizing whatever you do differently from others:

- Does the subject you are researching depart noticeably from the mainstream?
- Is your research method innovative or different from the ubiquitous secondary data sets, attitude surveys and interviews?
- Does your research propose new perspectives on theories that differ from what has gone before?
- Does it offer a convincing answer to the 'so what?' question?

You can see that these questions have somehow been answered in the rationale of your dissertation, where you identify the 'gap' in the literature, your aim and your objectives. All these have to be presented in an effective manner in the paper's introduction.

When writing the literature review for your paper, you can follow a structure similar to that provided by your literature map for your dissertation. However, you must remember that while in your dissertation you have gone into considerable detail to prove your competence in standard aspects of thinking, in a paper you do not have to repeat in detail concepts and theories that are already published in other articles. You will have to use your judgment here, to decide whether you are offering enough of a description to allow readers who are not very familiar with the concepts you are presenting to follow the paper while ensuring that others who do are not bored by reading something they already know.

The section regarding research design in your dissertation aims to show how well you know the relevant research methods literature, and you have probably gone into detail regarding the basic principles of research approaches and strategies, as well as the advantages and disadvantages of the various research tools that you have used in your study. In an article, this is not necessary. You simply need to talk about what you did, why you did it and how, and justify your choices with relevant literature. Your main consideration here is to ensure that enough detail is provided for your findings to be considered valid and reliable, and to enable the replication of your study by another researcher using the same techniques with the same (or a similar) sample.

In your dissertation your findings may be also quite extensive, but, as papers have space limitations, considerable editing may be necessary. Remember that this part of your paper serves two functions:

1. It reports the findings of the procedures described in the methodology section
2. It presents the evidence (i.e. the data, in the form of text, tables or figures) that supports the findings.

You will therefore need to decide which findings are important in answering your research question, and which can be left out. You should include only those findings that are relevant to the question(s) posed in the introduction to your paper. After deciding which findings to present, you should determine how best to present the supporting data – in text, as tables or as figures?

The discussion of these findings is the heart of the paper, and you may need to rewrite this section more than once, as it is the most important component of your paper (after the rationale for the research). You have to make sure that it fully answers the question(s) posed in the introduction, explains how the findings support the answers given, and how the answers fit within the existing body of knowledge. This is where you have the opportunity to express your own interpretations and views regarding the topic of your research and put your analytical and evaluative skills forward to be judged by your readers. Remember that, for the sake of your paper's clarity, you should keep your discussion as short as possible while at the same time offering full support to, explanation and defence of the answers that your study provides regarding the research question(s) of your paper. You need, however, to avoid mere reiteration of your findings.

For your conclusion, you can follow the structure offered regarding the concluding chapter of your dissertation. It is particularly important, though, that these conclusions relate to a broader context than your dissertation. A reviewer in Yuksel's (2006) study argues: 'far too many papers were very good at presenting statistics but were weak at discussing the bigger picture impacts of their research' (Yuksel, 2006: 444). Whereas in your dissertation it was acceptable to write conclusions about a specific context of study, for a paper (or journal article) you will have to think of more generalizable implications. You can always discuss your specific context in detail, but it is important also to offer evidence that the implications of your study apply in other contexts too.

Review questions

1. What is the generally accepted structure of a dissertation?
2. Which are the four questions that the abstract should answer? How can these be related to the sections of a structured abstract as presented in Box 11.1?
3. What are the three principles for engaging in a dialogue with the literature?
4. What are the four main components of the concluding chapter?

References

Barley, S. R. (2006). When I write my masterpiece: thoughts on what makes a paper interesting. *Academy of Management Journal*, 49(1), 16–20.

Day, R. A. and Gastel, B. (2006). *How to Write and Publish a Scientific Paper*. Cambridge: Cambridge University Press.

Emerald for Authors. Support and services. Available at: http://juno.emeraldinsight.com/vl= 5309899/cl=145/nw=1/rpsv/literaticlub/editors/editorialadmin/abstracts.htm (accessed 12 May 2007).

Eustathius (1970). *Commentarii ad Homeri Iliadem et Odysseam*. Hildesheim: G. Olms.

McNiff, J., Lomax, P. and Whitehead, J. (2003). *You and Your Action Research Project*, 2nd edn. London: Routledge.

Yuksel, A. (2003). Writing publishable papers. *Tourism Management*, 24(4), 437–446.

Index